ESSAYS ON CZECH MUSIC

Zdenka E. Fischmann

EAST EUROPEAN MONOGRAPHS, BOULDER
DISTRIBUTED BY COLUMBIA UNIVERSITY PRESS, NEW YORK
2002

EAST EUROPEAN MONOGRAPHS, NO. DCX

Copyright 2002 by
Czechoslovak Society of Arts and Sciences (SVU)

ISBN: 0-88033-508-4

Library of Congress Control Number 2002106641

Printed in the United States of America

Table of Contents

ACKNOWLEDGMENTS

Editors
Anne Palmer
Dagmar Hasalova White

We gratefully acknowledge the permission of various publishers to reprint the following articles: "Smetana Centennial," "Brod Centennial," "The Vixen Bystrouška and Her Champions," and "Music in Terezín," all originally published in the journal *Cross Currents;* "Max Brod's Life in Music," "Jewish Musicians with Roots in Czechoslovakia," "Some Jewish Musicians from Czechoslovakia," "Oscar Morawetz—Humanitarian Composer," all originally published in the *Review for the Society for the History of Czechoslovak Jews.* A shorter version in Czech of "Max Brod and his Music" appeared in *Proměny*; the article published here is taken from a more extensive draft in English. The remaining articles were given to us in draft form and have been edited for publication.

We are deeply grateful to Hannelies McFalls, devoted friend of Zdenka Fischmann and executor of her will, for making available to us Dr. Fischmann's articles and manuscripts for publication.

We are greatly indebted to Jiří Eichler from Prague, Czech Republic for the excellent and patient computer work for preparing these essays for printing.

INTRODUCTION

Dagmar Hasalova White

From the rich musical heritage of a small nation in the heart of Europe, Zdenka Fischmann chose many interesting and sometimes fascinating or little known subjects for her research and study. She wanted to acquaint the public through her lectures and publications with Czech music and her compatriots with their musical heritage. She was a tireless propagator of Czech music. As a positive contribution to musicology, the Czechoslovak Society of Arts and Sciences has published posthumously her work in this collection of *Essays on Czech Music.*

During great political upheavals many countries lose their brightest, most talented, and courageous citizens through exodus, imprisonment, or worse, which impoverishes the nation. This happended several times in the history of the Czech Lands. First, during the Thirty Years War after the Battle of White Mountain, again during the Second World War, and then again after the Communist takeover of the country. Some of those who left dispersed throughout the world and became assimilated. Others, although they made contributions to their new country with their talent and intellect, never forgot their origins.

To this second group belongs Zdenka Fischmann.

Zdenka Fischmann was born Zdenka Sedláková on Sept. 7, 1923 in Prague. Her father, Jaroslav Sedlák, was a teacher and school principal. She had a congenital hip malformation that did not respond to belated treatment. However, this condition did not prevent her from partaking of life fully and with great zest. She was musically gifted, studying voice and piano, hoping that after graduating from high school she would go to the university to study music.

When her country was occupied by the Nazis and the universities were closed she kept on studying music privately but bowed to the practical aspect and reality of the situation by taking commercial courses and waited.

In May 1945 Czechoslovakia was free again and Zdenka was able to pursue her dream of a career in music. She enrolled at the Charles University in Prague where she met Vítězslav Fischmann, her future husband and a student of psychology, sociology, and philosophy. Vítězslav Fischmann, or Slávek as he was called, was a survivor of the Auschwitz death camp. He was born on November 19, 1919 into a well-to-do Jewish family. Although born in Vienna, he had his domicile rights from his father in Moravia where he grew up in the town of Jihlava. There he went to Czech schools and became a sincere Czechoslovak patriot.

During the Nazi occupation Vítězslav was exposed to all the cruelty the Gestapo meted out to the Czechoslovak Jews, culminating in a transport to Terezín with his mother and sister. From Terezín they were sent to Auschwitz

1

where his mother and sister went directly to the gas chambers. Slávek survived by being selected for slave labor. His father had perished earlier in Auschwitz.

The year 1945 in a free Czechoslovakia was full of hope for Zdenka and Slávek. They were working hard preparing for their careers but still had time for their friendship to develop into love. They were married in October 1947. Slávek was proud of his Jewish heritage and Zdenka embraced the faith of her husband and converted to Judaism in the spring of 1949, taking the name of Ester. With her new faith, she developed a life-long interest in Jewish musicians with Czech and Slovak roots. She wrote and published many articles about these talented musicians and composers, whom she considered part of her national heritage as her articles in this book attest.

In October 1948 Zdenka Fischmann completed her studies and received a doctorate in musicology and sociology. But with the Communist takeover of Czechoslovakia her husband was prevented from completing his Ph.D. The young couple decided to leave the country and emigrate to Panama.

They settled in Panama City where they soon found jobs in their respective fields, Zdenka lecturing in musicology at the University of Panama, eventually becoming associate professor at that institution. Her husband worked as a clinical psychologist at a State Mental Hospital and maintained a private practice. His unfinished doctorate continued to bother him. So, finally in 1962 he received his doctorate from the University of Marburg, West Germany, which accepted all of his credits from Prague and a dissertation he wrote in Panama.

Because of the unstable political situation in Panama in 1964, the Fischmanns decided to move to the United States, settling in 1965 in Corona, California. Contacts with exile organizations in Los Angeles and elsewhere in the United States, the feeling of freedom in this enormous country, and access to information from the entire world helped the Fischmanns to settle down comfortably. Slávek found a postion as staff psychologist at a California Rehabilitation Center for Drug Addicts while Zdenka developed a second career as a music therapist and psychiatric group therapist with the Penal Code Patients at the Patton State Hospital, working there with great dedication until her retirement in 1984.

Zdenka Fischmann was diligently researching material for various studies and writing articles and book reviews for publication. She had many works published on psychotherapy but the bulk of her published and unpublished work is in the field of music. In her double capacity as a musicologist and psychologist Zdenka Fischmann gives us an inside analysis of a composer's personality, fused with his creative talent. This is evident in the essay "Janáček and Creativity," or the evaluation of Smetana's mental problems in the article "Smetana and Pivoda," or in the "Vítězslava Kaprálová and Martinů" article.

Zdenka Fischmann was one of the most devoted members of the Czechoslovak Society of Arts and Sciences (SVU). She was an active member of the Los Angeles chapter. In 1969 she became editor in chief of the *Los Angeles SVU Bulletin.* During the period 1980-82 she was editor of the *SVU Bulletin*, an English language counterpart of the Society's *Zprávy (News).* She was on the editorial board of *Kosmas,* the biannual scholarly journal of SVU, contributing articles on musicology.

In 1992 Zdenka Fischmann lost her husband of 45 years. A few years later she moved to Phoenix, Arizona, hoping for a new life and many cultural offerings in a city with a large Czechoslovak community. Sadly, her health was deteriorating steadily. She died at the age of 75 on May 14, 1999.

EDITORIAL REMARKS

Anne Palmer

After more than forty years as an émigré, Dr. Fischmann returned to Charles University in Prague to participate in the 1992 SVU conference and experience the euphoric atmosphere which followed the Velvet Revolution. Although she was old and frail, she brandished her cane as if it were a weapon and had the fiery pride of a Kostelnička. She had looked the events of the Holocaust and the Communist occupation of Czechoslovakia squarely in the eye, and was not about to be intimidated by mere musicologists!

She had pursued doctoral studies at Charles University in Prague and written a dissertation, *Vývoj a vzájemný poměr polyfonie a homofonie* (Development and Interrelationships of polyphony and homophony) in the fateful year of 1948. But like other emigres, she had to build an entirely new life, and thus, she joined her husband in a career of psychotherapy. She lectured at the University of Southern California and worked with convicted felons at the California Patton State Hospital. In addition to the papers in this volume, she also wrote on topics related to her work, such as the sociological aspects of criminal offenders and post-traumatic stress. Thus it is not surprising that she had an unusual ability to address the impacts of medical and psychological issues on music history.

Like many émigrés who experienced the First Republic, she had an indelible, elemental love for the Czech lands, and conveyed this love in her articles. However, she also realized that promoting Czech music in foreign countries implied that it would be judged objectively against the international repertory, and her articles also reflect this objectivity. She whole-heartedly adopted the remarkable tolerance exemplified by Max Brod. She demonstrated it in her article about František Pivoda, who is often vilified as Smetana's enemy. This tolerance seems to have been a source of strength to her as she faced the calamities of the twentieth century. She took as her example the brief moment in history when Jews, Germans, and Czechs were able to work together for common cultural goals, to promote the music of Janáček throughout the world. Perhaps as a result, she identified all musicians who flourished in Czech lands as part of the nation's heritage.

She was propagating the Czech musical tradition wherever and whenever she could, specifically to the émigré community as well as to the world at large. She translated, published, lectured, and influenced others to join her. Some of her articles honor those who shared this commitment.

Most of the articles were written within severe limitations. During the years of Communism, few secondary sources in Czech and Slovak music were generally available. In rural California she was far from libraries with major collections in Czech music, such as the Music Division of the Library of Congress and the music library of Indiana University, whose holdings reflect the tireless work of the Prague musicologist Paul Nettl. Dr. Fischmann, like many others, often had to rely on copies which were privately owned. Thus, it is understandable that her principal goal was to disseminate vital information which was not available in English rather than to do original research.

However, her activity led to an unusual opportunity. The Brno musicologist Leos Firkušný, brother of the pianist Rudolf Firkušný, had emigrated to South America. He brought photostats of part of the correspondence of Leoš Janáček and Rosa Newmarch with him, but died before he could publish it. His widow, Růžena Horákova-Firkušný, entrusted Dr. Fischmann with this valuable material. She contacted Rosa Newmarch's daughter Elsie, and obtained not only the remainder of the correspondence, but also Rosa Newmarch's personal file of newspaper clippings and other documents related to the correspondence. Dr. Fischmann edited and annotated this material, publishing it as *Janáček-Newmarch Correspondence* (Rockville, Maryland: Kabel Publishers, 1986, 1990). This publication represents her most significant achievement in the field of musicology.

As she would have wished, her very success has overtaken her. American-trained musicologists who followed her example began to read Czech. They made contacts with Czech musicologists and used Czech libraries, especially after the Velvet Revolution. They published in English - often with results which Dr. Fischmann could not have anticipated. Czech musicologists are now able to travel freely, and are lecturing more frequently at international congresses. Czech monographs are becoming more available in English translation. The first edition of *The New Grove Dictionary of Music and Musicians*, the first music reference work to contain extensive, authoritative articles in English on Czech musicians and music history, appeared after many of her articles had been written. The second edition of this reference work, which includes a far more authoritative summary of the history of Czech music than any American musicologist could have provided during the Communist era, has only come out in the last year.

Understandably, Dr. Fischmann's work is not always consistent with this avalanche of new information. Nevertheless, it provides a remarkable documentation of an era when emigres joined forces to ensure that the spirit of Czech music, the spirit of the nation itself, would endure.

MUSIC IS THE LIFE OF CZECHS

Our title refers to the well-known words "V hudbě je život Čechů" of Bedřich Smetana on May 16, 1868, spoken on the occasion of the ground-breaking ceremony for the National Theater in Prague. They certainly express the love of music characteristic of the Czechoslovak ethnic groups, and are applicable in any country where Czech and Slovak immigrants have found themselves.

Contributions to the musical life of host countries by emigré musicians from the Czech lands and Slovakia has been multi-faceted. However, it is often taken for granted rather than specifically documented. Even the well-established research concerning the eighteenth century migration of Bohemian musicians into many European countries has not yet exhausted all of the sur-viving primary sources. Dvořák's American years have been well researched, but information about other outstanding musicians of Czech and Slovak de-scent in America is often difficult to find in secondary sources in the English language.

A comprehensive pioneering study, "Czechoslovak Composers and Musicians in America," was published during World War II by a prolific, well-informed writer on Czech music, the emigré Jan Löwenbach (1880-1972). [1] He compiled a significant list of eminent Czech virtuosi, singers and conductors who either toured or where active in this country around the begin-ning of the twentieth the century. Detailed biographical and musical informa-tion is also given for three Czechoslovak composers whom Löwenbach knew, and were still alive when the article was written: Jaromír Weinberger (1896-1967), Jaroslav Ježek (1906-1942), and Bohuslav Martinů (1890-1959). Since 1943, additional information about this interesting but neglected topic has been published by Miloslav Rechcígl which brings additional musicians to light. [2] A well-documented article from the 1960's by Karel Boleslav Jirák (1891-1972), "Czechoslovak Music in the American Music Literature," pro-vides an update to Löwenbach's information. [3]

Such articles are valuable to us as we study Czechoslovak musicians in America, for reliable information is scarce. Czechoslovaks living in the United States generally deplore the lack of interest in Czech music by Ameri-can scholars; however, the scholarly community rightly points out that there is a lack of reliable data in English.

The nature of secondary sources for musicology also contributes to this dearth of information. Only highly specialized monographs can present thor-ough research results and detailed information. Any general musicological reference work - a general history, biographical dictionary or encyclopedia – is necessarily selective and incomplete, and often necessarily must give prefer-ence to well-known musicians.

Authoritative musicological sources in the Czech language are diffi-cult to find in America. To make matters worse, ideological repression in

Czechoslovakia during the Cold War has severely affected musicological information in print in the Czech language. The length and content of biographical information may reflect an ideological assessment of the person and may be based on non-musical factors. For example, many of the more than fifty names on Jan Löwenbach's list do not appear in *Československý hudební slovník osob a institucí* [Czechoslovak musical dictionary of persons and institutions], an important Soviet-era reference source in the Czech language. This two-volume dictionary lists Czech and Slovak musicians of historical importance, many of whom do not appear in English-language music dictionaries. However, it does not include musicians who were not in favor at the time it was compiled. Some of them were emigres who had left the country precisely because of this repression

Many Czechs and Slovaks have made contributions to the music of the United States according to Czechoslovak tradition: in order to promote the love of music in their adopted country rather than to achieve personal recognition – another reason why the secondary sources in English are not very informative. A great number of instrumentalists, vocalists, conductors, choirmasters, minor composers, music teachers, organizers, publicists, and simply music enthusiasts have exerted a wide, lasting influence through professional competence, steadfast musicianship and performance, constant dedication. However, the traces of their work tend to surface unexpectedly, and thus to illustrate the various ways in which these contributions were achieved.

The oldest documented mention of music performed in Czech which I have been able to find belongs to the pre-revolutionary era. On September 4, 1745, the Moravian Brethren congregation of Bethlehem, Pennsylvania sang the popular hymn *In Dulci Jubilo* simultaneously in thirteen languages. In alphabetic order they were: Czech, Dutch, English, French, German, Greek, Irish, Latin, Mohawk, Mohican, Swedish, Welsh and Wendish. [4] This community established and fostered a tradition of Moravian music in the New World.

Connections between Bohemian music and North America involve two famous American public figures. Both Thomas Jefferson and Benjamin Franklin are well-known for their interest and even personal involvement in music.

Jefferson's 1783 handwritten catalog of the music collection at Monticello includes an interesting item, "Wodizka's solos." The *Sonata III, Opus 1, in d minor* for violin and basso continuo by Wodizka is one of the compositions on the recording *Music from the Age of Jefferson* which was produced as a bicentennial musical contribution of the Smithsonian Institution using authentic instruments of the time from the Smithsonian's Division of Musical Instruments. [5] The notes for this recording do not provide much information about Wodzika beyond dates which are given as ca. 1715 to 1774. It is therefore a pleasant surprise to identify the composer Wenceslaus Wodizka (also written as Wodik) as Václav Vodička, a Czech composer and violinist born in Bohemia around 1720. His flute and violin sonatas opp. 1 and 2 were published in Paris in 1739. These works also appeared in London in 1740 and 1750. Vodička was engaged in 1745 as concert master in Munich and died there in 1774. The style of his symphonies and concertos resembles that of the Mannheim school – yet they contain Czech traits. This circumstance is not surprising, for the Mannheim style was in part established by Jan Václav Antonín Stamic (1717-1757), better known as Stamitz, who was also a Czech émigré. Whether Jefferson knew who Vodička was, whether he ever played his music or liked to listen to it is impossible to determine. Jefferson may acquired these scores through Dr. Charles Burney, with whom he corresponded. Or he may have bought them when he was residing in London.

During his stay in Paris (1776 to 1785), Benjamin Franklin became a very popular public figure as the representative of the newly-founded American Republic in France. He was approached by many, among them a well-known musician who inquired about the career possibilities across the Atlantic. [6] This composer and virtuoso player of viola and viola d'amore was Carl Stamitz (1745-1801); he gave concerts in Paris and London in 1778. However, Carl Stamitz did not cross the ocean to the American shores. Carl was the son of Jan Václav Antonín Stamic and was born in Mannheim of a German mother, but he still had uncles and nephews in Německý Brod.

The name of Sig. Charles Stamitz appears on a program announcing the music to be played at the opening of the new Federal Street Theatre in Boston program on February 3, 1794. [7] This entertainment was called *Yankee Doodle*. The opening numbers were a *Grand Battle Overture in Henry IVth* and *General Washington's March*. Between the acts of an unspecified work, several orchestral pieces were performed: *A Grand Symphony* by said Sig. Charles Stamitz, *Grand Overture* by Sig. Vanhall, *Grand Symphony* by Sig. Haydn and another *Grand Symphony* by Carlos Ditters - evidently Karl Ditters von Dittersdorf, who lived in the Czech lands for a time. It must have been a gala event. It is hoped that the ladies minded the request to "attend without hats, bonnets, feathers or any other high head dress, that the sight of the gentlemen seated behind them, may not be obstructed!" and that the serious music lovers did "prevent the thoughtless, or ill disposed, from throwing apples, stones etc., into the orchestra, that while they [the musicians] eat the bread of industry in a free country, it may not be tinctured with the poison of humiliation." [8] Such was the concern of the organizers who thoughtfully prepared a code of behavior for their theater goers in advance. It is a pity that the performed works were not been identified more precisely, for Wanhal (Jan Křtitel Vaňhal 1739-1813) is a well-known Czech composer.

Such entertainments must be viewed from a historical perspective. After 1770, the relatively rich musical life of the colonies had gradually been curtailed as political strife increased in intensity. The question of public entertainments came before the First Continental Congress in Philadelphia when a resolution was passed on October 20, 1774, with the recommendation, among other issues, to "encourage frugality" and "discountenance and discourage every species of extravagance and dissipation, especially all horse-racing, and all kinds of gaming, cock-fighting, exhibition of shows [sic], plays, and other expensive diversions and entertainments."

After the Revolution succeeded, music gradually began to take firmer hold in the Republic. Various theatrical British companies returned; but at first they had to be careful not to offend the still pervading spirit of austerity. One of these was the Hallam and Henry company, which performed in the mid-1780s in New York, Baltimore, Annapolis, Richmond, and in January 1787 in Philadelphia. Their program of January 19, 1797 includes the music of a Czech composer. [9]

"*A Concert of Music*, Vocal and Instrumental: Between the several parts of the Concert will be delivered *Lectures*, Moral and Entertaining.

FIRST ACT

Overture . . . . Kammel

PROLOGUE AND LECTURE

Song . . . . Mr. Wools

SECOND ACT

Simphonia . . . . Schwindl

LECTURE

Song . . . . Mr. Harper

CLARINET CONCERTO
(By Desire)

The Overture to Rosina, to which will be added, a Pantomime called 'Harlequin's Frolic,' in which will be introduced a Musical Entertainment, called 'The Reapers,' with original music."

Antonín Kammel (b. Běleč, Bohemia, April 21, 1730; d. London, ca. 1788, according to various editions of *Cyclopedia*) was a contemporary of Haydn. His one-page entry in the *New Grove* provides details of his life and a list of his instrumental works. The article questions whether he actually died in London and tentatively gives his death date as "by 1787." The work on this concert may have been one of the overtures for eight instruments from a collection published in London in 1773. [10]

All such evidence must be examined carefully. The opera *Arianne* was performed on March 28, 1791, in New York. Oscar Sonneck states that he first thought that it might be Jiří Antonín Benda's (1722-1795) famous melodrama *Ariadne auf Naxos* (1774). However, he later identified it as a French opera by the Alsatian composer Johann Friedrich Edelmann (1749-1794) which was performed in Paris in 1782. [11]

The Battle of Prague, a composition for piano, with violin, cello and drum *ad libitum* was popular during the early post-revolutionary period. The fifth edition of *Grove's Dictionary* describes this work as "that extraordinary and musically quite valueless descriptive piece" which caught the fancy of Londoners and Americans. *The New Grove* calls its composer, František Koczwara (also written as Kočvara, Kotzwara; b. Prague, ca. 1750), "something of a vagabond." His career led him to Ireland and then to London, where he died on September 2, 1791, apparently under rather scandalous circumstances.

The *Battle of Prague* was first published around 1788 in Dublin. According to Sonneck, it was played in Baltimore as early as February of 1791 in connection with the "elegant and fashionable pasticcio, the *Evening Brush*," which was produced by the Virginia theatrical company of West and Bignall.[12] Gilbert Chase states that *The Battle of Prague* was introduced to American music lovers by Benjamin Carr (1768-1831) who came from London in 1793.[13] The Carr family established music shops and music publishing houses in Baltimore, Philadelphia and New York. Even if Benjamin Carr was the first to print this composition in America, it could have been performed here before it appeared in an American edition. *The Battle of Prague* may have been an inspiration for battle pieces composed by James Hewitt (b. Dartmoor, England, 1770; d. Boston, 1827). It is not clear whether there might have been some relationship between this work and Hewitt's lost *Overture in 9 movements, expressive of a battle* which he and his ensemble of four more chamber players performed in their first concert in New York, where they arrived from England in September 1792. [14] The program for that performance includes a *Flute Quartetto* by Stamitz, without further identification of the composer or the particular work.

Hewitt's second martial composition was *The Battle of Trenton* for piano solo, composed in 1797. A modern, abridged version is available; it has been recorded in an arrangement for organ, and there is also an arrangement for band. [15] Imitation of bugle calls and drums, along with a patriotic tune – in Hewitt's work, *Yankee Doodle* – and references to revolutionary figures and places were naturally in harmony with the spirit of the times. Hewitt's piece apparently did not supplant Kočvara's, for it continued to be popular into the nineteenth century even after Beethoven composed his more dramatic but not less superficial *Wellington's Victory* in 1813. It is interesting to contemplate what significance *The Battle of Prague* may have had soon after the American Revolution.

A romantic figure of the first half of the nineteenth century was Anthony Philip Heinrich, who was born in Krásný Buk, near Děčín, on March 11, 1781, and died in great poverty in New York on May 3, 1861. [16] William Treat Upton's comprehensive biography, *Anthony Philip Heinrich,* [17] was Jan Löwenbach's source for his essay "Americký Beethoven" in his book *Hudba v Americe* [Music in America]. [18] Löwenbach considers Heinrich to be a loyal Czech and a good patriot and says that the Germans appropriated him and other composers born in German-speaking border regions of Bohemia. Löwenbach provide additional information about Heinrich's 1857 visit in Prague and the success of his works there. Löwenbach was also able to identify the author of a review of Heinrich's concert at Žofín. At that time, the cipher "Z" was used by Josef Leopold Zvonař (1824-1865). Upton reprinted this review, calling it the best evaluation of Heinrich's art. Zvonař wrote that Heinrich, "our worthy countryman," composed what became known as programmatic music; and that he was "so absolutely untouched by any fundamental art culture as is obtained through the study of theory and musical literature, but forced to rely solely upon his own exceedingly sensitive and innately expressive spirit ... Then, too, there are moments showing a well-

pressive spirit ... Then, too, there are moments showing a well-disciplined, consistent, logically correct musical diction, and a carefully worked out and originally conceived instrumentation ... " [19]

This trip to Prague took place when Heinrich was an elderly man. At first, he was a banker and businessman with musical aspirations, and music became his career only after a bankruptcy in the 1810s. He was often called the "Beethoven of America." He visited America for the first time in 1805 and returned in 1810. In 1820, Heinrich published a music collection *The Dawning of Music in Kentucky or the Pleasures of Harmony in the Solitudes of Nature*, and a complement to it, *The Western Minstrel*. Two volumes of *The Sylviad, or Minstrelsy of Nature in he Wilds of North America* followed between 1823 and 1826. After writing such songs as *Hail to Kentucky*, Heinrich declared himself an American "log-house composer." He also composed a considerable amount of chamber music and large orchestral works which remained in manuscript and may not have been performed during his years in America.

Heinrich was able to absorb local color; for example, he used elements of American Indian music, and often quoted American patriotic songs. He had a good sense of humor and the courage to seek special harmonic and orchestral effects. He wrote a *Monumental Symphony - To the Spirit of Beethoven - written for a grand orchestra. An Echo from America to the inauguration of the Monument at Bonn*, which was scheduled for the concert on May 5, 1846 at the Broadway Tabernacle in New York, but could not be performed because the large orchestra which the work required was not available. [20] Heinrich liked such long, descriptive titles for his musical works. His predilection for very large orchestras which are difficult to find and conduct is like Berlioz's – and both encountered problems in presenting such works.

A Heinrich benefit took place in the Tremont Temple, Boston on June 13, 1846. His *Tecumseh, or the Battle of the Thames - A martial Overture - for full Orchestra* and *Ouverture To The Pilgrims -Full orchestra, with Trumpet obligato* were played. Heinrich commented on the performance in a letter to a friend in Boston: "The musicians of Boston have in their zeal and refined accomplishment nearly chopped off my head ... Upon the imperfect, nay slovenly, confused execution of my orchestral works in Boston, I cannot accept any criticism or forecast of judgment on my musical ways -- in common justice beyond that miserable fact of instrumental bankruptcy with which I was cruelly served by many delinquent performers ..." In spite of the composer's unhappiness about the concert, "critical acclaim was again unanimous." [21]

Such compositions were inspired by his admiration of American Indians and by his patriotism related to the United States. Some of his imaginative, "most American" titles are *The Columbiad, Grand American National Chivalrous Symphony, Yankee Doodliad, Indian Carnival, The Mastodon, Manitou Mysteries* Although he wrote nostalgic music about Bohemia, he also paid tribute by his music to the Austrian Emperor, Queen Victoria - and even to *The Condor of the Andes and the Eagle of the Cordilleras* in his striking *Ornithological Combat of Kings* (Grand Symphony). No wonder his contemporaries sometimes found "Father Heinrich" somewhat eccentric and too modern.

The *Ornithological Combat* has been recorded [22] as well as a selection of songs and piano pieces from his *The Dawning of Music in Kentucky.* [23] Such original creations as *Barbecue Divertimento* for piano or *Epitaph of Joan Buff*, a lady who sneezed herself to death after taking snuff, are proof of his daring originality and are worth a hearing.

Dissertations on Heinrich's music were written during the 1970's at the University of Illinois and Indiana University. [24] At the beginning of the Bicentennial year his orchestral work *The War of the Elements and the Thundering of Niagara Capriccio Grande* was performed as *The Mighty Niagara* by the Buffalo Philharmonic Orchestra conducted by Michael Tilson Thomas, with favorable popular and critical success. [25] A symposium on Heinrich was part of the Bicentennial Conference of the Sonneck Society, "Two Centuries of Music in America," which took place on May 28-30, 1976, at Queensborough Community College, New York. The contributions of "Father Heinrich" to American music have been recognized: "Heinrich was merely one hundred years ahead of his time." [26]

The aftermath of the 1848 revolution in Austria-Hungary motivated the emigration of Balatka, Maretzek, and Strakosch. Hans Balatka was born on February 26, 1825, in Bouzov-Doly near Olomouc. [27] He studied music under Prosch, Sechter and others in Vienna. His participation in the 1848 revolution forced his emigration to America in 1849. He reportedly was in close contact with Vojta Náprstek in Milwaukee. He founded the Milwaukee *Musikverein* in 1851; in 1860 he became conductor of the Chicago Philharmonic Society and soon afterwards of another choral society, the Music Union. He conducted symphony concerts, introducing, for example, Beethoven's and Schubert's symphonies. He, gave concert tours with the Viennese soprano Eugenie Pappenheim (b. 1849; d. Los Angeles, 1924) and directed the Germania *Männerchor*. In Chicago he founded the Liederkranz and the Mozart Club and was conductor of the Symphony Society. His compositions *The Power of Song* for double chorus, the *Festival Cantata* for soprano and orchestra, and other choruses were performed. *ČSHS* identifies him as a Czech choirmaster. *Baker's 6* states that he played an important role in bringing German musical culture to the American Midwest.

Two very energetic and competent Moravians arrived in the United States in 1848: Max Maretzek or, in Czech spelling Mareček, and Maurice Strakosch. [28] Both became operatic impresarios -- and for some time worked together – and also conducted, composed, and were otherwise active in music. Maretzek, born in Brno on June 28, 1821, remained in America until his death in New York on May 14, 1897. Strakosch, born in 1825, returned to Europe and died in Paris on October 9, 1887. Both left autobiographical memoirs, in English and in French respectively, which are well worth reading for many details about the difficult conditions under which opera was established in the United States, and also in Mexico and Cuba.

Maretzek's opera *Hamlet*, written when he was nineteen, was performed in Brno on November 14, 1840. He made contact with Berlioz, Meyerbeer, Chopin and others during his sojourn in Paris, and met several English musicians - for example, Balfe - in London, where he temporarily resided before he crossed to the United States. His first U.S. engagement as manager and conductor was with the company at the Astor Place Opera House in New York, which was quite a large theater with a capacity of 1,800 seats. He describes his first seasons in the book *Crotchets and Quavers or Revelations of an Opera Manager in America* [29] The preface for the reprint was written by Jan Popper, professor emeritus of music at the University of California and director of the Opera Workshops in Los Angeles and Austin, Texas. Popper was a knowledgeable and dedicated promoter of Czech music in America, producing operas by Janáček, Kurka and others.

Maretzek wrote these reminiscences as a series of seven letters to his European friends with dates from July 5 to September 27, 1855, and adding "My Postscript to the Public" dated October 5 of the same year. He describes different aspects of his life and work to each one of the addressees: Berlioz and Fiorentino in Paris; L. Lablache, M. W. Balfe and Frederick Gye, Esq., in London; Professor Joseph Fischof and Carl Eckert in Vienna. In his introduction, he rejects the title "Napoleon of the Opera" and declares himself proudly as the "Don Quixote of the Opera," [30] a man who believes in this artistic form and valiantly struggles to make it available to all people, not only to the rich subscribers, even if it means that he may end his life in debt. [31] According to Jan Popper, Maretzek's battle cry was "Opera for the people, not only for the Upper Tendom." [32] His descriptions of temperamental Italian singers, an unfriendly press, adventures on a dangerous but financially successful Mexican tour, his description of his childhood - his parents allowed him to follow his musical inclinations only after he ran away from his first session in a dissecting room and refused to become a doctor or a lawyer - and many more interesting stories are amusing and informative. Maretzek described his later triumphs in his second memoir, *Sharps and Flats*, published in New York in 1890.

When Maretzek discovered Adelina Patti (1843-1919), she was a child in his neighborhood. He presented her in concert at the age of seven in New York. Strakosch married Patti's sister Amalia and managed some of Adelina's tours. In 1860, Strakosch let Maretzek wait in vain in Mexico City for Adelina; she was supposed to have sung principal roles in Maretzek's opera season. Milton Goldin writes: "Stranded in Mexico City without a prima donna, Maretzek devised a solution to his problem unique in the history of music. The impresario made roller skating popular. The skating scene in his production of Meyerbeer's *Le Prophète* was a sensation. "The Gran Teatro Nacional," writes Maretzek, "became a well-paying skating hall with a performance thrown in as an added entertainment for the same price of admission." [33] The career of an impresario was obviously not an easy one.

Another of Maretzek's discoveries was the American soprano Minnie Hauk (1852-1929), who made her debut at the age of 14 in his company, and created the role of Juliette in Gounod's opera *Romeo and Juliette* under his baton in November 1867. This performance took place at the New York Academy of Music, which was the most important opera house before the Metropolitan Opera was established. Maretzek and Strakosch were both associated with the Academy of Music, which was a theater inaugurated by Maretzek in 1854 with *Norma,* featuring Grisi and Mario. Among the operas which Maretzek introduced to America were works by Meyerbeer and early Verdi. He composed an opera, *Sleepy Hollow or The Headless Horseman* which was inspired by Washington Irving's legend; it was performed in New York on September 25, 1879. He gradually came to be known as "Maretzek the Magnificent." On February 12, 1889 the Metropolitan Opera staged a Golden Jubilee Gala benefit to commemorate Maretzek's 50th anniversary as an operatic conductor. One of the speakers said: "The year 1848 will forever go down in the history of this country as the glorious year in which the war with Mexico was concluded, gold was discovered in California, and Max Maretzek arrived in New York."

Strakosch was active as a composer, impresario, teacher and pianist as well as a conductor. He wrote two operas which were produced in New York: *Giovanni di Napoli* and *Sardanapalus.* The famous American pianist-composer Louis Moreau Gottschalk (1829-1869) was under his management for four years. His *Souvenirs d'un impresario* was published in 1887 and his *Ten Commandments of Music for the Perfection of the Voice* appeared posthumously in 1896.

The remarkable efforts of Maretzek and Strakosch to establish continuing opera seasons of high quality in New York and to perform their productions on tour have been recognized as a significant achievement in the history of operatic music in America.

Four more musicians will be briefly introduced here who are not mentioned in Löwenbach's article. Each contributed in a special way to the development of music in the United States.

Alois Reiser was born in Prague on April 6, 1884, and died in Hollywood, California on April 4, 1977. He studied violoncello at the Prague Conservatory of Music and was a member of several chamber music ensembles and of the Czech Philharmonic. He is said to have been a composition student of Dvořák, but so far this statement has not been verified in primary sources. He toured U.S.A from 1904 to 1906, returned to Prague and emigrated permanently to America in 1914. His *Quartet in E minor (*1916) won second prize in the first Berkshire Festival of Chamber Music at Pittsfield, Massachusetts; this festival was organized by Mrs. Elizabeth Sprague Coolidge and inaugurated in 1918. This quartet was later heard in Prague in 1927 during a chamber music tour sponsored by Mrs. Coolidge. He won the NBC Prize for his *String Quartet in C major* and several of his orchestral works were performed throughout this country and in Prague. His *From Mount Rainier* premiered in Philadelphia (1926); *Slavic Rhapsody* (1931), *Violoncello Concerto* (1933) and *Erewhon* (1936) were performed in Los Angeles. He conducted his own. Compositions. The *Violoncello Concerto* won second prize in the Hollywood Bowl competition. His early opera *Gobi* was performed in New York in 1923. Alois Reiser was a Czech-American musician who achieved a respectable stature in this country during his lifetime. [34]

Henry Holden Huss (b. Newark, New Jersey, June 21, 1862; d. New York, September 17, 1953 studied with his father and then in Munich with Rheinberger. He had a very active career as a concert pianist and gave joint recitals with his wife, soprano Hildegard Hoffmann. He lectured at Hunter College in New York, taught piano and music theory, and wrote many compositions for orchestra, chorus, chamber ensembles and piano. He received a prize from the National Federation of Music Clubs for his *Quartet in b minor* (1918), and an award from the Society for the Publication of American Music. [35] Howard describes him as "a composer of the elder contemporary group who wrote music of considerable charm in the romantic mold, even though he seemed to lack enough of the power of self-criticism to give his works endurance." [36]

Robert Dolejší was born in Chicago on June 7, 1892. He studied at the Vienna Academy of Music with Otakar Ševčík. From 1915 to 1917 he was the director of the Birmingham conservatory, and served in the United States Navy from 1917 to 1919. After the war, he lived in Chicago, playing viola in a quartet, teaching violin, viola and viola d'amore and giving recitals on the viola d'amore. He also wrote reviews and articles on music, some of which appeared in *Musical America*. The only biographical dictionary with an entry on Dolejší is *ČSHS*. His *Modern Viola Technique* (1939) is mentioned in the *Harvard Dictionary of Music*. [37]

Another American-born composer who spoke and read Czech was Robert Kurka, whose early death "brought to a close a career that showed great promise, even though the young man's talent had not yet reached its full development." [38] He was born in Cicero, Illinois on December 22, 1921 and died in New York on December 12, 1957 at the age of 36. He studied at Columbia University and at the Berkshire Music Center. Darius Milhaud and Otto Luening were among his teachers. He received a Guggenheim fellowship grant in 1951. The *Suite for Wind Orchestra* from his opera *The Good Soldier Schweik* was performed in New York as early as 1952, but the opera was premiered posthumously in 1958 by the New York Opera Company at City Center. Other successful premieres of his major works followed: *Second Symphony* in New York, 1959; Concerto for *Marimba and Orchestra* in 1959, performed by the Orchestra of America; and the *Ballad for French Horn and Strings* in 1961, performed in Fort Wayne, Indiana. His opera *Švejk* was performed in a Czech translation in Plzeň, Czechoslovakia, in 1960. The suite from this opera and his *Concerto for Marimba* have been recorded. He has a brief entry in *ČSHS*.

Many more important composers, conductors, performers and musicologists who were born in the territory of modern Czechoslovakia or are American-born and of at least partial Czech or Slovak descent. have been active on the North American continent. Many appear in the sixth edition of *Baker's Dictionary*. Some died in this country; others are alive and well, contributing to the current musical life. In alphabetical order, they are: Karel Ančerl, Rudolf Berger, Emmy Destinn, Rudolf Firkušný, Rudolf Friml, Karel Husa, Marie Jeritza, Karel Boleslav Jirak, Victor Kolar, Ernst Křenek, Rafael Kubelík, Gail Kubík, Pavel Ludikar, Oskar Morawetz, Václav Nelhýbel, Paul Nettl, Jarmila Novotná, Emanuel Ondříček, Paul Reif, Feri Roth, George Schick, Ernestine Schumann-Heink, Rudolf Serkin, Paul Stefan, Josef Stránský, Walter Süsskind, Tomáš Svoboda, Henry Swoboda, Arnold Walter, Hugo Weisgall and Charles Wels.

Notes

This article is an expanded version of a paper read at the Eighth Congress of the Czechoslovak Society of Arts and Sciences, Inc., Washington, D.C., August 1976. The theme of this Bicentennial Congress was "The Contribution of Czechs and Slovaks to North America."

Editor's note: Dr. Fischmann compared data from the following biographical dictionaries when gathering information for this paper: *Československý hudebni slovnik osob a institucí* [Czechoslovak Music Dictionary of Persons and Institutions], 2 vols. (Prague: Státní hudebni vydavatelství, 1963-65), abbreviated here as *ČSHS*. *Baker's Biographical Dictionary of Musicians*, 5th ed., 1958; Supplement, 1965, abbreviated as *Baker's 5*; 6th edition, 1978, abbreviated as *Baker's 6*; 7th edition, 1984, abbreviated as *Baker's 7*. *The International Cyclopedia of Music and Musicians*. Edited by Oscar Thompson (1887-1945), 5th edition, 1949, abbreviated here as *Cyclopedia 5*; 9th edition, abbreviated here as Cyclopedia 9; 10th ed., 1975, abbreviated here as *Cyclopedia 10*. *Grove's Dictionary of Music and Musicians*, 5th edition, 1954, abbreviated here as *Grove's 5*. *The New Grove Dictionary of Music and Musicians*, 1st edition, 1980, abbreviated here as *New Grove*. These were the biographical dictionaries which were readily available when the paper was written. Her comparison of these sources is, in part, an assessment of their usefulness and reliability for providing basic information about Czech and Slovak music – a task which she pursued with viligance for many years.

1)   Jan Löwenbach, "Czechoslovak Composers and Musicians in America," *Musical Quarterly* 29 (July 1943), pp. 313-328.

2)   *Czechoslovakia Past and Present*, ed. Miloslav Rechcígl, Jr., (The Hague: Mouton, 1968), vol. 2, pp. 1362-1375.

3)   Karel Boleslav Jirák, "Czechoslovak Music in American Music Literature."

4)   Gilbert Chase, *America's Music. From the Pilgrim to the Present*. Revised second edition (New York: McGraw-Hill, 1966), p. 61.

5)   *Six Solos For a Violin and Bass* was printed in London circa 1750. The Smithsonian Collection recording project was a program of the Smithsonian's Office of Public Service, Julian Euell, Assistant Secretary.

6)   I. Lowens, "Other Composers' Plans to Come to the U.S." *High Fidelity Magazine*, December 1975, p. 73.

7)   G. Sonneck, *Early Opera in America* (Reprint ed., New York: Benjamin Blom, 1963), p. 139.

8)   I. Lowens, "Music in 1776. A Dearth of Diversion, an End to Entertainment?" *High Fidelity Magazine*, July 1976, p. 47.

9)   Sonneck, pp. 73-74.

10) Krammer has only a sixteen-line entry in *ČSHS*. *Cyclopedia* has given him a five-line entry in editions since 1949. He does not appear in *Grove's 5* or in *Baker's*.

11)   Sonneck, pp. 197 and 201.

12)   Sonneck, p. 162.

13)   Chase, p.120.

14)   I. Lowens. *Music and Musicians in Early America* (New York: W.W. Norton & Co., 1964), p. 198.

15)   *Organ in America*, Col. MS-6161. E. Power Biggs. *Broad Stripes / Bright Stars*, Dept. of Defense Bicentennial Edition, 50-1776.

16)   Heinrich's nationality has been variously described. *Grove's 5* calls him "an American violinist and composer of German-Bohemian birth," while Thompson's *Cyclopedia* has kept the indication of "Czech-American violinist and composer" through several editions. *ČSHS* describes him as a Czech composer in America and lists compositions in a Czech patriotic vein, such as the *Prague Waltz*, *The Fair Bohemian*, and especially *Mým slovanským bratrům v Evropě* [To our Slavic brethren in Europe], a four movement piano elegy on the death of Josef Jungmann (1773-1847). The Czech title is Heinrich's, as well as the English subtitle *To My Sclavonian* [sic] *Brethren in Europe*. *New Grove* was the first biographical dictionary to list these works. It describes him as an American composer of German-Bohemian birth, and gives him a three-page entry. However, the work list take up almost two of the three pages.

17)   W. T. Upton, *Anthony Philip Heinrich: a Nineteenth-Century Composer in America* (New York: Columbia University Press, 1939; reprint ed., 1967).

18)   J. Löwenbach, *Hudba v Americe* [Music in America], (Prague: Hudební Matice, 1948). The full title of his essay (pp. 71-88) is "Americký Beethoven, Dobrodružný život českého emigranta Antonína Filipa Heinricha (1781-1861)" [American Beethoven. The Adventurous Life of the Czech Immigrant Antonín Filip Heinrich (1781-1861)]. Löwenbach mentions numerous manuscripts which Heinrich donated to the Prague Museum and adds: "Perhaps, one day, someone will discover them ..." (p. 87).

19)   J. T. Howard, *Our American Music*, 4th ed. (New York: Thomas Y. Crowell Co., 1965), p. 236. Zvonař does not appear in *Cyclopedia 10*.

20)   Lowens provides program notes for the "Monumental Symphony" in *Music and Musicians*, pp. 205-206.

21)   Ibid., pp. 207-210.

22)   New World Records. *Recorded Anthology of American Music*, NW 208, 1978. Syracuse Symphony Orchestra, Christopher Keene, conductor.

23)   Vanguard Everyman Classics, SRV.349 SD, 1975. The American Music Group, Neely Bruce, director and piano solo.

24)   These dissertations were: D.M. Barron, *The Early Vocal Works of Anthony Philip Heinrich* (University of Illinois, 1972); L.H. Filbeck, *The Choral Works of Anthony Philip Heinrich* (University of Illinois, 1973); *The Symphonies of Anthony Philip Heinrich. Based on American Themes* (Indiana University, 1973).

25)   Review by H. T., "Buffalo Phil: Heinrich premiere." In *Musical America*, May 1976, p. 24. *Baker's 6* does not mention this work, but cites a New York performance of the *Gran Sinfonia Misteriosa-Indiana* on December 2, 1975.

26)   Vanguard Everyman Classics. Notes by Neely Bruce.

27)   *Thompson's Cyclopedia*, up to the 10th edition, indicates March 5, 1827, as his birth date and identifies him as an "Austrian conductor and composer."

28)   Neither is listed in the first edition of The New Grove, 1980 ed., but Maretzek appears in The New Grove Dictionary of American Music, 1986 ed., 3: 174. Strakosch is listed in Cyclopedia 5, p. 1808; Cyclopedia 10, p. 2167; and Baker's 7, p. 2222. The dictionaries do not agree whether the protagonist of Strakosch's opera was Giovanni or Giovanna -- di Napoli.

29)   Max Maretzek. Crotchets and Quavers, (New York: Da Capo Press, 1966), reprinted from the original edition published by S. French in New York in 1855. This reprint edi-

tion includes Sharps and Flats (first printed New York, 1890). The date of the original edition of Crotchets and Quavers is erroneously given as 1885 in Cyclopedia 5, in ČSHS and other reference works; Baker's gives the correct date.

30)   Maretzek, *Crotchets*, pp. 57 and 335.

31)   Ibid., Preface, p. viii.

32)   Milton Goldin, *The Music Merchants* (London: Macmillan Publishers, 1969), p. 54.

33)   Maretzek, *Crotchets*, Preface, p. v.

34)   *Baker's 7. Cyclopedia 10* gives 1905 for his arrival in New York. *ČSHS* has a short entry. He is not included in *New Grove.*

35)   Huss is identified by *Baker's 6* as a descendant of Leonhard Huss, brother of the religious reformer and martyr Jan Hus. The article gives additional details about his ancestry. *ČSHS* ignores him completely, although it contains a lengthy entry on Jan Hus. *New Grove's* provides an eleven-line entry with a short list of selected works, but does not mention his relationship to Jan Hus.

36)   Howard, p. 359.

37)   *Harvard Dictionary of Music*, 2nd ed., 1969.

38)   Howard, p. 597. Kurka does not have an entry in the fifth edition of *Grove's Dictionary*. *Baker's 7* gave him a sixteen-line entry. *Cyclopedia 10* has a substantial article on him. *The New Grove*, 1980 ed., 10: 136, offers fourteen lines and a selective list of works.

A SPANISH MAESTRO WITH BOHEMIAN ROOTS
A CONTRIBUTION TO THE HISTORY OF MUSICAL EMIGRATION

The history of emigré musicians from the Czech Lands during the eighteenth century has been systematically explored by musicologists. Most of those musicians found good positions in Austria or Germany, and developed outstanding careers in exile. The migrating trend continued strong into the early nineteenth century but then seemed to subside, though some Bohemian and Moravian musicians were active in most European countries and even overseas. However, Spain remained a rather isolated and unexplored area.

Finding the name Skoczdopole [1] in connection with Spanish music naturally must catch the attention and curiosity of any Czech speaking person. That happened to me some twenty years ago when somebody brought up the name. At the time I only found a portrait of Juan Skoczdopole, conductor, and two mentions of his name in José Subirá's one volume *Historia de la música española e hispanoamericana* (Barcelona-Madrid: Salvat, 1953, p.715, 716, 725), in the chapter on *zarzuela* of the nineteenth century. Even though Subirá mentions (p. 694) his other book, *Historia y anecdotario del Teatro Real* (History and Anecdotes from the Royal Theater), that and other possible sources were not available to me - and the mysterious musician remained shelved but not forgotten.

His complete story came to my notice only in 1987, from an unexpected part af the world, Argentina, in a letter from Růžena Hořáková-Firkušný. [2] The Jičín born mezzo-soprano - soloist of the "Met of Latin America," the Teatro Colón in Buenos Aires - wrote about the Argentinian concert clarinetist, Juan Daniel Skoczdopole, whose 75th birthday and fifty years of his artistic and teaching activities had just been celebrated. And she offered more information.

The Skoczdopole story has been documented both in Spanish and Czech, but has not appeared yet in English, The Czech part of the story started in Prague. In 1954, the Prague filumenistic (matchbox) society was organizing an international exhibition. A collection of seventy-five matchbox labels that arrived from Spain caught attention of the organizers, František and Jiřina, Kodlovi. Two labels were of special interest: one had the word "Praga" over a portrait of "Julio Schulhoff, 1825;" [3] the second one had "Bohemia" superposed over a fully bearded "Skoczdopole, 1817-1877." Yet, inquiries addressed to knowledgeable music historians in Prague and the search in music dictionaries did not bring any information - until 1960.

That year the couple presented the mystery of the presumably Czech musician in Spain on their television program. They appealed to the viewers for any information and, after the answers started to come from several individuals, piecemeal at first, they published information about the Skoczdopole family in Bohemia. [4]

The musician was identified as Jan Skoczdopole, a son of the sacristan and bell-ringer Jan Skoczdopole, domiciled at Svatá Hora, near Příbram. He was sent to Prague to study music at the Conservatory, where Josef Slavík (1806-1833), the violin virtuoso, was among his teachers. He was doing very well but then, suddenly, he disappeared ... Dionys Weber (1766-1842), director of the Conservatory, wrote to the father that young Jan was chosen to substitute for an ill bandmaster of the touring Rienzi Circus. And there was Carmen, the beautiful equestrienne. In brief, Jan travelled with the circus all over Europe and ended in Madrid. By that time Carmen abandoned him and he was getting "tired of Gypsy life," as he later told his brother when he eventually contacted and visited his family back in Bohemia.

In Madrid, Jan became Juan Daniel Skoczdopole, keeping the original spelling of his name. He opened a music school, was appointed conductor of the Teatro del Circo (to 1848), Teatro del Museo (1848-1851) and Teatro Real (1851-65 and 1870-77), conducted many zarzuelas and operas, and composed a number of works very Spanish in style and spirit. He had a splendid artistic and social career. Among his private music pupils was the future wife of the French Emperor Napoleon III, Eugenia de Guzmán, Duchess de Tabas y Montijo, and her sister María Francisca, Duchess de Alba. The Spanish royal family favored him and awarded him some special privileges. One of his sons, José Skoczdopole (1843-1923) moved to Buenos Aires. The clarinetist Skoczdopole is José's grandson and the Madrid-Juan's great-grandson.

The original Jan Skoczdopole died in Madrid, on March 12, 1877. That date is certain. For his date of birth, however, the years 1811 and 1817 are given. According to the material from Czechoslovakia, gathered *in loco*, Jan Skoczdopole was born on December 28, 1811, and it is documented that that person later went to Madrid. Yet the Spanish sources consistently say he was born in 1817. [5)]

A doubt also exists about his marriage, for some of his known biographical data appear to have come from his oral statements that were later perpetuated in print or by his family. He did visit Příbram in 1860 and spoke with one of his brothers, his father having died earlier. At the time, he allegedly said that he married Manuela, a daughter of a royal official in Madrid and had two sons, both musically talented. The Spanish sources, including his obituary, speak about his wife Dona Eulalia Larsonneur who survived him and died in 1887. Six Skoczdopole children are known by their first names, three daughters and three sons. Maestro Skoczdopole may have been married twice but the details are not clear.

Some uncertainty concerns his exact arrival in Madrid but early 1840s seem most probable. His appointment as an established composer and conductor at the Teatro del Circo in 1845 is documented. After his pupil Eugenia became the French Empress in 1853, there may have been some plans of moving Maestro Skoczdopole to Tournay, Belgium. However, they did not materialize as is documented in Madrid in the 1850s. Except for conducting operas at the Théâtre Italien in Paris between 1865 and 1867, he remained active in Madrid.

As mentioned above, he visited Bohemia and also corresponded with his brothers. Genealogical research [6] in Czechoslovakia has uncovered quite a lot of information about the musical Skoczdopale family of Příbram. One brother, Josef (b. 1832, d. Prague, 1883) had a military career which led to Vienna and Trieste. There, in 1877, he was commander of the College for noncommissioned officers until his retirement two years later, after which he went to Prague. Another brother, Jiří (b. 1819, d. ?) remained in Příbram and directed the choir at the Jakub Church. František (1823-1907) canducted the miners' band in the same town and it was he with whom Juan Daniel from Madrid had most contact.

At least one letter each by František (1865) and Josef (1873) have been found. František in his letter expressed the desire to visit his famous brother in Paris. Josef asked even for a small monetary contribution "to buy a horse," needed for his current military position. Both letters appeal to and dwell upon their brother's successes abroad.

Juan Daniel Skoczdopole's professional career is documented in detail in Spanish musicological literature. He has been recognized as a significant conductor and composer. As conductor he was especially praised for his steady tempi and exact beat, described by Becquer thus: "The movement of that arm has the mechanical precision of a steam engine." This seems to tally with his earlier conducting experiences in providing musical support to the diverse acts of the Rienzi Circus. The thought of the band accompaniment to the aeralists' jumps, the tension underlying the moments of a "salto mortale," or the coordination of music: with the equestrian drills and other acts evokes an image of a very disciplined conductor. He must have developed quite a routine in which the timing and precision were the first concerns. Moreover, he is reported in the Spanish document as conducting festive dances and ballets, accompanying singers on piano in one specific concert (November 1844), and conducting several orchestral overtures from currently popular operas as well. This activity demonstrates his versatility and implies musical flexibility.

Juan Skoczdopole reportedly was able to play trumpet, violin, piano, cello, bass, flute and oboe. Such familiarity with many instruments came in very handy in 1849 when the premiere of Verdi's early opera *I Masnadieri* was scheduled for the Teatro del Museo, but a full orchestral score was not available. Skoezdopole arranged a viable orchestration from the vocal score (voice and piano) and conducted the work. When the Teatro Real was inaugurated in 1850, Maestro Skoczdopole conducted, among many other works, Verdi's *Rigoletto*, *Il Trovatore* and *Aida*; Arrieta's *Marina*, Mozart's *Don Giovanni*, Haydn's *Creation* and the first production in Spain of a Wagner opera. This first performance of *Rienzi* on February 2, 1876 is still considered a milestone in Spanish operatic history. It is a strange coincidence that this opera's title corresponds to the name of the Rienzi Circus.

Juan Daniel Skoczdopole also gained recognition as a composer. His arrival in Madrid coincided with the second revival and flourishing of the Spanish *zarzuela*. This special lyric form for the theater started in the seventeenth century as a type of comic opera, alternating singing with spoken dialogues. It eventually developed into the *zarzuela grande* in three acts which could be considered the Spanish national opera. [8] Skoczdopole knew the most outstanding composers in this genre whose zarzuelas he conducted and worked with the most popular singers who acted in them. He also took sides in the frequent rivalries between established composers and talented newcomers. Among them were the young Ruperto Chapí (1851-1909; *La hija de Jefte*), Miguel Hilarión Eslava (1807-1878), Emilio Arrieta (1823-1894; *Marina*), Francisco Asenjo Barbieri (1823-1894; *Pan y toros*) and others. The composer Cristóbal Oudrid was Skoczdopole's colleague as a conductor at the Teatro Real. Both died in March 1877 on consecutive days. This fact is repeated in several sources as a great loss for the Spanish theater music.

In 1858, Skoczdopole's lyric composition *Los majos en el rocío* [9] and his songs *La naranjera* and *¿Quién me verá a mí?* were premiered by principal singers of the Teatro Real. Other songs which he composed to Manuel de Palacio's lyrics were *La cigarrera*, *La florera del teatro*, *La abaniquera* and others. The songs and some of his dance music appeared in print.

One of his sets of dances for piano is entitled *Escala de amor* (Ascent of Love). Each dance has a subtitle: *Primera miradá* (first look), followed by *Billete expressivo* (Billet doux) and other steps, culminating in the lovers' *Felicidad* (Happiness). Skoczdopole used rigaudons, redowas, schottishes, waltzes, different types of polka, habaneras and other then popular social dances.

Another composition of this type was titled *Album astronómico* (Astronomie Album) in which Jupiter was represented by a set of waltzes, Vesta by a polka, Ceres by a polka-mazurka, Saturn by a schottisch, Venus by a habanera, Mars by *los lanceros*, La luna (Moon) by a redowa and Juno by the Virginia reel. Among his 19th century salon dances also belongs the early *Gran Wals* which was successfully premiered in the Teatro del Circo and was composed in the emerging Viennese waltz style.

Only the habaneras represent Spanish music in these suites of fashionable dances However, Skoczdopole was able to compose flamencos which were accepted as authentic by his Spanish born colleagues and critics. His best-known compositions in this genre are *Jaleo de Jérez,* [10] which is still performed, and the Andalusian *El Holé*. His adaptation to Spanish music could have been eased by familiarity with the Central European Gypsy music and its exciting, free, improvisatory character. After all, flamenco music is rooted in the typical rhythms, melodies, dances, and songs of the Iberian gitanería (collective term for the Gypsies) in combination with Andalusian folklore.

Juan Daniel Skoczdopole was characterized as a "most meritorious" musician who assiduously improved the technical functioning of the lyric theaters, promoted all genres of operatic repertory, and maintained high standards for the singers and actors with whom he worked. He was a serious and conscientious man, a good manager, dedicated to serving the Muses. One of his obituarists, Fernandez Brenson, called him the "Maestro de hierro," the master with iron constitution, who never missed a performance or rehearsal during his many years in Madrid theaters.

To commemorate the 100th anniversary of Skoczdopole's death, the Argentinian musicologist and critic Juan Pedro Franze compiled a study "Juan Daniel Skoczdopole, músico de España" (J.D.S., A Musician of Spain) in 1977. He had access to documents that the Buenos Aires clarinetist Skoczdopole had collected for many years, which included the compositions mentioned in the Spanish literature

The career of the Madrid Maestro's Argentinian great-grandson does honor to the family name. Juan Daniel Skoczdopole has played in the La Plata and Buenos Aires theater orchestras and in the Teatro Colon as a solo clarinetist since the 1930's. He has performed with various chamber music ensembles, taught at the Manuel de Falla Municipal Conservatory and the Superior Art Institute of Columbus (Colón) Theater, and has given clarinet recitals. Among his memorable experiences have been performances conducted by Arturo Toscanini and concert tours to Madrid, Paris, Rome, Washington D.C., and New York. In 1983 he taught master classes at the School of Music, University of Tokyo, Japan.

When the late Czech conductor Václav Smetáček had an guest engagement at the Teatro Colón in 1968, he met Señor Skoczdopole. The latter later visited Prague, and the Smetáčeks drove him to Příbram to see all the places where the history of his musical family had begun.

Special thanks go to Mrs. Růžena Hořáková-Firkušný and Maestro Juan Daniel Skoczdopole from Buenos Aires for the material they sent and the encouragement to present in English this "almost detective story" of the Spanish musician with Bohemian roots or another - Czech musician who did well abroad.

Notes

1) Skoczdopole, or in the modern spelling Skočdopole, literally means "Jump-in-the-Field," and is rather unusual. However, it can easily be identified as a Czech family name having to do with a rural environment.

2) Růžena Bendáková is the widow of the prematurely deceased musicologist and Janáček scholar Leoš Firkušný, older brother of the pianist Rudolf Firkušný. Leoš was born in 1905 and died on July 9, 1950, about a year after he and his wife settled in Buenos Aires. Ms. Firkušný was well known in Czechoslovakia under her name of Hořáková (her first husband's name). She concertized extensively in Argentina, introducing works from the Czech and other modern vocal repertories in her recitals. She sang many roles at the Teatro Colón, particularly in the Latin American premieres of *Jenůfa (*1950, 1963) and *Katya Kabanová* (1968).

3) Julius Schulhoff (b. Prague, 1825; d. Berlin, 1899) was a pianist and composer, Tomášek's pupil, living mostly in Paris, Dresden and Berlin. He was the great-uncle of pianist and composer Ervín Schulhoff (1894-1942), who perished in a Nazi concentration camp.

4) Kodlovi, František and Jiřina, "Případ Skočdopole - Historie téměř detektivní" [The Skoczdolopole Case - Almost a Detective Story] *Filumenistický magazín*, p. 92-101 (Tisková ediční a propagační služba místního hospodářství, Praha 1964)

5) It is not clear to me how this difference in dating could be resolved. It does not seem probable that Skoczdopole would lie about his age. Could there have been two sons born in Bohemia six years apart, both named Jan after their father? If so, the older one would have died in childhood, or the other baby would not have inherited the name - as often when many children were born and only a few survived. We simply do not know. All Spanish references give this date, which would make him 60 years old at the time of his sudden death.

6) The existence of the Argentinian Juan Daniel apparently came to light when the Czech Nonet toured Buenos Aires in 1961. The flutist Václav Žilka wrote an article for *Lidová demokracie* after his return, stating that the only Czech family name he found among the orchestra members of the Teatro Colón was Juan Dl. [Daniel] Skoczdopole and wondered who this "Honza Skočdopole" might be. This led to inquiries by Jindřich V. Bezděka, a genealogist from Příbram. Contact was made and there was correspondence between Argentina and Czechoslovakia. Their communication was facilitated by members of the small Buenos Aires Czech colony who translated the letters from Czech to Spanish and Spanish to Czech.

7) "The famous professor" Liszt seems to have participated in this concert, playing several fantasies on operatic tunes and a Hungarian Melody (Subirá, *History of Music*).

8) The word *zarzuela* is derived from *zarza* (bramble, ostružiník). The *Zarzuela grande* had three acts and sometimes was embellished by changing the spoken dialogue into operatic recitatives. Zarzuelas were similar to comic opera, but large-scale ones might utilize more dramatic, even tragic libretti, reflecting developments elsewhere. The *zarzuelita*, also called *género chico* (the "small" genre) had one act. These works were performed as comic intermezzos or short operettas. Both types of *zarzuela* were performed in Skoczdopole's theaters.

9) The titles of Skoczdopole's compositions can be translated as follows:

Los majos en el rocío - The *majos* in the Dew. The word *majo, maja* has no direct equivalent in English; "flashy young men and women" or "idlers" are the descriptive terms in the Spanish-English dictionaries. Goya painted them, Granadós immortalized them in his music later, and Skoczdopole dedicated his lyric theater work to them.

La naranjera - a female selling oranges; the song was dedicated to the prima donna Marietta Gazzaniga of the Teatro Real who saved the autograph for posterity.

¿Quién me verá a mi? - Who will see me?

La cigarrera - a female selling or making cigars and cigarettes, perhaps in a tobacco factory.

La, florera del teatro - a female seller of flowers in the theater.

La abaniquera - a female making and selling fans.

These songs seem to have been individualized portraits of and tributes to typical Spanish characters seen by Skoczdopole in Madrid and elsewhere in Spain.

10) The Andalusian town and port of Jérez has been one of the important centers of the authentic "cante hondot" (deep song) in the past and today. A chair in flamenco studies was established there in the mid-1900s. Gypsy, Spanish and Moorish elements contribute to the richness of flamenco.

Jaleo is a flamenco dance. It derives from the verb *jalear*, to stimulate the dancers and singers by hand clapping and various encouraging shouts. "El Holé" (Olé!) is another Andalusian song / dance.

References

Diccionario Enciclopédico Espasa-Calpe.

Diccionario de la música Labor, H. Anglés and J. Pena, eds. (Barcelona: Editorial Labor, 1954)

Bécquer, Gustavo Adolfo, "Ensayos y esbozos."

Franze, Juan Pedro, "Juan Daniel Skoczdopole, músico de España."

Molina, Ricardo, *Cante flamenco* (Madrid: Taurus, 1965)

Subirá P., José: *Historia de la música* (Barcelona, 1946; 2 volumes)
Historia y anecdotario del Teatro Real (Madrid: Edición Plus Ultra, 1949)
Historia de la música teatral en España (Barcelona; 1946) .
Historia de la música española e hispanoamericana (Barcelona-Madrid: Salvat, 1953)

VÁCLAV JAN KŘTITEL TOMÁŠEK'S POETIC PIANO PIECES

This paper discusses only certain aspects of a composer who has been identified as an important forerunner of the Czech national school of music. We shall focus on Tomášek's life-long interest in piano playing and his internationally recognized contribution to the piano music literature in the form of characteristic or poetic pieces which had chronologically proceeded Schubert's *6 Moments musicaux*, Op. 94 (composed c.1823-27) and *4 Impromptus*, Op.142 (composed 1827).

Tomášek wrote an autobiography in German, which was published as a series from 1845 to 1850 in the almanac *Libussa* under title *Erinnerungen* (Memoirs). A Czech translation by Zdeněk Němec along with a worklist of his compositions and a bibliography was published in 1941 as *Vlastní životopis V. J. Tomáška* (*Autobiography of V. J. Tomášek*). This translation is the major source of information for this article.

The autobiography unfortunately ends with the events of the year 1823 when the author was 49 years old, and therefore does not mention the music or the personalities of musicians whom he might have met when they visited Prague: Paganini (1828), Wagner (repeatedly since 1826; his works performed in Prague beginning in 1832), Clara Schumann (1837), Liszt (1840), Berlioz (1846), and others. Since it was written not long before Tomášek died, the enthusiastic opinions of his youth are seasoned by the very critical, rigid and sometimes even sour attitudes of his solitary and rather embittered older years. This ambivalence makes for interesting reading, and can be observed in descriptions of Tomášek by his contemporaries. Whether he was a respected "patriotic Master" or the archconservative musical pope - the Dalai Lama of Prague, as he was called by his student, the internationally respected music critic Eduard Hanslick - is today beside the point. He was an important musician of the transitional period between the classicism and romanticism who made a valid contribution to the music of his country and his time.

Tomášek candidly states in his autobiography that he was self-taught. He began to study singing and violin at the age of 9 in the town of Chrudim, with the choir director Pavel Josef Wolf, returning after two years to his hometown of Skuteč. There his older brother, knowing that the youngster wanted to play "a keyboard instrument which would reveal my innermost feelings through harmony," [1] gave him a little clavier and found him a local teacher with whom Tomášek took a total of three lessons. In the first one the teacher gave him a sonata by Wagenseil with instructions to figure out the right hand as 5 notes up from the alto clef and left hand as 7 notes down, and left him to his own devices. The budding pianist managed to decipher eight measures before the teacher came back from a tavern and found him wanting. The second lesson ended with a slap in the face and in the third one the teacher kept hitting him with a ruler across the fingers. When the father saw his bleeding fingers, he stopped the lessons - and the clavier was locked up in a room. But

Tomášek continued practicing on his own in secret, during his father's absences, learning how to read piano music. A school friend gave him an explanation of the rules of general bass and thus enabled him to delve into harmony.[2]

At the age of 13, he was sent to the Minorites high school in Jihlava, where he was a choirboy. He had the opportunity to play piano for two friendly elderly ladies, but his music teacher, Brother Donat, refused to teach him organ. By pretending he lost his voice, he left Jihlava and in 1790, with the help of his other brother, managed to settle in Prague. He says that "the little clavier [in the Czech text, *pianinko*], my constant companion, made my every free moment sweet," [3] but he feared that painful, recurring chilblains would ruin his fingers for ever. At the time, his favorite composer was Pleyel, but he soon turned to Mozart. As violinist he took part in quartet playing, yet improvement in piano improvisation and composition were his goals. "My first attempts were twelve Hungarian dances for pianoforte; I wrote them without having ever heard any Hungarian folk tune; therefore they were characterized by originality" he informs us. [4] At about this time, 1791 or 1792, he had a painful experience. A schoolmate made him improvise on his good piano and expressed astonishment seeing that Tomášek played every scale using only the thumb and index finger. Then he proved it was a wrong fingering by showing him Georg Friedrich Wolf's piano method, *Kurzer aber deutlicher Unterricht im Klavierspielen* (2 vol., 1783, 1789). Tomášek's reaction was characteristic: "I was completely crushed ... But I did not lose my spirit; I immediately bought this book and studied scales day and night." [5] He also acquired Georg Simon Löhlein's book on general bass, Daniel Gottlob Türk's *Neue Klavierschule oder Anweisung Klavierspielen für Lehrer und Lernende* (1789) and the *Anweisung zum Generalbass-spielen* (1791); with these references, he was able to overcome his technical problems. After school, homework, tutoring for money, study of harmony, piano practice, and some composing, he had about three hours left for sleep. No wonder his brother worried about his health and suspected that he had tuberculosis. During 1794 and 1795, he played Mozart's overtures and other works arranged for four-hand piano with his brother, and worked through Fux's *Gradus ad Parnassum*. His plan to study counterpoint with Jan Antonín Koželuh (1738-1814) did not materialize for practical reasons. He also "decided that from now on I should teach piano. I tried it with the son of a count's servant; he made such progress in a short time that the count became aware of it, and consequently I soon became piano teacher in many aristocratic families." [6] He continued to compose, but burned his compositions because "blindness and vanity were foreign to me, and I criticized my own work much more strictly than others would have done." [7]

In 1797 he entered the school of law but counterpoint, canon, fugue and Sulzer's *Allgemeine theorie der schönen Kunste* interested him more. His piano playing improved, reaching a bravura level and his chilblains were cured by a special ointment. A crushing blow to his self-esteem occurred the following year when he heard Beethoven play in Prague. Nevertheless, Beethoven's pianistic and improvisational skill spurred Tomášek to harder work.

Although Tomášek graduated from law school and continued his general education, music gradually became his only career. His *10 Variations for pianoforte on a theme by Winter* were published as opus 1 in 1800. In 1806, Tomášek accepted the position of a composer and music teacher in the family of Count Georg August Buquoy (1771-1851), who had been his piano pupil for some time. This position gave him financial security and time enough for composing, but meant that he had to renounce a career as a pianist-composer. Nevertheless, he often attended recitals of such performers and systematically assessed their strengths and weaknesses.

The *Autobiography* provides detailed descriptions which are often in an anecdotal and sarcastic vein of recitals of pianists visiting Prague, for example Daniel Steibelt (1765-1823), Josef Wölffel (1773-1812), Muzio Clementi (1752-1830), Jan Ladislav Dusík (1760-1812), Jan Nepomuk Hummel (1778-1837), and others whom Tomášek heard on his trips to Vienna, particularly during the Vienna Congress in 1814. Tomášek learned something from each by shrewdly evaluating technique, touch, interpretation, programming, skill in improvisation, compositional flair, stage presence, and other traits - and by comparing his own capabilities with theirs. In 1816 and 1819, after he left the service of Count Buquoy, he clearly defined his reactions to "the plentiful crop of virtuosos who travel throughout Europe with a few well-practiced etudes by Chopin or a few so-called fantasies by Thalberg; not to honor the art but to call attention to themselves as something exceptional which has never been experienced here ... Where can they find necessary time to perfect themselves? They are never home, they are continually travelling and occupied with programs for performance; they have no time to study anything new, so that their programs are mostly only repetitions of the previous ones, except that the compositions are played in a different order. This experience, which I have verified by observing many traveling artists, was the cause of my decision not to lead the Divine Art hither and thither on a leash for money, because in that manner I would only get farther and farther away from its mysteries." [8]

His resolution to serve the art of music, his interest in poetry as documented by his extensive output of songs, his frequent criticism of the superficial programming by virtuosos, and the circumstance that smaller works were practical for his performing and teaching requirements led to the invention of the new forms of poetic piano pieces which are the basis of the recognition he is given today.

He explains the origins of his inventions in the Autobiography, using a literary style which sounds somewhat ponderous and more romantic than the compositions themselves. The first mention of eclogues is from 1807, when the Count left for his country mansion and Tomášek stayed in Prague, composing his *Symphony in D*, Op.30; *Fantasy for Glass harmonica*, Op.32; and several vocal works.

He says: "An incomprehensible indifference has long prevailed with regard to the piano sonata and orchestral symphony. Endless variations had to take the place of the sonata for pianists as the orchestral overture has taken the place of the symphony. This shallow taste of the time forced me to seek refuge in poetics, to determine whether one could transplant some of the many poetic genres into the realm of tones and thus expand the limitations of musical poetry. The first attempt was the *Six piano eclogues* which were then published as Op.35 by Kühnel in Leipzig. These musical compositions, which were soon to win popularity, are a kind of pastorales, but differ very much in melody, harmony, and rhythm from older pastorales; therefore, I will provide at least a bit of explanatory advice about their interpretation. I had in mind shepherds whose life style is indeed simple, but who have to endure hardship, as all humans do. To their feelings about diverse life conditions through music was a difficult task which I set for myself and - judging from the general interest - which I successfully accomplished with appropriate expressiveness. Many foolhardy and, alas, frustrated attempts by others show that it is not easy to compose eclogues. Eclogues require a simple but very sensitive interpretation to transport the listener into an idyllic world without overlooking here and there easily resolved, interesting passages. First of all, it is necessary to respect meticulously all precise indications of *tempi* and dynamic shadings; otherwise that which is precisely is the specific trait of this kind of composition could be lost through careless interpretation. So far, I have not had the pleasure of hearing my *Eclogues* interpreted properly by anyone except my own pupils." [9]

Tomášek's composed seven volumes containing six eclogues each (Op. 35, 39, 47, 51, 63, 66, 83) and performed them frequently with great success. Eclogues evoke a lyrical atmosphere. They are written in concise A-B-A form and are characterized by uncomplicated harmony, occasional rhythmic shifts, and flowing pianistic style. They are moderately difficult.

In 1810, the initial success of the eclogues motivated Tomášek to compose another set of poetic piano pieces which he called rhapsodies. Again he explains his inspiration: "I also wanted to attempt compositions in which prevailing tenderness would be combined with forcefulness and virility. As if by a touch of magic, Antiquity and its rhapsodies came to my mind; in my imagination I heard entire passages of Homer's *Iliad* recited in an irresistible manner. I reflected why music, the queen of the emotional universe, could not express specific sensory impressions through tones, even if only by suggestion. To find an answer to such an important question, I composed *Six Rhapsodies pour le Pianoforte* Op. 40, published by Haas in Prague, now available in a second edition published by Marco Berra. I wanted to prove that the essence of musical works is not only determined by form, but that their inherent nature depends upon poetic thought. Thus I chose the form of eclogue without worrying whether these distinctive compositions would confuse listeners. I was not wrong; they are inherently distinctive in performance. As a rule, the eclogue requires tenderness and charm, whereas the rhapsody almost always represents something powerful and decisive and emphasizes the technical, even the bravura aspect of pianism. The rhapsodies were highly valued, especially by able pianists, who encouraged me to write the *Six Rhapsodies for Piano* Op. 41, published by Kühnel in Leipzig." [10] He wrote another three rhapsodies which were published as opus 110.

In 1818, Tomášek discusses the origin of another type of poetic composition. In his articulate manner he says: "An objectively vital work of art holds its own even in shifting contexts, but trifles which pay homage to bad contemporary taste share the fate of ephemera. My eclogues and rhapsodies, still sought after by serious pianists, prove to me daily that this opinion is not in error. Guided by this certainly correct opinion, I again examined the poetry to see whether I could use something more for music? And lo! - It was the dithyramb which I chose for musical activity, and I immediately composed *Tre Dithyrambi per il Pianoforte*, published as Op. 65 by Marco Berra. The first dithyramb is harsh in expression, as the Romans had been, while the second reminds us of Greeks by its sensitivity and charm; both elements are combined in the third.

Since few pianists know what a dithyramb is, I was encouraged to write a preface to the work, a short explanation in German and Italian in which I concisely indicated how these compositions should be interpreted. It is absolutely improper that the publisher should have omitted the explanation in the second edition, probably for reasons of economy. By doing so he made the work unintelligible for many.

It must be clear to anyone at first glance that a pianist can use them to display brilliant technique and ardent interpretation. Berra told me that this work is often asked for as 'Tomášek's tortures for pianists.' Something like this may amuse some, but such a gross ignorance can only sadden the author and justify his not too high opinion of the literary erudition of the majority of pianists." [11]

The dithyrambs are longer, more elaborate, and somewhat more dramatic and fantasy-like than the eclogues are. The dithyrambs apparently did not achieve the popularity of his eclogues.

Tomášek created these new genres as the result of a rational decision to enrich the current pianistic repertory. He left 42 eclogues, 15 rhapsodies and 3 dithyrambs, all of which were published during his lifetime. Some of the were reprinted in albums of Czech piano music before World War II. He is represented in the volume 20 (1954) and volume 29 (1956) of the scholarly series *Musica antiqua bohemica*. One of his dithyrambs appears in Pohanka's *Dějiny české hudby v příkladech* (*History of Czech Music in Examples*, 1958). Urtext editions of his *Ausgewählte Klavierwerke* (1971) by G. Henle Verlag offer a representative selection of Tomášek's works: a set of *Variations* Op. 16, *Six Eclogues* Op. 35, *Tre Ditirambi* Op. 65, and *Tre Allegri Capricciosi di bravura* Op. 84.

Tomášek wrote a second *Piano Concerto in E flat major* which remains in manuscript. The two concertos and the two symphonies were composed in 1805, when Tomášek hoped to organize concerts and present pairs of own compositions, for example the *Concerto* and *Symphony in C*, in all tonalities. During this year, he was still hesitating between careers in law and music.

Several of his *Grandes Sonatas pour le Pianoforte* belong to the same period; they were probably influenced by contact with Ladislav Dusík.

The piano works provide only a partial image of Tomášek, an ambitious and self-reliant man who stayed in Prague instead of seeking fame in Vienna or elsewhere despite opportunities to do so. He remained true to his chosen motto, "Truth is the only diadem of art" (jen pravda je diademem umění) which is inscribed on his tombstone at the Košíře cemetery in Prague. He served music with sincerity and dedication.

AMS Annual Meeting
October 1975
Los Angeles, CA

Notes

1) *Vlastní životopis V. J. Tomáška*, edited and translated by Zdeněk Němec (Prague: Editio Topič, 1941), p.14.
2) *Vlastní životopis V. J. Tomáška*, pp. 15-17.
3) *Vlastní životopis V. J. Tomáška*, p. 27.
4) *Vlastní životopis V. J. Tomáška*, p. 32.
5) *Vlastní životopis V. J. Tomáška*, p. 33.
6) *Vlastní životopis V. J. Tomáška*, p. 37-38.
7) *Vlastní životopis V. J. Tomáška*, p.191.
8) *Vlastní životopis V. J. Tomáška*, p. 207-208.
9) *Vlastní životopis V. J. Tomáška*, pp. 82-83.
10) *Vlastní životopis V. J. Tomáška*, pp. 101-102. Marco Berra (b.1784 in Italy, d.1853 in Prague) was trained in Vienna and was a music publisher in Prague from 1811.
11) *Vlastní životopis V. J. Tomáška*, pp. 196-197.

THE FIRST CZECH OPERA:
FRANTIŠEK ŠKROUP'S "DRÁTENÍK" (THE TINKER)

On February 2, 1826, a special event took place at Stavovské Divadlo (Estates Theatre) in Prague. [1] On that day, the young musician František Jan Škroup (b. June 3, 1801 in Osice near Pardubice, Bohemia; d. February 7, 1862 in Rotterdam, Holland) premiered his first work, entitled Dráteník [The Tinker] and initiated what has been called the history of Czech opera.

It is often said that Dráteník is the first Czech opera, but this statement is open to question. Several Bohemian composers wrote operas before 1826 – but these operas were not intended to express a national spirit. Many of these composers lived outside of the Crownlands of Bohemia and Moravia, and they often wrote operas in the Italian style. [2]

Although Josef Kohout (b. 1736 in Bohemia; d. 1793 in Paris) spelled his name according to French orthography as Kohault, and composed French comic operas for the Comédie Italienne, he was of Czech origin. The respected teacher and theoretician Antonín Rejcha (b. 1770 in Prague; d. 1836 in Paris) also composed operas in Paris. In German-speaking areas, Jiří, better known as Georg Benda (b. 1747 in Staré Benátky; d. 1795 in Köstritz, Saxony), Leopold Koželuh (b. 1747 in Velvary; d. 1818 in Vienna), Pavel Vranický (b. 1756 in Nová Říše; d. 1808 in Vienna), Vojtěch Matyáš Jírovec (b. 1763 in České Budějovice; d. 1850 in Vienna) and others created many Singspiels and operas. The successful composer of Italian operas, Signor Venatorini, might have concealed his less euphonious name of Josef Mysliveček (b. 1737 in Prague; d. 1781 in Rome) but was undoubtedly proud of his sobriquet "Il divino Boëmo." Jan Ev. Koželuh (b. 1738 in Velvary; d. 1814 in Prague), a cousin of Leopold, spent his life in Prague and his Italian opera Alessandro nell Indie was performed there in 1769. This opera and his second opera Demofoonte (performed in Prague in 1772) are written in the Neapolitan opera style. His Italian oratorios were also frequently performed in Prague. After 1770, he dedicated his best efforts to sacred music.

These composers should be given full recognition as Czech composers, just as Handel's Italian operas and English oratorios are recognized as a German's contribution to international music history.

One should also note that operas with Czech subjects were composed before 1826. Opera was introduced in Bohemia by Count František Antonín Sporck (1662-1738). This illustrious aristocrat was owner of three palaces in Prague and an important summer estate in Kuks; he was a student of philosophy, a well traveled patron of all arts, and an avid hunter who brought French (hunting) horns into Bohemia. His serious interest in music was so well-known that Johann Sebastian Bach dedicated masses to him. In 1724, Count Sporck hired the opera company of the Venetian impressario Antonio Denzio, which performed in his private theatres in Kuks and in Prague for the next ten years.

One of the operas which was highly successful was *Praga nascente da Libussa e Primislao* with music by Antonio Bioni (b.c. 1698 in Venice). This operatic setting of the legend about the foundation of Prague by the Queen Libuše and her husband Přemysl, performed during the last season of Denzio company's Prague stay (he left in 1735) precedes Smetana's *Libuše* by almost 140 years. The librettist for Bioni's *Libussa* may have been Denzio himself. Škroup's *Libušin sňatek* (*Libussa's Wedding*) on Chmelský's libretto (performed in 1835, second version in 1850) is also written on this theme. No one could wish for a subject which was more Czech; nevertheless, the opera was written in the Venetian baroque style.

A few years earlier, a work of similar caliber was written and performed in the provincial town of Jaroměřice, the Moravian seat of the Viennese aristocratic family of Questenberg. Music particularly flourished at Jaroměřice Castle during the life of Count Jan Adam Questenberg (b. 1678 in Vienna; d. 1752 in Jaroměřice) who was a sophisticated connoisseur of music and a good lutenist. The Jaroměřice castle was thus a perfect setting for the 1730 performance of Míča's *L'origine di Jaromeritz in Moravia*.

František Václav Míča (b.1694 in Třebíč; d. 1744 in Jaroměřice) was certainly a Czech musician; he spent most of his life in his homeland. He entered Count Questenberg's service as a valet. He became member of his Count's Viennese orchestra in 1711 and returned to Jaroměřice probably before 1723. He wrote operas, cantatas, oratorios, arias, some smaller orchestral works and allegedly the *Sinfonia in Re*. Incomplete manuscripts of his operas, some without titles, have been found in Bohemia, Moravia, and Vienna.

Míča wrote other operas on Czech subjects during the season of 1731/32 and in 1737. Since these works have been preserved only in fragments, their musical quality cannot be fully assessed; nevertheless, he may have been the first operatic composer to write in the Czech language. Jan Antoš' *Opera de Rebellione Boëmica Rusticorum* (also called *Opereta o sedlskej svobodě aneb rébelírování*) on the subject of one of the Czech peasant rebellions, was performed in Bohemia in 1775. Czech musical comedies were performed in Bohemia and in the Haná region of Moravia. The composer Josef Pekárek (1758?-1820), an elementary school teacher, used the Haná (region of Moravia) dialect for his music comedies. These dramatic plays and comedies with music achieved popularity in cities as well as in the smaller towns where Czech survived as the language of daily communication, even during periods of strong Germanization.

Many Moravian towns and courts, including Brno, Holešov, Strážnice, Olomouc, Kroměříž, had periods of flourishing musical activity. If one concentrates only on prominent musicians in Prague, an incomplete image of the musical life in Bohemia, Moravia, and Slovakia emerges. This performing tradition had a direct influence on Škroup and *Dráteník*.

Škroup was strongly nationalistic from the beginning of his career. At Škroup's suggestion, *Dráteník*'s libretto written by the patriotic poet Josef Krasoslav Chmelnický (b. August 7, 1800 in Bavorov; d. January 2, 1839 in Prague). Chmelnický studied philosophy and law in Prague. He was appointed as a judge in 1829. He died of tuberculosis. Theatre and literature were his avocations, and he was prominent in Czech intellectual patriotic circles.

Dráteník was performed during the initial enthusiastic phase of Czech national revival in Prague, the center of the nationalistic movement. Therefore, it was logical that Dráteník was acclaimed as "the first Czech opera" without regard to strict historical truth. The work had enough merits to attract a special attention, and the general spiritual and emotional atmosphere at the moment was favorable for it. It could be said that the work received just the right publicity to become well-known and to fill the need of the moment.

Škroup and Chmelnický called Dráteník a Singspiel or, in Czech, zpěvohra (drama with music), a work which uses spoken dialogue instead of recitatives. This form was used for serious and comic opera alike: the original versions of Beethoven's Fidelio, Weber's Der Freischütz, and Mozart's Die Entführung and Zauberflöte used spoken dialogue, which were translated into Czech by the writer and poet Simeon Karel Macháček (1799-1846) and Jan Nepomuk Štěpánek (1783-1844), administrative director of Stavovské divadlo. Dráteník was written in Czech, the national language, partly as a reaction against the prevailing Italian import of opera seria. Another consideration was that the Czech language and the popular and folk-music styles which Škroup utilized were familiar to the audience.

Dráteník can be considered to be the first truly Czech opera, because it ws a precursor of the Czech operas which were written to express the national spirit. Some of these operas were: Smetana's first opera, The Brandenburgers in Bohemia, composed in 1862/63 and performed in the Provisional Theatre in 1866; Žižka's Oak (1847), written by Jiří Macourek on a libretto by Klicpera; Jan Bedřich Kittl's Bianca und Giuseppe oder die Franzosen von Nizza on a libretto by his friend Richard Wagner, which was performed in German in 1848 and in Czech translation in 1875.

In 1823, Škroup organized the first Czech company, which performed at the Stavovské Divadlo. Its first production was Weigl's Singspiel Die Schweizerfamilie. Other operas in its repertory included Cherubini's Les deux journées, Weber's Der Freischütz (1824), and Mozart's Don Giovanni (1825). Škroup worked as organizer, coach, singer, and conductor. He was only twenty-five years old when Dráteník was premiered. Although this work is his first major composition, it seems surprisingly mature and self-assured.

Dráteník was obviously a labor of love and enthusiastic ambition. The basic story is simple. The protagonist is a poor Slovak house-to-house tinker. As the opera begins, he is repairing pots at the house of the rich merchant Květenský in a small Bohemian town. Květenský announces that his pretty daughter Růžena must marry a man of his choice. She refuses to marry an "unknown man." She is in love with young Vojtěch Lána, and he with her. The parlor maid Liduška helps the young lovers to meet and the tinker's help is also enlisted when the gruff and scared manservant Kul does not dare to let Vojtěch into Květenský's house. After the usual buffa confusion of identities (the tinker and Vojtěch exchange clothes) and Květenský's drinking bouts with his friend, young love triumphs.

Chmelenský's text seems rather stiff and clumsy by modern linguistic standards but has a certain old-fashioned charm. It is especially noteworthy that tinker uses the Slovak language, and thus becomes an authentic folk figure. This role was sung by Škroup himself in the premiere. The combination of Czech and Slovak is unusual and original, and is reinforced by the tinker's words "že Slováku bratr Čech" ("the Czech is the Slovak's brother"), apparently a reference to the Panslav ideal. Květenský sings "what could be sweeter than Czech wine in combination with the Czech language," which is echoed by the young pair as "what could be better than a Czech boy in a love with a Czech girl." The tinker also expresses his lyrical yearning for beautiful, far-away Slovakia and his bride, but this is personal rather than patriotic nostalgia which is is appropriate for his character and for the plot.

The libretto and the score mix elements of French opera comique, German Singspiel and Italian opera buffa. The music generally conforms to current fashion. The solo parts are very singable and sometimes catchy; ensembles are well constructed; accompaniments are rather simple, and the overture and orchestral interludes are more elaborate; the orchestration is basically Mozartian. In brief, *Dráteník* is well-written and not especially demanding.

When the tinker appears, the character of the music changes. One suddenly hears bagpipes in the accompaniment, the rhythm and melody change subtly, and the whole atmosphere becomes decidedly Czech. Škroup does not use actual folk-song material, but the tinker's solos do resemble the sincere, idealistic songs (*obrozenecké znárodnělé písně*) which became popular and influenced folk music.

The vocal score of *Dráteník* which was consulted for this article was the centenary edition published by Umělecká beseda; it was awarded a prize in 1927. This piano score contains the overture and fifteen musical numbers; it does not include Chmelenský's spoken text. The first edition, also published by Umělecká beseda, appeared in 1913.

The Overture, in which a short initial Andante con moto leads into an Allegro vivace, uses the melodic material of the music to come. The second act has an introduction of twenty measures. The tinker opens the play with few phrases which are followed by a lively ensemble of two to five voices in which the elements of the plot are described. In the second number, a bass buffo aria, Květenský complains that young girls, with all of their thoughts and questions about love, are troublesome merchandise to keep. Růžena and Liduška then sing a recitative and duet about the pleasures and the tribulations of love. Numbers 4 and 7 are lyric solos by the tinker. Vojtěch sings of love in number 5, and Růžena expresses feelings ranging from bashful confusion and melancholy to a dramatic, imaginary jealousy in her two solos. Liduška also has a solo. The other numbers are ensembles for various combinations of voices. The concluding number is written for five independent voices sung by seven singers. Bass parts are also doubled in the sextet. There is no chorus and no ballet. Škroup uses da capo and strophic song forms for the arias Růžena's second act solo (number 9) could perhaps be classified as a cavatina.

Škroup's treatment of the text is not always consistent; accents of words and music sometimes clash. This problem is, in part, due to that fact that an important linguistic issue had not been resolved for setting Czech texts to music - the problem of metric prosody versus accent prosody. Chmelenský and Macháček took the position that the classic metric structure of poetic forms should be used for music. The theory that the natural accents of prose were more suitable for the Czech language gained strength in Smetana's era. It is well known that Smetana (1824-1884), under the influence of the aesthetician Otakar Hostinský (1847-1910), was extremely scrupulous about the adjustment of his vocal line to the used text. The historian František Palacký (1798-1876) favored accent prosody, recommending folk-songs as best models for a correct, unadulterated fusion of text and music.

Since the work was written for a particular opera company, and Škroup had to consider the capabilities of his principal singers. Thus, the music provides information about their capabilities. Some of the members of the original cast had successful operatic careers. The bass baritone Ferdinand Pohl (1794-1832), who sang the role of Vojtěch Lána's father, was later active in Graz, Austria. Sporano Kateřina Kometová (1807-1889) began her opera singing career at the age of 12; she taught voice after retiring from the stage in 1849. Among her many roles were Agatha, Rosina, Donna Anna. She took part in the Berlioz Prague concerts in 1846. Kometová stayed in Prague her entire life in spite of offers from the Vienna opera. She married the tenor-baritone Matyáš Podhorský, who sang Vojtěch's role to her Růžena in Dráteník's premiere, thus transforming the stage romance into reality. Matyáš Podhorský (1800-1849) was the first Czech Don Giovanni, and also sang this role very successfully in German. Magdalena Forchheimová (1803-1870) began to act when 16 years old. At Škroup's suggestion she also took up singing. The first Liduška was the actress-singer Magdalena Forchheimová, who later married the distinguished Czech writer, journalist and dramatist Josef Kajetán Tyl (1808-1858), who was closely associated with Škroup's Czech opera group. He is the author of Fidlovačka, a popular satiric farce with incidental music by Škroup. Further information was not found about Michalesi, Šimek and Chauer, who also took part in the first performance.

Dráteník was an immediate hit and was often repeated in following years. Škroup was officially appointed as the second conductor of the Stavovské Divadlo in 1827, and was the principal conductor of that theater from 1837 to 1847. He introduced the operas of Verdi (Nabucco and Ernani in 1849) and Wagner (Tannhäuser, 1854) to Prague. He composed other Czech operas (Oldřich a Božena 1828, Libušin sňatek 1835) and German operas (Der Nachtschatten 1827, Der Prinz und die Schlange 1829, Die Drachenhöhle 1832, Die Geisterbraut 1836, Drahomíra 1848) none of which met the success of Dráteník. His German opera Der Meergeuse (1851) was successful in Rotterdam (1861), but Columbus, composed in 1855, was not performed until 1942, and then in a Czech translation. Of his incidental music, Fidlovačka

(1834, piano score 1952) is the best known. He composed and edited many Czech songs; the rest of his work (cantatas, church and synagogue music, chamber music, and several orchestral works) is of secondary importance. He accepted the position of conductor at the Rotterdam Opera in 1860. Josef Plavec's comprehensive monograph *František Škroup* was published in 1941.

Škroup is remembered chiefly as the composer of *Dráteník* and of the incidental music to Tyl's *Fidlovačka*. Among the numbers of *Fidlovačka*, the song "Kde domov můj?" ("Where is my home?") was singled out by popular enthusiasm to become Czech national anthem. This song has given Škroup an emotionally charged, permanent place in the history of Czech music.

Notes

Editor's note: Additional information about Škroup's career as a conductor and his role in establishing Wagner's operas in Prague can be found in "Rückblick: Die Wagner Festwoche in Prag 1856," in *Besuch bei Cosima: eine Begegnung mit dem alten Bayreuth mit einem Fund der Briefe Cosima Wagners*, edited and annotated by Vladimír Karbusicky (Hamburg: von Bockel Verlag, 1997), pp. 36-43.

1) Stavovské Divadlo (Estates Theatre) was the name given in 1798 to the well established Nostitz Theatre (founded in 1783; Mozart premieres in 1782, 1786 and 1787). The Italian repertory prevailed until a German company took over the theater in 1807. Czech performances, alternating with the German repertory, were introduced in 1823 (cf. note 2). In 1949, the theatre was renamed Tyl Theatre.

2) Emil Axman (1887 - 1949), *Moravian Operas in the XVIIIth century* (1912); Vladimír Helfert (1866-1945), *Musical Baroque in the Czech Castles* (1916) and Music in the Jaroměřice Castle (1924); Paul Nettl, *Music-Barock in Böhmen und Mähren* (1927). Bibliographical information on unpublished dissertations and recent articles in Czech can be found under various headings in *Československý hudební slovník osob a institucí* (*Czechoslovak Music Dictionary of Persons and Institutions*), 2 volumes, Prague 1963 and 1965.

SMETANA AND PIVODA

Although Bedřich Smetana is recognized as a founder of the Romantic school of Czech national music and as one of the greatest of the Czech composers, he has at times been the center of bitter controversy. At the beginning of the twentieth century, Antonín Dvořák was proclaimed as Smetana's opponent and the ideal representative of the Czech national school of music, initiating a bitter conflict which needlessly divided Czech musicians, musicologists and others into two irreconcilable camps for several decades. Another controversy arose during Smetana's lifetime. He is often depicted as being persecuted, martyred and even destroyed by the villain František Pivoda. This view has persisted in histories of Czech music and biographies of Smetana. Few have cared to find out what Pivoda's side of the story might have been.

Ironically, Smetana and Pivoda were born the same year, on March 2 and on October 19, 1824. It is also ironic that Pivoda's literary and musical legacy is held in the Smetana Museum in Prague. The Pivoda holdings consist of his published and unpublished compositions, materials for his extensive pedagogic activities, his personal documents, autobiographical fragments, song books which he edited and compiled for various school levels (which were used in elementary and high schools and teachers' colleges as late as 1927), extensive correspondence consisting of letters he received and the copies of those he mailed, and his apology for his part in the Smetana controversy.

Let us examine what these men had in common. Both were born in small towns - Pivoda in Moravia and Smetana in Bohemia. Their musical talent was discovered early, but Smetana appears to have been more precocious, having shown natural ability for piano playing and composition since his childhood. He studied with Joseph Proksch in Prague from 1843 to 1847 and became a virtuoso pianist. As early as in 1843 Smetana wrote in his diary: "By the grace of God and with His help, I shall one day be a Liszt in technique, a Mozart in composition." [1]

Pivoda's musical education took another direction. As a boy, he was a chorister in Brno (1839-40) and studied at the teachers' colleges in Moravia. He went to Vienna for further study in 1844 and began to compose there, but his principal interest was always vocal pedagogy. He became versed in Italian methods of singing and adhered to them for the rest of his life.

Both men moved toward recognition and a firmer financial basis through positions as teachers in aristocratic families. Smetana taught five hours a day in the family of Count Leopold Thun in Prague and in its country seats between 1844 and 1847. He then made several concert tours, established a music school in 1848, accepted a post in Göteborg, Sweden in 1856, and began to write a remarkable series of compositions with the encouragement of Franz Liszt. He returned to Prague in May 1861 without prospects of a secure position.

In 1844, Pivoda went to Vienna, where he became active in local Czech cultural activities, including the theater. He entered the service of Prince Karl Khevenhüller-Metsch in 1853 as a music teacher, dividing his time between Vienna and Komorní Hrádek near Chocerady in Bohemia and making short visits to Prague. Pivoda was popular within the Czech community of Vienna. Johann Strauss Jr. performed his dances *Tatran-Mazur* and *Prostějovka-Polka* at a ball there in 1851. Pivoda would eventually compose and arrange at least 134 works, mostly songs and choral arrangements, as well as salon pieces and transcriptions and a *Fantasy* for violin and piano. [2] According to Horák, there was a rumor that Pivoda intended to write a Czech opera. His unfinished opera *Radmila* is dated 1862. [3] Could he have intended to enter it in Count Harrach's competition for a new, definitively Czech opera – the competition which was won by Smetana?

In 1860, Pivoda moved to Prague and began to make a career in Czech musical circles. Pivoda's Pěvecká a operní škola [School for voice and opera] was formally established in 1869 and became a permanent success. It continued until 1940. Karel Kovařovic, composer of operas and later the opera director of the National Theater, a man of strong convictions about the stylistic direction of Czech opera, succeded Pivoda. Kovařovic's successor as director of the school was Pivoda's niece and student Marie Pivoda (1862-1940), who also had a career as a coloratura opera singer in Germany.

As he describes in his *Method*, Pivoda strictly adhered to the Italian school of voice production, applying it to singing in the Czech language as well. He was very much against Wagner, calling him "the destroyer of voices." One of Pivoda's cherished plans was to prepare singers for Prague operatic performances and, in fact, many of his pupils sang at the Provisional Theater and the National Theater. Yet, he wanted to determine the repertory of these theaters. He proved to be a musician of limited horizon, declaring himself in favor of domestic productions of certain traditional foreign operas and of simple Czech operas which were untainted by echoes of Wagnerian opera reform. Despite the controversy which arose as a result, Smetana praised Pivoda's voice students who had leading roles in the operas he conducted. Pivoda stressed the value of building vocal technique slowly and carefully, remarking: "The voice which I have trained continues to sing for an aging artist - even two weeks after his death." He could easily demonstrate the results of his pedagogical approach, for he was able to sing effortlessly into his seventies. [4]

Both men were ambitious artists and had severe setbacks in their musical careers. Both were sincere Czech patriots and wanted to contribute to the development of Czech musical life. They were among the founders of the new organization of Czech Artists, Umělecká Beseda in 1863 and worked together in its Music Section; Smetana was its first chairman, and was succeeded by Pivoda during 1866 and 1867. It is documented that Pivoda sang a Schubert song and one of his own songs under Smetana's baton in 1862 as part of a concert series intended to improve the musical taste of Prague audiences. Smetana received help from Pivoda in 1865 when applying for the directorship of the Prague Conservatory of Music. The Provisional Theater was opened in 1862, Maýr was appointed as conductor, and Smetana succeeded Maýr in 1866 with Pivoda's support and approval. [5]

Both musicians became music critics. When Smetana wrote for *Národní listy* in 1864, he was very critical of the lack of interest in good contemporary music by the Prague public. He severely chastised Maýr's practices in opera presentations and made derogatory remarks about Maýr's musicianship. The sharpest rebuke followed the interpolation of the one-legged dancer Julian Donato between the acts of Rossini's *Otello,* and similar events that were very much appreciated by the general public. Maýr and his friends did not forget Smetana's reviews and later took revenge.

On the other hand, Pivoda favorably reviewed the premiere of Smetana's first opera, *Brandenburgers in Bohemia,* in the German-language publication *Politik.* The performance took place on January 5, 1866 in the Provisional Theater, and Smetana was the conductor. Pivoda noted that Smetana had given up an excellent position abroad to serve his nation. The premiere of the first, simpler version of *The Bartered Bride* on May 30 of the same year was greeted by Pivoda as the birth of a true Czech opera. However, his enthusiasm decreased when Smetana revised the work.

Smetana's *Dalibor* was first performed on May 16, 1868. This opera became a *cause celebre* which ignited Pivoda's hostility to what he identified as Wagnerian traits in Smetana's music. It may be relevant that the vocal style of this opera did not correspond at all to the Italian bel canto style, and that the title role was sung by Lukes, a operatic tenor who had frequently sung the title role of Dratenik with outstanding success, and whom Smetana had entrusted with coaching the opera singers – a position which Pivoda had wished to have for himself. Pivoda had given up his career as an opera singer in 1861 after a performance in Škroup's opera *Drátenik*. His tenor voice was reportedly cultivated and pleasant but too small for the theater. His lack of height would also have been a handicap on the operatic stage.

Pivoda became the foremost member of the anti-Smetana camp. To be fair, we must note that some of the invectives which have been associated with his name actually came from his supporters, and the underlying political conflict between the Old and Young Czechs exacerbated the controversy to an unhealthy degree which is difficult to understand fully today.

John Clapham provides valuable source material for the journalistic battle between the Smetana and Pivoda camps, and for the background of political and cultural struggles between the Old Czech and Young Czech parties. He includes English translations of the most important attacks which appeared in the Czech press and musical journals. [6] Brian Large gives a detailed description of the controversy in his biography of Smetana. [7] In addition, the lists of operas produced and conducted by Maýr and by Smetana during their tenures at the Provisional Theater which Clapham and Large provide are useful in clarifying the stylistic motivation of the anti-Smetana attacks.

Accordingly, he concentrated on training singers, many of whom had brilliant careers, and on his ambition to be a prominent, vocal arbiter in Prague music circles. He found a niche in the Old Czech party, which was led by František Rieger (1818-1903), a writer and a politician as well as the Intendant (theater manager) of the Provisional Theater. Pivoda followed the party line against the Young Czechs, which included Smetana and his adherents. [8]

By 1870, the differences between Smetana and Pivoda had crystallized and their antagonism had become a public issue. Their aesthetic positions were irreconcilable. Pivoda corresponded with Eduard Hanslick and generally accepted Hanslick's ideas on aesthetics, including his dislike of the music of Liszt and Wagner. Hence Pivoda's criticism of Smetana's "Wagnerism" may also be an echo, a local variation of the larger aesthetic battles which raged at the time. Smetana wanted to create Czech music that would equal the compositions of Liszt and Wagner, which were interpreted by some as "non-Czech" and "non-Slavic," and by others as revolutionary.

Smetana's objections to the prevalence of the popular, mostly Italian, operatic repertoire were misrepresented by Pivoda – champion of the ideals and techniques of Italian vocal music - as an attempt to Germanize the Czech musical style which was just beginning to emerge. Pivoda's contention that folk music should be the only basis of a truly national music was too severe a limitation for the development of Czech music, even at the time. On this point history has proved Pivoda wrong. But personality differences also fueled the controversy, as Brian Large points out. He depicts Pivoda thus: "He seems to have been a narrow-minded, mean and selfish man, who was nicknamed 'Orpheus' by his enemies because he was always singing his own praises to further his own ambition." [9] This harsh description may be unjust to Pivoda as well as to Orpheus.

Horák provides detailed information about Pivoda's generosity to his father and other family members, and offers comments from some of his numerous pupils who found him an understanding and quite lovable father figure, even though he liked prestige and authority. Perhaps as a result of his years in service to the Prince, he liked elegance and polite social communication, and had a touch of a grand seigneur. [10] But the tone of some of his invectives against Smetana is anything but polite. The most hateful attacks were published in 1874, at the very time when Smetana had to resign his position at the Provisional Theater. The timing was most unfortunate, for everyone - including Smetana - hoped that his loss of hearing was temporary. These attacks were later considered to be the cause of Smetana's breakdown.

It is not surprising that the wrath of Smetana's friends and supporters was concentrated on Pivoda and that he felt a need to justify himself. But he waited too long. Between October and December of 1897, while already seriously ill, he wrote down the seventy pages of "K objasnění" [An Explanation]) and "Mé dojmy z prvních styků se Smetanou" [My impressions from my first contacts with Smetana]. Pivoda died on January 4, 1898, and his apology was not published until 1970. [10]   .

Pivoda begins "An Explanation" by referring to articles in the journal *Dalibor* from 1884 and 1895 concerning two of those who assured Smetana's eventual recognition - Otakar Hostinský and Adolf Čech - and the ban which

prevented students from Pivoda's singing school from performing in the National Theater. [11] He explains that he did not wish to protest, because he
would have to touch upon the memory of the late Smetana once more, and that
he wanted Smetana to be viewed as a thoroughly noble being by posterity,
although he had - as a man - many social and ethical faults.

He then describes an occasion in 1894 which turned out badly for him.
He tried to collect money to keep the manuscript of the piano score of *The
Bartered Bride* in Bohemia – the manuscript which Smetana had presented to
his friend and publisher, Emanuel Starý. A collector from abroad had apparently offered to buy it, and Pivoda's initiative was criticized as inappropriate
just because it came from him. However, he also says that "a brief is being
prepared to destroy me," and continues: "This affair will probably be the part
of Smetana's biography and of the history of Czech music in which my name
will play a sad role. – It's a pity it will appear only after my death. How it
would have amused me ... It will be a heroic deed when they courageously
attack - a corpse." And he wonders why no one had ever asked his opinions,
for he had been in direct contact with Smetana for many years. He resented
being called the man who "persecuted Smetana to death," continuing: "That
has an odor of murder, of public accusation." Hence he decided to break his
silence and document his impressions of Smetana, even if they would contradict the idealized image of the composer of *The Bartered Bride.* [12]

Let us now summarize a few of the highlights of the "Impressions."
When Smetana first settled in Prague, Pivoda did not know much about him
and his achievements in Göteborg. It seems that he gave Smetana the benefit
of a doubt and was more than willing to get acquainted. However, a social
faux pas was apparently made at the very outset. Smetana did not give Pivoda
a formal invitation to his musical soirees, but asked one of his piano pupils, a
sister of a Pivoda student, to invite him verbally. When the two men were
eventually introduced, Smetana said: "Well, Maestro, I invited you to my soirees, but you didn't come; should I have made the invitation in tails and a top
hat?" which was Pivoda's usual daily attire. Pivoda answered: "Don't do that,
Mr. Smetana. I would not visit you anyway, you are too rude for me." After
that exchange, they did not speak to each other all evening. When they met in
the company of others, Pivoda was shocked when Smetana spoke very bitterly
about the problems of unappreciated, poor artists and complained that his former aristocratic pupils now ignored him. Pivoda continues: "I had an impression of unrestrained hatred, resentment and envy. I concluded that Mr.
Smetana's disposition was dominated by dissolute passions of vanity, self-
love and megalomania - the furies that can destroy the roots of mental health,
if there is no rational mind that could master and control them." He felt that he
never could have a harmonious relationship with such a person. [13]

Nevertheless, Pivoda recognized Smetana's compositional ability and
felt that Smetana was the chosen one among those who were called. Thus he
was willing to suppress his personal feelings and to give help. He writes in
detail about Smetana's unsuccessful quest for the directorship of Prague Conservatory, and about his recommendation of Smetana to the Provisional Thea-

ter. He reproduces a conversation with a member of the Theater Association who wondered why Pivoda would want that "bore of Smetana," to which he answered: "You asked me whom I would recommend for a conductor, not with whom I am in love." He protests against Jan Neruda's comparison of Smetana with "towering Petřín Hill" in whose shadow a tiny Pivoda disappears; he considers it absurd to compare an opera composer with a singing teacher. [14)

After Smetana was appointed, Pivoda thought that he could become his personal friend, but other conflicts followed: over a singer, Pivoda's pupil; about Smetana's revision of *The Bartered Bride* - an opera Pivoda admired although its composer referred to it as "only a toy" - and most importantly, over Wagnerism.

Pivoda explains that he was a staunch anti-Wagnerian, but believed that he had been tolerant to those who disagreed with him. He endeavored to be true to his maxim: "Heed any opinion, defend your convictions decidedly, until you come to the conclusion that they are wrong." Obviously, he never changed his opinion about the school of composition which included the German composers Liszt and Wagner - and that was his right. He then suggests that Smetana "imitates Wagner in everything;" including "[Wagner's] world-famous 'martyrdom.'" And he continues: "Well, where there is to be a martyr, a torturer is needed. And for Mr. Smetana that [torturer] was anyone whom he hated, begrudged and persecuted. And because Smetana hated *me* above all others, everyone will understand why Mr. Urbánek called me Smetana's principal torturer in his journal *Dalibor*. Smetana's martyrdom was of two kinds. One kind, which is not without irony, was caused by his aroused passions; the other, his really tragic suffering, was allotted to him by merciless fate." He suggests Dvořák's success was a blow to poor Smetana, who "had to live to see Dvořák's fame. No wonder that his mind started to cloud. And his friends talked about the possible catastrophe of - insanity." As Pivoda had been one of the first critics to praise "the victory" of Dvořák and to claim that Dvořák's musical style was based on Czech elements in Smetana's *Bartered Bride*, his apology on this point sounds somewhat hollow. Smetana usually spoke favorably about Dvořák and said he was happy to have such a rival; Czech music needed stimulating competition to grow and flourish. [15)

Pivoda concludes his "Impressions" on a personal note. "As long as the abyss of insanity did not completely engulf Smetana, I used to see him once in a while during my strolls. Whatever the cause of his suffering was, his suffering was so great that just the thought of it made my blood congeal ... Each time I was so moved by the sight of the poor man, that I had an urge to approach him and try to give him a word of sympathy and comfort. Perhaps it would have been right to do so. Why did it not happen?

"Well, a certain fear that I would be rebuffed kept me from it. I regret that I did not act spontaneously, as my heart was telling me. It would not have harmed me, had I experienced something unpleasant. I feel that today I would be happier with the memory of a rejected approachment than I am with the knowledge that I obeyed the voice of untimely sensibility. –

Smetana died in an asylum.

On his casket I placed a wreath with the words:

To the Creator of *The Bartered Bride*.

He is buried in sacred Vyšehrad. May his rest be easy – easier than the conscience of those who exerted their disastrous influence on him and kept him in a constant turmoil, instead of caring for his inner peace and good state of mind, of which he had an utmost need for his work and for the benefit of his nation." [16)]

With these words Pivoda ends his artistic testament. He seems to imply that if Smetana not rejected his friendship, he - Pivoda - would have given the composer the love and care he deserved.

It no longer matters whether we can accept Pivoda's apology as sincere or self-serving. It also is beyond the point to what extent the controversy was a personality clash, a power struggle or a created conflict. Pivoda deserves to be heard - and his above writings are interesting documents. Although his merits as a founder of Umělecká Beseda and as a contributor to the Czech art of singing are recognized today, he is still perceived as the villain in the Smetana affair.

But it is said that it takes two to tango, and it certainly takes two to keep up a controversy. And thus we should also discuss Smetana's illness as a possible contributing factor.

Smetana's death certificate reads *Dementia Senilis*. Professor Jaroslav Hlava performed an autopsy and diagnosed Smetana's illness as progressive paralysis. Let us briefly review a few facts that may throw light on Smetana's illness. Since 1857, the medical profession had suspected that there might be a connection between syphilitic infection and a general paresis that sometimes developed many years later. The discovery of the infectious agent and of the three stages of syphilis took place between 1905 and 1910, and the trepomena pallidum (or spirochete) was found in paretics brains in 1913. Artificial fever, arsenical Salvarson and serological tests were discovered shortly thereafter. Today, serological tests are a sure method of distinguishing the syphilitic paralysis from other brain diseases. Various types of neurosyphilis were established, referring to the affected parts of the brain. The symptoms and the course of deterioration depended on the focus of the neurological damage. [17)] During the 19th century, the only procedure which was effective for some patients was the Schmier mercury cure, which Smetana seems to describe in his diary and letters from 1875. But then it would have been too late for this cure to have any effect on his destroyed hearing.

A permanent cure became possible only after the introduction of penicillin in 1943. Since then syphilis has been considered a chronic physical illness which causes unpredictable brain damage. It is not madness or psychosis. However, patients develop psychotic symptoms in the untreated last stage, as Smetana did a few months before his death when he had to be admitted to the Prague asylum. His symptoms had already become severe.

We know that Smetana suffered the complete loss of his hearing in the course of a few months in 1874. Clapham mentions an annotation from

Smetana's diary from July 1874, stating that Smetana had an ulcer, throat problems and a rash, and his ears became blocked at that time. Smetana also described an instance of auditory hallucinations in August. By September he was deaf, and he resigned his position at the theater. Dr. Jan Löwenbach quotes a letter of March 11, 1862 from Smetana to his wife Bettina, in which he states that he had experienced an episode of auditory hallucinations in Copenhagen. [18] The date of 1862 conforms much more closely to the usual course of the illness, which develops over five to fifteen or more years after the primary infection, manifesting occasional, insidious symptoms alternating with remissions, often giving the impression of a vague neurasthenia before serious and irreversible neurological damage emerges. During the latent stage, characterologic changes take place and the so-called organic personality develops.

Young Smetana was often described as a vital person, full of *joie de vivre*, enthusiastic, outgoing, sociable, a tireless dancer, a rather happy-go-lucky fellow, and something of a ladies' man. He was able to bounce back in the 1850's after having lost two daughters and his first wife, remarry in 1860 and start another family. But Pivoda was not the only one who found him somewhat difficult in social contacts during the 1860's. In the above-mentioned article, Clapham says that "Smetana was liable to confuse issues, misunderstand meanings and misconstrue innuendos," though he contributes it to Smetana's clumsiness "when he wrote in Czech." Clapham also states that Smetana had several faults: he "was a man of strong prejudices, vulnerable to verbal attacks, whose anger was easily roused," and "it was easy to rub him up the wrong way." [19] Such behavior could be construed as increasing rigidity, hypersensitivity, hypervigilance, and less controlled irritability, all of which are characteristics often found in the organic personality. A decrease of Smetana's physical stamina and a tendency to become easily fatigued had been noticed in connection with his concert work and conducting before he lost his hearing. Of course, euphoria alternating with depression, grandiose feelings and slight eccentricities are such common features of the temperament of creative artists that they might escape notice unless they became extremely exaggerated – as would the occasional touch of paranoia that often is an intrinsic part of the competitive artistic environment, especially where the opportunities are limited and contact with opposing cliques is unavoidable.

I suggest that Smetana must have developed organic symptoms which became progressively more severe, and that these symptoms have contributed to his problems with his contemporaries. He would have encountered increasing subtle difficulties in his daily life, and would have gradually become less effective under levels of stress which had not bothered earlier. Taking into consideration the state of medical knowledge of his time, no one, Pivoda or anyone else, could have either saved or destroyed Smetana by spoken or printed word, for it would have been impossible to stop his illness and avoid his final, total collapse.

It was a miracle that his diseased brain allowed him for so long to play piano and compose, by sheer strength of his indomitable spirit, before it ceased to function properly – only a few months before his physical death on May 12, 1884.

Smetana was indeed a genius - and Pivoda was not his murderer by any means. He misused his abilities as a critic to incite Smetana's furies instead of taming them by his song, as the Orpheus of the legend would have done. Nevertheless, the end result would have been the same.

To make a proper evaluation of the effect of Smetana's illness on his life and music, his diaries, letters, manuscripts, sketches and similar archival sources would be have to be submitted to expert analysis.

Notes

A major source for the biographical and other factual data in this article was *Českoslov-enský hudební slovník* [Czechoslovak Music Dictionary] 2 vols. (Prague: Státní hudební vy-davatelství, 1963-65). Dr. Fischmann made the following assessment of the information she found there, with the implication that the length of articles about particular figures somewhat reflected the extent to which they were in political favor at the time this biographical diction-ary was compiled:

"Assuming that the length of the entries in music encyclopedias gives some indication of biased or objective views, it was deemed useful to peruse the *Československý hudební slov-ník* from that perspective. Volume II (1965) dedicates approximately two columns (one page) to František Pivoda, and adds another column about his well-established school of singing. Smetana's entry has thirteen full pages and Dvořák (Volume I, 1963) has nine pages of text. Of the other persons involved in the controversies around 1870, the longest article in the dic-tionary (three and a half pages) pertains to the aesthetician and music historian Otakar Hostinský from the pro-Smetana faction. Jan N. Maýr, Smetana's precursor at the Provisional Theater, is represented by slightly over one column. Other contemporaries who contributed as defenders or opponents of Smetana - or whose names were drawn into the controversies - are mentioned in the *Slovník* proportionately to their accomplishments as musicians, music critics, literary men, authors of personal Smetana reminiscences, and so on, as may be each individual case."

Editor's note: material related to Pivoda's singing school, the stylistic reasons for his opposition to Smetana, and the controversy itself have been taken from Dr. Fischmann's draft article "The Year in Czech Music" (1974).

In this and other articles by Dr. Fischmann, "National Theater" refers to Národní di-vadlo in Prague, and "Provisional Theater" refers to Prozatímní divadlo, the interim theater which served the Czech nationalist movement until the opening of Národní divadlo. The pre-sent stage of Národní divadlo occupies the space where the Provisional Theater once stood, the space where Smetana's early operas were first performed.

Národní divadlo is, among other things, a gallery of art which represents a pantheon of Czech music. Smetana is honored in that pantheon as the man who did more than any other to establish Czech opera in the difficult early years of Czech nationalism.

Background information about the political context of the Smetana-Pivoda controversy can be found in Bruce Garver, *The Young Czech Party 1874-1901, and the emergence of a multi-party system* (New Haven: Yale University Press, 1978).

1) "Jsem nástrojem vyšší moci. S pomocí a milosti Boží budu jednou v technice Lisztem, v komponování Mozartem." František Bartoš, ed. *Smetana v vzpomínkách a dopisech* (Prague: Topičova edice, 1948), p. 16.

2) Vladimír Horák, *František Pivoda: Pěvecký pedagog* [František Pivoda, Voice Pedagogue] (Brno: Universita J. E. Purkyně, 1970), p. 18. Horák provides a work list of Pivoda's compositions and arrangements, pp. 123-132.

3) Horák, pp. 143-144.

4) Horák, p. 149. Horák lists singers trained by the Pivoda method, pp. 135-142.

5) Umělecká Beseda, founded in 1863, had three sections: music, literature, and fine arts. It sponsored concerts, lectures, exhibitions, and publications. Its Shakespeare celebration in 1864 was one of its early projects to honor a special occasion. Smetana was the first chairman of the Musical Section; Dvořák held the position in 1880. The Prague Conservatory of Music was founded in 1811. Jan Bedřich Kittl (1808-1868) was its first director from 1843 until his resignation in 1865. He was the composer of the opera *Bianca und Giuseppe* (1848), whose libretto was written by his friend Richard Wagner. Josef Krejčí (1821-1881) was appointed as his successor. Jan Nepomuk Maýr (1818-1888), Czech bandmaster and conductor, studied singing and organ in Prague and Vienna, was active abroad, and in Prague after 1846. He was the conductor at the Provisional Theater in 1862-66 and 1874-81.

6) John Clapham, "The Smetana-Pivoda Controversy" in *Music and Letters*, vol. 52 no. 4, October 1971, pp. 353-354.

7) Brian Large, *Smetana* (New York, Washington: Praeger Publishers, 1970).

8) Horák, p.145.

9) Large, p. 233.

10) Horák, pp. 152-181. Horák prints these documents in their entirety for the first time. Mirko Očadlík's article "Smetanův nepřítel" [Smetana's enemy], in *Lidové noviny*, Nov. 24, 1940, included only a brief quotation.

11) Adolf Čech (1841-1903) was a conductor at the Provisional Theater under Maýr during the 1864 / 65 season and from 1876 until he moved to the National Theater. He conducted Smetana's premieres after *Libuše*, premiered the entire set of symphonic poems known as *My Country (Má Vlast)* in 1882 and presented a complete cycle of Smetana's operas in 1893. He conducted *The Bartered Bride* in Vienna (1892) with resounding success. Several of Pivoda's pupils had leading roles in that performance. Otakar Hostinský (1847-1910) taught aesthetics at the Prague University since 1877, history of music at the Prague Conservatory (1882-86), as well as history of art and of acting at other schools. He was a firm supporter of Smetana.

12) Horák, pp. 154-155.

13) Horák, pp. 157-158. The sisters were probably Gabriela and Marie Roubal. Gabriela (1843-1922) studied with Pivoda. He fell in love with her and wanted to marry her. She had a career in Italy under the name La Boema and married Raffael Steffani. She died in Melbourne, Australia, where she taught singing. Pivoda remained a bachelor. Marie studied piano with Smetana and taught in his piano school.

14) Horák, p.161 ff. Jan Neruda (1834-1891), Czech poet, writer and critic, was Smetana's friend and his stanch defender. Many of his poems have been set to music.

15) Horák, p.164. František Augustin Urbánek (1842-1919) published the journal *Dalibor* (1879-1899) and was its editor from 1883 to 1893. The Urbánek publishing house was an important cultural institution until its nationalization in 1948.

16) Horák, p.180-181.

17) Arthur P. Noyes, M.D., & Lawrence C. Kolb, M.D., *Modern Clinical Psychiatry* (Philadelphia-London: W.B. Saunders Co., 1963). Miroslav Velek, M.D. & Paul Marks, "How Dark, O Lord, Are Thy Decrees - General Paresis as Reflected in the Lives and Work of Some Musicians" (unpublished).

18) Jan Löwenbach, *Bedřich Smetana, Genius of a Freedom-Loving People* (Washington, D.C.: The Volta Bureau, 1943) Reprint from the *Volta Review*.

19) Clapham, p. 364.

THE SMETANA CENTENNIAL

"The pelican might well be the symbol for his life, which was a perpetual sacrifice of his musical genius to his patriotism."

This metaphor from the pen of William Ritter, [1] the French-Swiss writer and an connoisseur of Czech and Slovak arts and culture around the turn of the century, is a striking comment on Smetana. The legend of the pelican who, by offering its breast to nourish its young, dies in the process, is well known, but to connect it with the fate of the creator of the Czech national music is an ingenious idea worthy of closer examination.

Smetana apparently decided to become a truly Czech composer during a visit to Weimar, probably in September 1857. [2] When, at a gathering of musicians, the Viennese composer Johann Herbeck commented that Bohemia only produced fiddlers and other performers but not original composers, Liszt came to the rescue by playing Smetana's recently published early piano pieces as an example of purely Czech music of a high caliber. On his way home, the happy Smetana solemnly swore that he would dedicate his entire life to his nation and his country's art. He was at that time engaged in Göteborg and later informed his friend, Dr. Ludevít Procházka, that he "tried to give the symphonic poem *Wallenstein's Camp*, composed in Sweden in 1858, a national character." [3] To the same correspondent he wrote on another occasion: "I need hardly repeat that I am Czech, body and soul, and it is my pride to be the heir to our glory." [4]

After his return to Prague in May 1861, Smetana concentrated on fulfilling his vow. Eight completed operas, the cycle of six symphonic poems *My Country*, the two series of *Czech Dances* for piano, the cantata *Czech Song*, the *String Quartet in e minor* "From My Life," the duo *From My Homeland* and numerous other works were the steppingstones in his efforts to develop a characteristic national style.

He once remarked that the highest mark of originality was achieved "when it is possible to say after a few bars: that is Mozart – that is Chopin," and expressed the wish: "If only one day it were possible to say after a few bars: that is Smetana ..." [5] Generations of his countrymen have been able to do so since then.

This year Smetana's double anniversary is being celebrated: one hundred-sixty years since his birth on March 2, 1824 and a hundred years since his death on May 12, 1884. In his native country his position of the founder of Czech national music is indisputable. Abroad, his complete work is largely unknown to the average music lover and even to scholars, unless they specialize in Czechoslovak music. The Smetana celebrations in Prague, following last year's centennial in the National Theater, consisted of "festival performances of the complete body of his works, including such less familiar operas as *The Kiss*, *Libuše*, *Two Widows*, and *The Secret*." [6]

All of these operas, of course, are very familiar in Czechoslovakia. *Libuše,* Smetana's fourth opera, composed between 1869 and 1872, was premiered on June 11, 1881, to inaugurate the National Theater in Prague, and was again performed after the fire to open the rebuilt theater on November 18, 1883. By the specific wish of the composer that this glorious tableau "be used only for festivals which affect the whole Czech nation" [7] and not be scheduled as a repertory opera, *Libuše* has been reserved for the principal Czech opera houses. It has mostly been staged on only very special occasions, such as the liberation of the country, the inauguration of a state president or on Smetana anniversaries. The composer never signed a contract with the directorate of the National Theater and adamantly wrote in 1883: "For the sake of a few gulden I shall not allow my work, the only significant one in our literature, to be dragged along in the society of songs made to be whistled." [8]   The special position of Parsifal which was reserved by Wagner for Bayreuth only comes to mind, even though the Metropolitan Opera in New York produced it, despite litigation, on December 24, 1903. Nothing like that has occurred with *Libuše,* and consequently it is an unfamiliar opera abroad.

Interestingly, Smetana's fifth opera *Dvě vdovy* (*The Two Widows,* 1873-74), was performed in Hamburg as early as December 28, 1881, with changes that greatly displeased the composer. [9] He felt his opera "in a distinguished salon style" was there treated in a "degrading" manner, as if it were a comic opera by an Offenbach or a Delibes. He rejected such success on principle and commented: "I have lost the wish to see my operas performed abroad; in my modesty I am content with the recognition of my nation, and the applause of the Czech public has rewarded me in full measure for my attempts – pure, sacred, and truthful!" [10] This work has become a part of the semistaged repertoire in English of the Pocket Opera (San Franscisco) directed by Donald Pippin, and has been reportedly doing well with the public since 1980.

Hubička (*The Kiss,* 1875-76) is Smetana's sixth opera, the first one he composed in complete deafness. It was first performed on November 7, 1876 at the Provisional Theater, with an enthusiastic response from the public of Prague and other localities throughout Bohemia. Smetana wrote about the premiere to Charlotte Valentin in Göteburg: "I have been called the founder of national music and all kinds of distinctions have been conferred on me. Unfortunately I was the only one in the packed house who did not hear a single note of the music, my own music into the bargain!" [11]

In conversation Smetana revealed that he subjectively considered Vendulka's meditation in the first act of *The Kiss* as "the most beautiful passage of my dramatic works, whether with regard to the most perfect harmony of words and melody or the most complete expression by the orchestral accompaniment, of the melancholy which reigns in Vendulka's soul." [12]   However, Smetana also expressed doubt about the lasting success of this opera. He was wrong; *The Kiss* has become his second most popular repertory opera in Czechoslovakia and has reportedly been performed in Austria and Germany under such conductors as Gustav Mahler.

The world premiere of his seventh opera, *Tajemství* (*The Secret,* 1877-78) on September 18, 1878 in the New Czech Theater "went off in an atmosphere of jubilation and sincere joy. Smetana, obviously moved, expressed his thanks after every act and received laurel wreaths and bouquets." [13] This opera stylistically resembles *Hubička* but has not been staged as often. The Supraphon recording of *The Secret* also includes the fragment of Smetana's last, unfinished opera, *Viola.*

Andrew Clark reviewed the Smetana festivities in Prague for the *International Herald Tribune.* [14] He begins this review with a question: "To what extent was the nineteenth-century composer Bedřich Smetana politically aware?" Clark then provides background information about Smetana's first opera, *Braniboři v Čechach* (*The Brandenburgers in Bohemia*), written 1862-63, and reports on the memorable 1945 production which was stylized as a modern allegory of the Nazi occupation. He mentions that the opera was withdrawn from the repertory after August 1968 and was staged in a traditional setting for Smetana's centennial. The reviewer states that *The Brandenburgers in Bohemia* deserves attention as an ensemble opera and that "the composer makes it clear that he sympathizes with the people, one more reason why his credentials as a Czech national composer have remained so impeccable."

Smetana received the libretto for *The Brandenburgers* from Karel Sabina in February 1862 and noted in his diary: "I am setting to work with great pleasure." [15] On April 23, 1863, he completed the third act and entered the score into Count Harrach's competition for a Czech national opera, under the motto: "Music – the language of feeling. Words – the language of ideas." [16] He also tried to have the opera performed. In the fall of 1865 he was asked to rehearse and conduct this opera himself. The premiere on January 5, 1866 at the Provisional Theater was very successful. Shortly afterwards, on March 27, 1866, he was notified that he had been awarded six hundred gulden as the first prize in the Harrach competition for *The Brandenburgers.*

1866 was a momentous year for Smetana. On May 30, he conducted the premiere of the first version of *The Bartered Bride,* on which he had worked since 1863. On July 3, the Prussians defeated the Austrians and occupied Prague. As Jan Löwenbach wrote, "*The Brandenburgers in Bohemia,* with its historical background was, in the war year of 1866, an artistic and political credo of almost uncanny foreboding." [17] Smetana, fearing possible reprisals now that "Brandenburgers" had actually come to Prague, sought safety with his family in the countryside. After his return at the end of the summer, he was engaged as the principal conductor of the Provisional Theater. By that time, he was well into work on his third opera, *Dalibor* (1865-67).

Peter G. Davies has commented: "Obviously there is something about *Dalibor* that resonates in the Czech soul but the rest of us can appreciate only from a distance." [18] *Dalibor* has been performed occasionally in the German-speaking areas of Europe and in Spain with a degree of *succes d'estime* but has never become popular outside of Czechoslovakia. It is somehow ironic that this opera at the time of its premiere on May 16, 1868 – held to celebrate the laying of the cornerstone of the National Theater – caused so much bad blood between Smetana's supporters and opponents. *The Brandenburgers* had sometimes been criticized as neo-German, but "Dalibor Wagner" became the focus of the most violent controversies about Smetana's Czechness. The comment by the music historian August Wilhelm Ambros that Smetana was "a whale in a fishpond" [19] pertains to this period, the era of the anti-Smetana campaign.

Davis also discusses *The Kiss*: "I can imagine this charming opera coming to life in a sensitive production with a superb cast of singing actors." He praises the literary quality of the libretto by Eliška Krásnohorská and Smetana's inventive treatment of it. "Arias, duets and ensembles grow organically from a seamless symphonic fabric, which gives the impression of having been composed in one breathless moment of inspiration."

Yet not even *The Kiss* has been a serious rival to *The Bartered Bride* (*Prodaná nevěsta*, 1863-66; final version 1870). The title is the composer's for Sabina's libretto is untitled. Smetana did not care much for this opera, despite the fast growing success of the revised versions, and formulated his ideas thus: "*The Bartered Bride*, gentlemen, is actually only a toy. I composed it, not out of vanity, but out of spite because after *The Brandenburgers* I was accused of being a Wagnerian and not capable of doing anything in a lighter, national style." [20] These words were spoken at a banquet celebrating the sold-out hundredth performance of *The Bartered Bride* on May 5, 1882, one of the highlights of that time for the ailing composer. In comparison, *The Brandenbergers* was performed only twenty-six times during his lifetime. On another occasion he protested, "When I hear *The Bartered Bride* loudly praised, I have the feeling that people are insulting my other operas." [21]

The Bartered Bride is the only Smetana opera which is regularly performed internationally by the most renowned opera houses and academic opera workshops. During his lifetime, the opera was produced abroad twice: in St. Petersburg in January 1871, and in Zagreb in October 1873. The National Theater performed it on tour in Vienna in 1892. Gustav Mahler introduced it in Hamburg and later conducted it in Vienna (also *Dalibor*). A German company played it in England at Drury Lane in 1907; Chicago saw the opera in Czech in 1893, and the Metropolitan Opera produced it in German on February 19, 1909. The thousandth performance at the Prague National Theater was celebrated in 1927, and two thousand performances were attained in 1953. [22] There is no need to give further proof of *The Bartered Bride*'s fully established popularity.

Smetana's eighth opera, *Čertova stěna*, (*The Devil's Wall*, 1879-82), which was somewhat of a failure at its premiere on October 29, 1882. Smetana was very hurt and was overheard to complain: "So I am too old, so I am not to write any more, they don't want anything else from me!" [23] However, the first complete performance of his cycle *Má Vlast* (*My Country*, 1872-79) on November 5 of that year scored another triumph for the composer.

The first complete cycle of Smetana operas was produced at the National Theater in 1893, Adolf Čech conducting; Kovařovič mounted the cycle twice, in 1904 and 1905; the centennial of Smetana's birth; the cycle produced during the Ostrčil era was a special occasion; in addition to the eight operas, the incomplete fragment of Viola was performed (May 12, 1924). Smetana's operas had a total of 302 performance before his death; in the decade of 1945 to 1955, the National Theater staged 1673 performances. [24]

Much more should be said about Smetana's work. He consistently used Czech subjects, shaped from local history and based on old national legends. In 1879, Smetana rejected a libretto called *Ahasver* as being "too cosmopolitan for me, and the choruses of the Jews and the Romans could not be carried out in any Czecho-Slav (sic) style." He thought that perhaps Dvořák or Fibich could undertake this "difficult task. Both are fresh and young." [25]

Illness prevented him from accomplishing more than a fragment of the first act of *Viola*, his setting of a Shakespearean libretto. The movements *My Country* which have the closest relationship to Czech history - *Šárka, Tábor, Blaník* – are the least performed abroad, while the imaginative *Vltava* (*Moldau*) has captured everyone's fancy without regard to its national origin. Smetana insisted on the Czech language and eschewed universal and traditional texts such as the Stabat Mater and Requiem Mass, which paved the way for Dvořák's international recognition. He did not write any oratorios in any language or genre which might have had wider appeal than his many choruses, which are well-beloved in Czechoslovakia and often limited to that country.

Smetana himself stated: "I am, according to my merits and according to my efforts as a composer, a Czech and the creator of the Czech style in the branches of dramatic and symphonic music – exclusively Czech." [26] His loss of hearing in 1874 and deteriorating health made impossible any expansion of his musical career. He continued to nurture his Czech-centered art with great determination while his strength declined. He regretted his fate but did not seem to feel it as a sacrifice. He gave his all to his people, remaining true to the works he pronounced while the founding stone of the National Theater was laid: "Music is the life of the Czechs," including Smetana.

Smetana celebrations in Czechoslovakia are taken for grated; but the Smetana Centennial: An International Conference and Festival of Czechoslovak Music in San Diego, California, was a one-of-a-kind occurrence. It took place on March 29 - April 8, 1984 at San Diego State University. The National Endowment for the Humanities, Skaggs foundation, and numerous other organizations and individuals supported the event. Scholars from Canada, England, Czechoslovakia and various parts of the United States participated in six academic sessions. Papers on Smetana's life and work, his predecessors and contemporaries, supporters and antagonists were presented. The Czech-American compose Karel Husa evaluated Smetana's heritage for modern composers and also conducted several of his own works; he composed a *Smetana Fanfare* (1984) for the occasion. The violoncellist František Smetana gave one of the recitals of Czech music. The university opera workshop, with the assistance of the Czechoslovak Sokol Dancers of Los Angeles, produced

The Bartered Bride.   The Finnish conductor Paavo Berglund led the San Diego Symphony in the complete cycle *My Country* - and there were still more musical events at the festival. Canadian-born Jaroslav Mráček, Professor of Music at San Diego State University, was the director of the entire enterprise. It was a dignified salute to Smetana's genius. [27]

Notes

1) Francois Marie William Ritter, *Frederic Smetana* (Paris: Alcan, 1907).

2) František Bartoš, *Bedrich Smetana. Letters and Reminiscences.* (Prague: Artia, 1955), pp. 45-7.

3) Ibid., p. 51.

4) Ibid., p. 59.

5) Ibid., p. 270.

6) Vernon Kidd, *International Music Festivals 1984*, p. 14.

7) Bartoš, p. 273.

8) Ibid., p. 274.

9) Ibid., p. 247.

10) Ibid., p. 250.

11) Ibid., p. 173.

12) Ibid., p. 175.

13) Ibid., p. 199.

14) Andrew Clark, review in the *International Herald Tribune* (June 6, 1984).

15) Ibid., p. 66.

16) Ibid., p. 77.

17) Jan Löwenbach, *Bedřich Smetana. Genius of a Freedom-Loving People* (Washington, D.C.: The Volta Bureau, 1943), p. 6.

18) Peter G. Davies, "Smetana's Opera: The Bartered Bride and Beyond" High Fidelity, August 1983).

19) Bartoš, p. 111.

20) Ibid., p. 254.

21) Ibid., p. 256.

22) *Československý hudební slovník* (Czechoslovak Music Dictionary), vol. II (1965).

23) Bartoš, p. 263.

24) *Československý hudební slovník*, vol. II.

25) Bartoš, p. 202.

26) Ibid., p. 250.

27) SVU Bulletin v. 1 (January 1984), v. 2 (May 1984).

GUSTAV MAHLER AND BOHEMIA

Gustav Mahler died at the early age of 51 of infective endocarditis, leaving his *Tenth Symphony* unfinished. We cannot know how his music style, his esthetics and his *Weltanschauung* might have developed if he had lived longer. He did achieve the main goals of his life, becoming an internationally renowned opera and concert conductor as well as a prolific composer, though the deserved appreciation of his creative work did not materialize during his lifetime. His career and life were complex, full of personal struggle and conflict with reality. He has been aptly described as an "eternal exile." Because of his many career moves and also because of his "internal exile," he never felt fully at ease wherever he lived. He was superficially assimilated to his world, but inwardly torn.

Max Brod describes the composer as a paragon of Jewish music in his book *Die Musik Israels* (Tel Aviv, 1951; 2nd ed. Bärenreiter, 1976) and in his frequent lectures on Mahler in Israel. He says: "Mahler wanted to write non-Jewish music; he did not succeed" (2nd. ed., p. 39). Brod made contact with the music of the Hasidic refugees in Prague during and after World War I, and found similarities in Mahler in rhythms (particularly in the march-like passages), certain harmonic features, and cantillation-like melody. Brod published several musical examples in this book and would play these on the piano during his Mahler lectures. He calls Mahler's symphonies "operas without words." Brod's own songs, composed in the early 1900s, have been described as Mahlerian in style and spirit. Moreover, Brod as a Prague music critic correctly predicted Mahler's future recognition and popularity as a composer whom he, in his own words, adored.

Another important factor is Mahler's familiarity with his Bohemian background. In 1871, when he faltered in his studies in Jihlava, he was sent to Prague to continue his studies at a gymnasium there. Young Gustav lived as a boarder with the Gruenfeld family, which produced two virtuosos, a pianist and a cellist. These two boys, Alfred and Heinrich, were several years older and more boisterous than the frail boy from Jihlava. Gustav's stay in the capital of Bohemia was very short; his scholastic grades did not improve. Soon thereafter he went to Vienna to study music at the conservatory and later combined music with humanities courses at the university – but for self-knowledge rather than an academic degree.

Mahler never forgot his Czech and, according to those who were familiar with Viennese German, had a Bohemian accent. The German spoken in Jihlava, a town which had the status of a *Sprachinsel* (a language island) was not *hochdeutsch* but a dialect, reportedly of Swabian origin.

Among Mahler's early, relatively brief engagements as a conductor was the theater at Olomouc (Olmütz, 1882-83) in Moravia and at the German opera in Prague 1885-86 and again in 1887-88). He gained experience and knowledge of the specific problems in conducting staged operas and enlarged his repertoire, though he did not yet have the freedom of choice to perform the works he personally preferred. He had to submit to the authority of the opera directors. Conflicts with singers, opera managers, music critics and the prevalent tastes of the public hounded Mahler in all his temporary stints, for he was uncompromising and a perfectionist in his conducting tasks. On the other hand, when Mahler had the opportunity to conduct Beethoven's *Ninth Symphony*, he was happier on the concert stage than in the theater. He also became acquainted with several Czech musicians.

He made stimulating, lasting contacts with Bohemian musicians between the years 1893 and 1897 in Hamburg. Mahler made a successful debut there at the end of March, 1891. He would have a hectic schedule of guest conducting throughout Europe for the next several years, meeting a number of prominent visiting musicians, premiering new operas in addition to the traditional repertoire, and composing as his time permitted. But he still was relatively unknown and largely unperformed as a composer.

In 1893, the Prague soprano Bertha Foerster-Lauterer (1860-1908) was engaged by the director Bernhard Pollini to sing Eva in *Die Meistersinger* in Hamburg. Her husband, the composer and music critic Josef Bohuslav Foerster (1859-1951), arrived with her, and both spouses soon made the acquaintance of Mahler.

Foerster discusses Mahler in several chapters in his book *Poutník,* translated into German as *Der Pilger. Erinnerungen eines Musikers (*The Pilgrim. Memoirs of a Musician; Prague: Artia, 1955). The meeting of these three Bohemian-born musicians could not have been more opportune, for Smetana's *Prodaná nevěsta* (The Bartered Bride) was in rehearsal and the opera, conducted by Mahler, with Bertha Foerster-Lauterer as Mařenka, was premiered on January 17, 1894 and became a hit. The Czech basso Vilém Heš (1860-1908) sang the role of Kecal in the reprises. Mahler produced other Smetana operas there that season. *Dvě vdovy* (Two Widows) and *Hubička* (The Kiss) were performed but did not find favor with the audiences or with the critics, and soon had to be withdrawn. *Dalibor* was presented on January 11, 1896 without much success; Mahler also conducted this opera in Vienna on October 4, 1897. Smetana's *Vltava* (usually known as The Moldau) and prelude to *Libuše* were on one of Mahler's concert programs in 1900.

The friendship between the Foersters and Mahler eventually became very close and lasted until Mahler's death in 1911. The most important result of this association was the artistic growth of both composers. As peers of the same age, they played new compositions for each other, knowingly discussed their creative aims and supported each other at disappointing and difficult moments. Foerster later wrote that Mahler needed to have just one person who would publicly stand behind him at all times. He also summarized Mahler's existential stand in these words: "The conductor Mahler was the embodiment of will, a commander and a leader; he was energy and power, a taut string stretched to the extreme ... The composer Mahler was the embodiment of the will to love. His entire life, his entire work knows only one goal in manifold variations: the yearning for love ... but he does not find love ... for perfection is God." Foerster championed his admired friend Mahler in Czechoslovakia where he returned after 1918 to become the director of the Prague Conservatory. He survived Mahler by forty years.

Mahler seems to have conducted Dvořák's music more frequently than Smetana's, even during his Vienna era. He conducted Dvořák's symphonic poems *Píseň bohatýrská* (Heroic Song) and *Holoubek* (The Wild Dove) in 1898 and the *Serenade in D*, op. 44 in 1901. Negotiations about the opera *Rusalka* were initiated and, in a letter dated May 4, 1901, Mahler expressed the hope that he would be asked to conduct it. A translation into German was then available but the talks took another turn and were broken. *Rusalka* was not performed in Vienna until 1935, and then at the Volksoper.

Another Czech composer of the same generation of post romantic innovators, Leoš Janáček (1854-1928), invited Mahler for a performance of the just-premiered *Její pastorkyňa* (Jenufa) in Brno. Mahler's brief answer, dated December 9, 1904, has survived. It reads: "Dear Sir, As I have explained to Baron Pražák, I am unable to leave Vienna at the present time, but as I would be very interested to get to know your work, I beg you to be kind enough to send me the vocal score with German words. Yours sincerely, Mahler." (J. Vogel, *Leoš Janáček. His Life and Work.* Prague: Artia, 1962; p. 234). The score could not have been sent, for the first German translation was made in 1916 by Max Brod after the Prague première of the opera. Vienna first heard it on February 16, 1918 in Brod's translation.

Mahler and Janáček had the opportunity to meet each other in April, 1880, but apparently did not do so. In that month, Janáček arrived in Vienna to study at the conservatory. As we have mentioned above, Mahler re-enrolled at the university at precisely this time after finishing his conservatory studies. Moreover, Mahler and Janáček both studied under the same director, Josef Hellmesberger. Mahler's professor of piano was Julius Epstein, Janáček's teacher was Josef Dachs, and neither of them became a concert pianist. Franz Krenn taught both students composition and counterpoint; Mahler also opted for the classes given by Anton Bruckner. Both students were considered very talented but somewhat rebellious and willful. Neither had found an easy route to recognition and success of their then unusual expression of strong creative personalities. And both are very famous today.

We must remember that Mahler's belated recognition after the end of World War II was a consequence of the politics of the 1930s. Being labeled by the Nazis as a degenerate Jewish musician, his music was prohibited in Germany, Austria and all the Nazi-occupied countries. A personal recollection may serve as a further illustration.

In 1962, on a trip to Europe, I had the opportunity to check out some holdings of the Westdeutsche Bibliothek, then located in Marburg / Lahn. While looking for Jewish music, I found books by Jadassohn and also copies of Mahler's published works. An interesting surprise was the fact that every page had been stamped with a swastika and that each swastika had been crossed out in ink, obviously by hand. Thus the music books seemed to be permanent documents of the twentieth century's history, after being hidden out of circulation until the end of the war. Whether the deletion of the Nazi stamps was intended to indicate Mahler's symbolic "rehabilitation" or "liberation" from having been silenced between 1933 and 1945, I do not know. At least the printed materials were saved.

Alma Rosé, Gustav Mahler's niece and a professional violinist, was less fortunate. She became the conductor of the girls' orchestra at the Birkenau death camp. She did not survive, as Fania Fénelon tells us in her book *Playing for Time* (New York: 1st Berkley edition, 1979). But that is another story.

MASARYK AND MUSIC

A minor aspect of the "Masaryk legend" and of the emotional attachment of many Czechs and Slovaks toward Masaryk as a benevolent father is
his involvement with music. Looking back, it seems that every child attending
school in the First Republic knew that certain songs were favorites of "tatíček
Masaryk" - just as they knew that he approved of studying, loving the truth
and the Republic, and working diligently. The idea of linking musical instruction in schools with good citizenship certainly is in agreement with Ko-
menský's pedagogical principles, which Masaryk supported, and has roots in
ancient Greek concepts about *ethos* in music.

Three folksongs in particular are firmly associated with Masaryk, to
such an extent that some of us disillusioned grownups may discount them as
an expression of undesirable sentimentalism and unfashionable softhearted-
ness. But who can hear or sing these songs without thoughts of Masaryk, and
without regretting that his optimistic ideals were lost in the reality of the 20th
century? This is a natural reaction, for music often sharpens and enhances diverse affective associations. And, after all, Czechoslovaks do consider themselves an eminently musical nation.

In any case, whether we treat them with aloofness or affection, these
three songs are: "Ach, synku, synku" ("Oh, my son, little son"), "Teče voda
teče" ("The water flows") and "Tatíčku starý náš" ("Our dear old daddy").
According to the soprano Jarmila Novotná, only the first of these songs was
actually Masaryk's favorite, perhaps because of its practical work ethic which
President Masaryk described thus: "This is my song; when anything gets broken, it must be fixed." The second song may have had an emotional affinity
with Masaryk's Moravian-Slovakian origins, and the third one has become
prophetic: all went reasonably well with Czechoslovakia while the old father
Masaryk lived, and when he died, his country and whole Europe sank into the
degradation of the Second World War.

And thus these songs became part of the popular charismatic legend of
Masaryk. The legend was complemented by his contacts with music in his
intimate family circle, as well as his position as head of the State. He attended
official musical events and prominent Czechoslovak composers dedicated
compositions to him.

The musician of the Masaryk family was, first of all, Mrs. Masaryk.
Born Charlotte Garrigue in Brooklyn, she began in 1874 to study piano in
Leipzig where she met Liszt and other musicians. Although she had to give up
her aspirations to become a professional pianist because of problems with her
hand, she kept her musical interests alive all her life. After she married Tomáš
Masaryk in 1878, she developed a sincere appreciation for Czech music, especially Smetana. In the 1890's she published a series of articles on: Smetana
which were re-issued in 1950 in book form. *Československý hudební slovník*
gives full recognition of her contribution to Smetana research.

It is generally accepted that she influenced her husband's interest in music. Their son, Jan Masaryk, was a fine pianist and friend of many musicians, and assisted them during his diplomatic career.

For example, when Leoš Janáček visited London in 1926, Jan Masaryk, then Czechoslovak ambassador to England, was very helpful. Bohuslav Martinů was Jan Masaryk's personal friend; he lived with him occasionally in Paris during the twenties and later returned the hospitality when Masaryk came in the spring of 1945 to New York for the inauguration of the United Nations. Moreover, Martinů's *Third Piano Concerto* of 1948 was composed in response to Jan Masaryk's tragic death; a quotation from Dvořák's *Requiem* appears in the second movement.

Perhaps Jan Masaryk's best-known contribution to music is the recording *Songs of Lidice,* made during World War II, in which he improvised accompaniments for Jarmila Novotná, member of the Metropolitan Opera. Václav Dobiáš notated these improvisations from the recording, and prepared the songs for publication in Czechoslovakia in 1947. Jan Masaryk, then Czechoslovak Minister of Foreign Affairs, wanted to publish these songs for performance and write an introduction. But then came the events of February 1948 and his unexpected death on March 10. Only a few copies of this publication survive. It was reprinted twenty years later during Prague Spring of 1968 with comments and texts in Russian, English, and German as well as Czech. Herberta Masaryková's 1948 introduction gives an interesting description of music in Masaryk's home: "Jan Masaryk used to come home from abroad; in the residence of the old President, he would talk of the world outside his country but play the music of his own country. The evenings were spent in the music room when Jan was at home, and there was music, singing, playing and merry-making. The old President was very happy than and used to beat time with his toe to Jan's livelier pieces. Those were the happiest days of Jan's busy and cheerless life."

President Masaryk was interested in the careers of musicians and often helped them with advice, recognition, moral and even financial support. Some were invited for musical evenings to the Castle or to the Lány retreat, as Jarmila Novotná gratefully remembers. Leoš Janáček dedicated his opera *Excursions of Mr. Brouček* to President Masaryk, "the Liberator of the Czech Nation." His correspondence with the office of Dr. Alice Masaryková from May 1919 has been preserved and confirms the acceptance of the dedication. The two men met at least once, during the concert of Janáček's works performed on December 8, 1924 in Prague, at the occasion of his 70th birthday. The President was present and invited Janáček to his box for conversation. He also sent him a personal letter when Janáček retired next year from his teaching post.

In 1918, Vítězslav Novák composed two choral works on texts by Machar under the title *To T. G. Masaryk.* One of them is called "Masaryk's March" and has been arranged for various ensembles, including band. We could also mention K. B. Jirák's *Salute for T.G.M.*, composed for the celebration of Masaryk's eightieth birthday on March 7, 1930.

Another such work is the cantata *Blahoslavený ten člověk* (Blessed Is the Man), op. 23, by Ladislav Vycpálek. The composer conceived the idea of a cantata, tentatively called *Vůdce* (The Leader), immediately after the end of World War I. He planned to use psalm texts and contemporary poetry celebrating the Independence of the Czechoslovak Republic and President Masaryk. However, he shelved the work for ten years and finished it in modified form under the new title in 1933. It was first performed on March 5, 1934 in Brno. Although it uses psalm texts, *Blahoslavený ten člověk* is not a truly religious work but signs the praise of a morally strong, just, humanistic man (and mankind) who can withstand the pressures and dangers of life without compromising himself. Vycpálek's dedication of the cantata to T. G. Masaryk is the only direct outcome of his original plan. Spiritually the whole concept is very close to Masaryk's idealism.

In 1939, Otakar Jeremiáš began to compose third cantata, *Zpěv rodné země* (Song of Our Native Country), using a poem by Josef Hora. He finished it in 1940 and received the first Melantrich prize for it in 1941. The work which ends with the words: "And thus we all, dead, alive and yet unborn, we march keeping watch," remained unperformed until March 7, 1946 when it was broadcast as a special program to commemorate Masaryk's ninety-sixth birthday. It seems also appropriate to mention that there is an unpublished vocal work among Jeremiáš's manuscripts entitled: "In us the grateful country sings to you;" these words are directly related to President Masaryk's teachings.

More compositions dedicated to Masaryk or connected with him in some way could undoubtedly be found, and other names should be mentioned. However this modest sample seems sufficient to support the initial statement that Masaryk and music are firmly associated in the hearts and minds of his people.

SVU meeting
Masaryk Symposium
Los Angeles, October 1975

VÍTĚZSLAVA KAPRÁLOVÁ (1915 – 1940)

Bohuslav Martinů went to Paris in 1923 at the age of 33 to study composition. He remained there for the next seventeen years, and became a recognized and performed composer. However, his career goal throughout all his adult life was to teach composition, preferably at the Prague Conservatory of Music. Such an appointment was prevented first by World War II, and then by the aftermath of his serious accident in July 1946, and after 1948, by the opposition of the communist regime in Czechoslovakia against him as a "foreigner." Martinů was unable to accept such early offers of a professorship and then was unwanted, not even invited for a short visit to his beloved native country. There seem to have been only two Czech composers who were Martinů's direct pupils.

One of these was Jan Novák (b. Nová Ríse, Moravia, 1921: d. West Germany, 1984) who studied composition with Martinů in 1947 in New York and with Aaron Copland at the Berkshire Music Center.

The other was Vítězslava Kaprálová. She was Martinů's pupil in Paris in the late 1930s, before her early death at age 25 and Martinů's adventurous flight from France to the United States, where he and his wife arrived on March 21, 1941. Vítězslava means Victoria in English; her nicknames were Vitulka and Vitka.

I was impelled to write this short paper to the memory of the woman composer Kaprálová by two factors. First of all, there has been a tendency in the United States during the past decades to identify women composers from different countries, such as Fanny Mendelssohn, Maria Szymanowska, Nadia Boulanger and others. New material was collected to organize full-length concerts and radio programs presenting their creative work, and to write articles about them. But as far as I was able to determine, Vítězslava Kaprálová is, for the most part, not known in this country except among Czechoslovak exiles or in connection with a special occasion connected with Czech music, such as a November 1989 concert at a university in Oklahoma in which her *April Preludes* for piano were performed.

The other factor was the appearance of a biography by Jiří Mucha. The author, a poet-son of the celebrated painter Alfons Mucha (1860-1939) married Vitka Kaprálová on April 23, 1940. At the time, he was enlisted in the exile Czechoslovak Army in France. After almost half a century, he gathered material from his personal memories and the surviving correspondence from the hectic prewar period in Paris up to Vitka's death on June 16, 1940, the day France capitulated.

The life story of this talented daughter of the Brno composer Václav Kaprál (1889-1947) and her precocious creativity deserve to be made known to American musicians and the public. It would be worthwhile to arrange a concert of Czechoslovak women composers, for Kaprálová is not the only such composer.

The short but fruitful life of Kaprálová can be summarized briefly. She was born in Brno on January 24, 1915. She started to compose at 9, entered the Brno Conservatory of Music at 15, and earned her degree by conducting the first part of her *Piano Concerto in d minor*, op. 7 (1934-35), with Ludvík Kundera as the soloist. The complete concerto won her the František Neumann Prize. In 1935-37 she studied at the Prague Master School and then, late in 1937 and again in 1938, she received a scholarship to Paris for the Ecole Normal de Musique.

Her composition teachers were Vilém Petrželka (1889-1967) in Brno, Vítězslav Novák (1870-1949) in Prague, and Martinů in Paris, though she was also enrolled in composition and orchestration classes with Mme. Boulanger. However, Boulanger was away for most of the time; she was invited to conduct in the United States and stayed there for the duration of the war.

In conducting - an unusual specialty for a young girl at that time - she was instructed by Zdeněk Chalabala (1899-1962) in Brno, Václav Talich (1883-1961) in Prague and Charles Munch (1891-1968) in Paris.

Her compositional output comprised 25 opus numbers. The last work was *Deux ritournelles* for cello and piano; she did not finish the second piece. She composed many other pieces which were performed and published, but considered them less important than the works to which she gave opus numbers.

Vitulka Kaprálová achieved an outstanding success when she conducted the Czech Philharmonic Orchestra in her *Military Sinfonietta*, op. 7, on November 27, 1937, at Lucerna Hall. She traveled from Paris to Prague for this special occasion, which was attended by President Beneš. This annual gala concert was sponsored by the Czech Women's Council and arranged by Senator Františka Plamínková (executed by the Nazis in June 1942). K. B. Jirák conducted the other two works: Dvořák's overture to *Šelma sedlák* and Suk's *Asrael Symphony*. In his book, Mucha gives interesting details about that concert and about the acceptance of the *Sinfonietta* for the 1938 International Society for Contemporary Music (ISCM) Festival London. Martinů accompanied Vitka to London and reported in a letter to her parents that she conducted her work very well. The London performance gained Vitulka an entry in Slonimsky's reference work *Music since 1900*. The *Military Sinfonietta* received the Smetana Jubilee Fund Prize in 1939.

Shortly before the trip to London, on June 2, a concert of Czech music took place in Paris, presenting Smetana, Janáček, Novák, Martinů, Suk and Dvořák. It was a special cultural program to honor Adolf Hoffmeister and his art. Josef Páleníček participated and Kaprálová conducted along with other French musicians. These successes took place within the still relatively carefree atmosphere of friendship between France and Czechoslovakia before the Munich pact changed the course of Czechoslovakia's history. One person who did not return to Prague after Munich was Jiří Mucha, a journalist on tour to England with the Czech Philharmonic, who settled in Paris permanently - and eventually met Vítězslava Kaprálová, in April 1939.

It would be interesting to learn more about the Czech colony in the Paris during the 1930's. Among the artists, musicians, diplomats, writers, journalists, politicians, students and - after March 15, 1939 - refugees from occupied Czechoslovakia we could mention Rudolf Firkušný, František Smetana, Jarmila Vavrdová, Rudolf Kundera, Miloš Šafránek, Egon Erwin Kisch, Otakar Kraus, Jaroslav Stein, Ivan Spaniel, Vláďa Clementis, Adolf Hoffmeister, Antonín Pelc, Rudolf Šturm, František Langer, the Osuskys, Julius Firt, Hugo Haas, the painter Diviš, Friedrich Torberg, and others. Some of them lived in Paris for years; others left for other countries as soon as possible, or joined the Czechoslovak Armed Forces in Exile, which was formed at the beginning of World War II.

But we should focus on our protagonists, Kaprálová and Martinů, and the narrator Mucha. It is interesting that before the *Strange Loves* appeared, Kaprálová's name was usually omitted or briefly mentioned in Martinů biographies, usually in connection with her *Military Sinfonietta*.

ČSHS alludes to the "artists' friendship" which developed between them. Mucha adds details which were not previously available. He married Vitka, but the marriage lasted only two months; her fatal illness - miliary tuberculosis - was discovered. Mucha was deeply hurt; only after several decades had elapsed was he able to study Vitka's diary and correspondence with Martinů as well as with her parents and "significant others" in her short life. Then he published his book.

According to Mucha, Martinů found the embodiment of his dream in Vitka - Juliétte, his musical alter ego, the person for which he had waited all his life, his Czech "Písnička" (little song), as he soon started to call her. She called him Špalíček (child's toy top, or children's folk rhymes), He was twice Vitka's age, and had been married since 1931 to Charlotte Henahen, a French seamstress whose dedicated care and work enabled Martinů to dedicate himself fully to composition, without and regular job. They led a rather Bohemian life; neither sought luxury, social status or comfort. Those who knew Martinů describe him as serious, basically shy and introverted, a creative loner, not too sure of himself despite his successes. Vitulka Kaprálová was his opposite in many ways. She was youthfully self-assured, unafraid to voice her opinions, even fresh with her elders, attractive and moody. Mucha says, "it was easy to fall in love with her and with her talent." And that is exactly what several men did - Martinů and Mucha as well.

Mucha tried to find the real Vitka through his research. In retrospect she was more complex a personality than he had known during their courtship and marriage. He comments that she "was able to be faithful to several persons at a time and, at that quite sincerely. She loved with her body, but also with her head." [1] Elsewhere he expresses this thought by alluding to her musical way of thinking and feeling: "The polyphonic voice-leading which Novák had taught her allowed her to manage two or three emotional relations simultaneously, usually without serious disharmony." [2] Mucha also introduces other rationalizations to explain how Vitka could write loving letters to several suitors while Martinů was asking her whether she would like to be with him forever - because it was decided in heaven that Písnička and Špalíček had to meet and never part from each other. [3] Martinů also wrote to her about their destiny to compose music, "a hard but beautiful obligation which can be a fulfillment of one's whole life." [4]

Music was a strong tie, but their personal relationship endured crises who were intensified by the political upheavals in Europe during 1938 and 1939, and the growing insecurity about surviving in France.

I wish to go beyond Mucha's speculations and make a more clinical analysis of "Strange Loves." It seems that this relationship has to do with dynamics of identification, symbiotic and dependency tendencies and, particularly, with transference-counter transference phenomena. These terms are often used in connection with the patient-therapist relationship but also apply to such dyads as those of teacher-pupil. We all are familiar with the infatuations of school girls for their teachers.

But, while such transference usually remains healthy - and it helps to develop imitation of skills and identification with a model of a profession - the admired idol is not supposed to return the affection and get entangled in a an actual relationship- for example, wanting to marry the patient or the pupil.

In the Špalíček-Písnička relationship, Martinů apparently was more persistent in pursuing his dream of bliss, while Vitka tried to go free after the initial intense contact. The documents bear this out. She wrote to her parents in April 1939 that she had nobody to talk to except Martinů but that she feared he would grasp how much she depended on him. [5] Her way to break the spell was to be cool rather than nice to him. She became engaged to Rudolf Kopec, an engineer, but she broke off with him before their wedding, which she had already postponed. She rejected another Czech in Paris, had a brief affair, and finally married Mucha. She discussed all these relationships with Martinů in letters to discourage him, but there were some brief reconciliations and there was even a notion that she might go to American with Martinů and that Charlotte would remain in France.

However, she wrote a long letter to Kopec in January 1939; among other things, she mentioned that she cried long into the night for a strange reason that she did not understand: she felt she did not love Martinů anymore... And she confessed how painful it was to see Martinů suffer. And on March 26, 1939, when she knew she did not want to return to the Protectorate – alhtough Kopec was waiting for her there, happily adjusting to the new Nazi regime - she wrote in her diary: "The most difficult day. I'm going to pieces."

It was a difficult time for Martinů too. After the Munich crisis, he felt that "Everything of mine is crumbling, all is collapsing ... All is sort of abandoning me and I am losing everything, my písnička ..." He wrote these words to Vitka from Schoenenberg, Switzerland, where he was writing *the Concerto Grosso*. Then Kaprálová received another scholarship and returned to Paris. Several Martinů letters in the book included various drawings or verses, very intimate, very sincere and even playful, not what one might expect from such a serious man. However, this story had to be told. The general tone of

Mucha's book is unsensational and his facts are well documented. It is hoped he found peace with the past through writing this book.

Vítězslava Kaprálová died in Montpellier, France. After the war, her ashes were transferred to her family domicile at Tři studně (Three Wells) in the Czech-Moravian Highlands. In 1946 she was made a member of the Czechoslovak Academy of Arts and Sciences, *in memoriam*.

Bohuslav Martinů died of stomach cancer on Aug 29, 1959, in Liestal, Switzerland, and was buried at the Sachers' estate. A few days before his death, he was married by a priest to his faithful Charlotte, who survived him and preserved his legacy. On August 27, 1979, he was reburied in his native Polička. The words "I am home" are on his tombstone and a plaque marks his birthplace. In 1941, Jiří Mucha married Geraldine Thomsen of London, a daughter of two musicians who had composed since her childhood and is a member of the Union of Czech Composers. The Muchas have lived in Czechoslovakia since 1945.

If you would like to know more, read Mucha's book, which provides many other important details.

Notes

Editor's note: Vítězslava Kaprálová has received increased attention in the last decade as an outstanding woman composer. Mucha's chronology and conclusions have been questioned on the basis of archival evidence. However, it is clear that her relationship with Martin had a decisive impact on his compositions as well as hers.

1) Jiri Mucha, *Podivné lásky* [Strange loves] Prague: Mladá fronta, 1988, p. 230.

2) Mucha, p. 374.

3) Mucha, p. 194.

4) Mucha, p. 170.

5) Mucha, p. 229.

"WITH EXTINGUISHED STRENGTH AND HEART IN THE DUST AS A TREE THAT HAS BEEN UPROOTED …"
A STUDY OF JANÁČEK'S CREATIVITY

Leoš Janáček's music has gained international acceptance since his death. Aspects of his music which seemed controversial, harsh, eccentric and ultramodern during his life are seen in retrospect as mellow and inherently lyrico-dramatic when compared with today's avant-garde music. Works that were initially criticized or rejected as impossible to play and sing have developed a relatively comfortable performing tradition, which can be accessed through numerous performances and recordings as models and stylistic guides by anyone who wants to try them for the first time. Nevertheless, the complete critical edition of Janáček's oeuvre has not been published.

Janáček research continues to increase in Czechoslovakia as well as in other countries. Although a great amount of valuable bibliographic material has been published since the end of World War II, most of it is available only in Czech and the primary sources are not yet exhausted.

The details of Janáček's personal and artistic biography have been narrated so many times that one should avoid superfluous repetition. Therefore we will refrain from a systematic biographical sketch and from listing his works, on the presumption that this data is readily available. In order to commemorate the 50th anniversary of Janáček's death and to introduce certain aspects of his creative life for further discussion, let us begin with a brief resume of his last weeks.

On July 1, 1928, Janáček went to the Luhačovice spa for three weeks to take the cure for rheumatism. He celebrated his 74th birthday there and returned to Brno thinner by fifteen pounds, tired and dispirited, yet eagerly looking forward to his planned vacation at Hukvaldy. He usually liked to be there alone and work quietly, but that year he had an additional guest room constructed, and Mrs. Kamila Stösslová accepted his invitation to visit him there.

He met Kamila, her husband Daniel Stössl and one of their sons on July 29 in Brno, and took them to see an exhibition of paintings by the Moravian Joža Úprka (1861-1940), who was a friend of Janáček, and the newly built Exposition Hall. The next day was the birthday of his wife; nevertheless, he and the Stössl family left at noon by train for Hukvaldy. At the last moment before leaving his house, he reportedly packed the third act of his manuscript of the opera *The House of the Dead,* which he wanted to revise, closed his piano and said in a soft voice: "I am done with everything; it feels as if I might not return." His goodbye to his wife was quite strained, for she had suffered much from his relationship with Mrs. Stösslová and strongly disapproved of this joint vacation. [1)]

Mr. Stössl left Hukvaldy after a few days, and Janáček remained with Kamila and the young boy. The composer had long wanted to show her all of the beloved places of his native Lachian region. They hiked, made excursions to surrounding points of interest, and met Janáček's good friends; he enthusiastically discussed his musical plans for the future with them. Then on Monday, August 6, Janáček caught a cold while frantically looking for Kamila's son, who seemed to be lost in the woods. His ears began to bother him seriously on Thursday, and the physician who saw him recommended hospitalization as flu developed into pneumonia. But Janáček refused to go until Friday, when an ambulance was called to transport him to the clinic of Dr. Klein in Ostrava. Despite high fever and worsening cardiac condition, he remained conscious on Saturday and strongly opposed the idea of informing his wife Zdenka about his illness. He started to fail in the night and died on Sunday, August 12, 1928 at exactly ten o'clock in the morning, after a series of heart attacks and a brief coma.

Zdenka Janáčková received a cable that he had been hospitalized only after his death. She went to Ostrava to arrange the transfer of his body for burial in Brno. The solemn, official funeral took place on Wednesday, August 15, which was also the birthday of Janáček's deceased daughter Olga. Then a mistake was discovered about the location of the grave, and Janáček had to be reburied quietly two days later, accompanied only by his wife and few close friends.

In her reminiscences, Zdenka wrote: "I looked at Leoš through the glass in the top of the casket. His face was sardonically contracted, angry looking. Olga and my mother smiled in their coffins, daddy had a peaceful expression on his face; but looking at Leoš I had to think: You hated to die, you fought death. I could not say goodbye to him with a hug and a sign of cross; there was that glass wall between us. At least I planted a kiss upon it. I felt like choking to death at the moment of that sorrow, tearless, wordless." [2] Unfortunately, a death mask was not made, as was customary at the time when prominent persons died.

Among many problems Zdenka had to face after her husband's sudden death was the erection of a suitable tombstone. The Moravian artist Eduard Milén, who had created the designs in 1924 for the world premiere of *The Cunning Little Vixen,* was asked to design the tombstone at the suggestion of Osvald Chlubna, who had been one of Janáček's students in composition. Milén described his inspiration thus: "I came to the conclusion that the (design for the) stone had to be resolved ideologically, simply, without a statue. Janáček did not follow conventional taste; he was like a hard boulder, a column growing out of the earth and giving light. And so I said to myself: I'll build a column, I will put notes on it and let it stand there like a strong rock, light in color, glowing." [3] Brno musicologist Vladimír Helfert liked the idea and chose the quotation. Zdenka liked it as well: "That tombstone is not intended to mean anything more than to express how I saw Janáček." The tomb was not finished until August 15, 1929, for the stone had to be ordered and the musical notes created difficulty for the stonecutter. A quotation from Tagore which also appears at the end of Janáček's chorus *The Wandering Madman* was chosen as the title of this study. Milén's depiction of the composer, whom he knew very well, is certainly significant and appropriate. It can serve as a starting point for our exploration of Janáček's creative personality.

Much material - almost too much - has accumulated about Janáček's creativity. A large part of it is centered on exegesis of his art from many different aesthetic points of view. Janáček also often wrote and talked about this topic, to defend his artistic credo against his detractors as well as to formulate his feelings and thoughts about himself and his composing. His self-revelations were sincere, spontaneous, frequent and unsystematic. They are scattered throughout his articles, feuilletons, voluminous correspondence, information about his compositions and personal life, and also appear in interviews and informal conversations preserved in writing by his friends or enemies.

In his letters, Janáček typically wrote about whatever musical or other matters concerned him at the moment. He would abruptly insert such ideas between completely unrelated statements about his state of mind as a person and / or a composer without further elaboration. One of the many examples which could be cited is his short letter dated May 7, 1921 to Otakar Ostrčil, who was then the opera director of the Prague National Theater. [4] Janáček begins by referring to Ostrčil's letter of May 5, 1921, which explains why a performance of Janáček's opera *Brouček* must be postponed. Janáček then quotes a Czech adage "You can't buy a hare in a sack - and I don't want to sell it that way anyway," or more idiomatically in English, "don't buy a pig in a poke," in reference to the proposed premiere of his recently finished *Katya Kabanova* at the Prague National Theater. But immediately afterwards he writes: "Now I am like an out-of-tune piano that had been played too much. The stormy ocean must feel just as rotten when it begins to settle down into a lazy quietness." He then returns to more prosaic matters: "So you don't know anything about last nominations for the Academy." Two more lines about the Academy nominations and a salutation conclude the letter. From other letters of that time, we can in this case deduct that this train of thought most probably indicates his anticipation of a vacation rest after a hectic, eventful and productive winter season. In other instances, and there are such revealing personal statements remain isolated - enigmatic and more meaningful through their expressively suggestive value than by any manifest content. His writing style mirrors some of his musical characteristics, and *vice versa*, especially a tendency to be lapidary and abrupt. On the other hand, he makes a great effort to be objective and scientific in theoretical works such as his harmony textbook, sometimes with almost pedantic results which contrast strongly with his expressive compositions and his free, poetic, and aesthetically stimulating writings.

Janáček's interest in psychology of music and aesthetics is well known; it began during his student years. His sources were Wundt, Helmholtz, Zimmerman, Durdík, Skuherský, Herbart, Riemann, Hanslick, Hostinský and a others who generally represent the state of knowledge of the third quarter of the nineteenth century. With this background of physiological and formalistic

theories, Janáček attempted to explain his creative processes and aims, antici-
pating the development of music in the latter decades of the twentieth century.
One can only speculate how acquaintance with dynamic psychology might
have affected Janáček's introspection, and in turn would have facilitated our
interpretation of this complex man and highly autonomous artist. Max Brod,
his early biographer, was the only one at the time who explicitly saw
Janáček's perplexing paradoxes and symbolism in the frame of the ideas of his
fellow Moravian Sigmund Freud. Brod was often able to write about the
composer in a very insightful manner which seems far ahead of its time.

Let us consider Janáček's creative personality on the basis of *Creativity. The Magic Synthesis* (1976) by Silvano Arieti, an American psychiatrist of
Italian origin, using Janáček's remarks and related material as illustrations. [5]
We are fortunate that Janáček, although primarily a musician, was also observant and very articulate.

Arieti outlines a very comprehensive theory of creativity and its multiple factors, which he generally applies to literature, visual arts, sciences and
philosophy. Mortimer Cass comments on the applicability of Arieti's theory
to music. [6]

In the introduction to the book, Arieti provides the following summary,
supporting his statements with references to his previous publications in the
field of psychology: "A sharp distinction must be made between the creative
process and the creative product. In contrast to what could be said about the
creative product, the creative process is shorn of newness and sublimity; to a
considerable extent it consists of ancient, obsolete, and primitive mental
mechanisms generally relegated to those recesses of the psyche that are under
the domain of what Freud called the primary process.

"The primary process, for Freud, is a way in which the psyche functions, especially the unconscious part of the psyche. It prevails in dreams and
some mental illnesses, especially psychoses. The primary process operates
quite differently from the secondary process, which is the way of functioning
of the mind when it is awake and uses common logic. Primary process
mechanisms reappear in the creative process also, in strange, intricate combinations with secondary process mechanisms, and in syntheses that, although
unpredictable, are nevertheless susceptible of psychological interpretation. It
is from appropriate matching with secondary process mechanisms that the
primitive forms of cognition, generally confined to abnormal conditions or to
unconscious processes, become innovating powers. I have proposed the expression tertiary process to designate this special combination of primary and
secondary process mechanisms. For accuracy's sake, I must point out that in
a certain number of creative processes the matching is not necessarily between
primary and secondary process mechanisms, but between faulty or archaic and
normal mechanisms, all of which belong to the secondary process. For these
combinations, too, I have used the name tertiary process.

"In making the distinction between primary and secondary process and
in stressing the role of symbolism in general, the reader will soon recognize

how much I owe to Freud and also, how much I differ from him. The concept of tertiary process does not exist in Freudian theory. Freud has the great merit of having stressed the importance of the psychic reality as something to be distinguished from the reality of the external world. But he insisted that the two realities must remain distinguished, lest psychic reality be used as an escape from external reality ... However, when we deal with the problem of creativity, a different prospect is desirable. The tertiary process, with specific mechanisms and forms, blends the two worlds of mind and matter, and, in many cases, the rational with the irrational. Instead of rejecting the primitive (or whatever is archaic, obsolete, or off the beaten path), the creative mind integrates it with normal logical processes in what seems a "magic" syntheses from which the new, the unexpected, and the desirable emerge." [7)]

Elsewhere, Arietti states: "the creative person − for some reasons not fully understood − maintains a greater than average accessibility to imagery, metaphor, emphatic verbalization, and other forms related to what he calls the primary process. According to Croce, art is intuition (or intuitive knowledge) that produces "images," not concepts ... "Inspiration" is the faculty by which a creative person finds a primary-process form that will hold the content of the secondary process ... The artist must put together many elements of different origins to make syntheses of higher orders − that is, to create artistic unities. The word "poet" derives from the Greek *poietes*, the maker. And yet often the artist seems to uncover unities rather than to make new ones ... Once the unity is formed by the artist, it is easily apprehended by others. The concordance of various elements, or the confluence of the various levels of cognition and affects, makes it easy to grasp the unity or at least to respond aesthetically to it. The new unity enlarges our world and our capacity for experience. Without it, life seems impoverished." [8)]

The intuitive knowledge of the artist produces 'images,' not concepts. What is popularly termed 'inspiration' means that through the primary process, the creative person finds certain material that will become the content of the secondary process.

The secondary process provides the screening and elimination of many suggestions and partial representations of the primary material. This is the logical, conceptual, intellectual second step of the creative process. Then comes what Arieti calls "the magic synthesis," the true creative moment of the tertiary process which provides the "click" or match between the primary and secondary processes, and a new unity comes into existence - a technical invention, a poem, musical composition or a new theorem. An important characteristic of such a new unity, in our case a new aesthetic whole, is the condition that it be formed from disparate elements which have never before perceived as congruous or combined in this particular way.

This complicated mental mechanism in the act of aesthetic creation requires, paradoxically, an unusual level of passivity and an increased level of activity on the part of the creative person, and also explains stages of indeterminate activity, search for form, groping, and preparation, below the level of awareness as well as on the conscious level. This explanation may suffice as a general theoretical framework.

This terminology would undoubtedly have been alien to Janáček. Yet many of his communications clearly indicate that he was usually sensitive to his mental processes and was able to describe them, usually in a metaphoric and aphoristic manner, especially toward the end of his career when he had achieved much personal and artistic maturity and inner security. He said about composing, for example: "How to find the beginnings of works, already known, in that ball of thread in my brain. It's not possible anymore. It is certain that each one of my operas was growing for a year or two in my mind without my hindering its growth by a single note. Each one of my works was a big headache for a long time." [9] He gave advice in a letter to Max Brod: "First of all, it is not good to write immediately after [having received] strong impressions. When those impressions are overlaid by another layer of living [experiences] the ideas become richer - and flow up more urgently like an Artesian well." [10] He confessed to F. S. Procházka: "It's my custom to put a finished work aside - until another flood of moods passes over it. After some time, one gets other eyes. The work must not absorb one completely, [absorb] all of one's mind." [11]

Janáček's treatment of texts has often been under fire for being repetitive as well as not being repetitive enough according to structural rules of traditional musical forms. This situation became apparent, for example, in translations made by Brod, who tended to eliminate repetitions of words or short phrases by enriching the text. Yet Janáček sensitively used the repetition for his dramatic, psychologically sound goals - for musings of a distressed protagonist, somewhat inarticulate exclamations under the press of emotions, the threefold fateful pronouncements, a instantaneous stutter on erotically charged words. In the course of an extensive section on the use of language in poetry, Arieti says: "... repetition of words or of special patterns of words increases the semantic effect It indicates that the matter dealt with should penetrate the heart of the reader" [12] and, we can add, one who listeners to music. "Often plays on words, assonances, alliterations, and so on are considered artificial techniques; poets are thought to indulge in these technical refinements at the cost of losing spontaniety and interest in the content. Nothing could be farther from the truth. Inasmuch as the poet has much easier access to these primary or archaic mechanisms, compared to the average person, special phonetic structures occur spontaneously to him ... The poet choses only those that fit with his secondary process and with the general need of his tertiary process." [13] Janáček's many fragments and the sources connected with new works in various stages of development are a rich source of information about the creative impulses that were not developed to the level of magic synthesis.

He worked for two years on the song cycle *The Diary of One Who Vanished* (1917-1919) and commented: "Regularly every afternoon several themes for the lovely verses about gipsy love come into my mind. It might make a nice musical novel - there would be some of the atmosphere of Luhačovice in it." [14] In a feuilleton for *Venkov* (2-5-28) he spoke about the long period of germination between the first stimulus and the moment when he could use it in a composition. His concluding words were: "Those were the secret pathways over which composer's vision roamed." [15] He described the moment of creative crystallization for *The Makropulos Case* thus: "It gripped me. The third act, I'm rather proud of that. It flows, there is a feeling of suspense. That is what I felt, what I wanted. I worked on it for about a year. Before that I carried it within myself, kept thinking of it - but then it went fast - like a machine!" [16] A comment on *The House of the Dead* in a letter to Kamila Stösslová describes the compositional process itself: "I am hurrying with the new opera like a baker throwing buns into the oven," he wrote. [17]

These and similar statements are important for our understanding of Janáček for two principal reasons. First, they clearly negate the frequent criticism that discussed his style and compositions as something crude, primitive, unfinished, hastily thrown on paper in the throes of a momentary, passionate inspiration. The second reason has to do with medical theories that tend to equate genius and insanity. [18] Arieti makes the following distinction: "... phonetic devices that are common in schizophrenic languages are also exploited by poets for artistic effect. But whereas in schizophrenic language these mechanisms constrast with the common meanings of the words and thereby confer bizarreness, in poetry they add charm and significance and agree with the meaning, which is carried by secondary-process mechanisms. In art, these phonetic mechanisms do not represent a regression to the primary process, but the emergence of the tertiary process ... The poetic work may show many and unexpected dimensions, some belonging to the primary process and some to the secondary process; but they are concordant, not discordant, and the whole attains new and unexpected results." [19]

It is generally understood today that the creative genius and the psychotic both have access to their primary processes. However, the psychotic becomes overwhelmed by them so that his mental processes disintegrate, but the genius explores them through the secondary process and in this way controls his creative *daimon*, to use a term that had been applied to Janáček more than once. Janáček's remarks like: "I drink Nature in, but will not drown in it,"[20] or the previously mentioned opinion that one must not get completely absorbed, or possessed, by the composition he is working on, as well as metaphors that he liked to use, such as "being on fire, but not burning up," seem to indicate his awareness of certain inherent psychological dangers and the need to gain considerable emotional distance from the original stimuli so that he could mold them into a new aesthetic whole. In this sense, his needs to theorize coldly and be objectively scientific - and perhaps even his "down to earth" involvement with folk music - have to be seen to a great extent as necessary and effective defenses against an excess of emotional overstimulation and enthusiasm.

Even though Janáček often proposed "a scientific method for composition," he said in a speech at the opening of the Brno Conservatory in 1919 "Who would want to teach the finches how to sing? Who would want to train someone to be a composer? He who composes was born for it. It is impossible to teach anybody how to compose musically," i.e., artistically, beyond a mere acquisition of technical knowledge and skills. And he continued: "Create your composition by yourself: Respect the secret of the effort and the motivation in creating it." [21] This statement corresponds to Arieti's opinion that "the creative person remains the keeper of the secret of what makes his personality creative - a secret that he cannot reveal to himself or others." [22]

Janáček seems to have come close to describing the undescribable in his feuilleton *Silence*. During a quiet summer day in his native village, he mused: "Even thoughts become silent: from one to another a lengthening emptiness - and suddenly a 'ringing' in your ear. Such a fine tremolo of tones ... Those are the tones leading to a thought. That mysterious pathway! ... I think it is the life-music at the point when it changes into mental, intellectual activity and when all emotional strings are loosened... We hear it from an inner, *central* stimulus... It is not that kind of 'ringing' as when we say 'somebody is thinking about me' ... It is the tone of silence, of creative inactivity; of laziness, emptiness; of tiredness, inwardness ..." [23]

It is perhaps logical that Janáček as a musician par excellence should discover such a central auditory core or focus within himself in a moment of what sounds like a description of a twilight state, that state of full relaxation when all defenses are down and when free associations, dreamlike mental activity, stream of consciousness type of productivity and potential awareness of what is today called 'gut feelings' are facilitated. It is to his credit that he was able to notice all his perceptions of such a moment, remember them, concretize them through verbalization, and transfer them onto paper.

We offer a systematic resume of the path from the general creative process to musical creativity per se: The musician's primary material are auditory images, concretized and objectified as an acoustic medium. Melody and rhythm are elemental 'universals' that antedate any form of cognition and have strong physiological concomitants. Melody has never lost its original function as means of expressing emotion; it also implies expressive verbalization on the cognitive level, whereas the rhythm is a sensory motor level. Harmony approximates states of tension and release, and is less essential. Timbre is the chief supplier of aural pleasure. The four mentioned musical components, originating at different levels of the psyche are fused by form which obeys Arieti's secondary-process principles of logic and balance. [24]

Whether it was meant as a compliment or a condemnation, Janáček was always recognized as a strong personality and an original artist – willful, rebellious, somewhat strange and "dissonant," not fitting into any existing category. Despite his strict, traditional training, he gradually modified all musical elements and developed them into a specific personal musical language in which he could express himself. We must not forget that he was almost 49 years old when he finished his first important large work, the opera *Jenůfa,* which possesses most of the characteristics of his distinctive style. He went through years of preparation to find what he wanted and needed, and then struggled with the composition of *Jenůfa* for nine years before he was satisfied.

To shape his melodic and rhythmic material, he developed his controversial theory and practice of *nápěvky* (speech melodies), short motifs that were derived from human speech, sounds of the nature, voices of animals, mechanical noises; in fact, any stimulus which Janáček perceived through his extraordinarily keen sense of hearing or created through his rich musical imagery. Janáček's *nápěvky* can be considered to be an unusually strongly elaborated example of Arieti's concept of implied expressive verbalization applied to melody. He wrote: "in the telephone receiver, in the dust of ancient writings; in the flag which flutters over the castle in frantic eddies; yes, everywhere the tone resounded in a motive heavy saddened with tears, stabbing in revenge, aggressive, torn apart in anger, broken by an argument. Tame as a dog, predatory as a vulture, dry as a wilted leaf; gurgling like the breakers, spluttering like a fire consuming green wood. Echoing every movement of the mind - even speechless in holy silence." [25] And in an interview, he said: "*Nápěvky?* For me the music inspired by the instrumental sound or literature is not truthful – be it even a work by somebody like Beethoven. You know, it was rather strange when somebody spoke to me; maybe I did not take in what he said, but that sequence of tones! I knew immediately what to think of him; I knew what he felt, whether he lied, or whether he was excited; and when such a person spoke to me – it was quite conventional talk – I felt, I heard, that he was inwardly crying. Sounds, tonal inflections of human speech, the voice and sound of any living creature, have always held for me the most profound truth. This, you see, was now my life's deepest need ... They are my small windows that permit me to look into the souls of others. I would like to emphazies the fact that they are extremely important, especially for dramatic music." [26] Because he could hear the hidden music in human speech, he was able to make all of his music speak. The exact meaning of his own music was always crystal clear to him, although it was at times misunderstood by his listeners and even more frequently misinterpreted by his critics.

He did not want simply to annotate what he heard, but intended to express all that he experienced through sound. He seemed capable of transforming the input of all his senses into auditory images. Thus he spoke, for example, about "the charm of rhythms caught by eye, ear and touch" [27] and also stated that: "When you see well, only then you hear well." [28] In a letter to Max Brod he wrote: "You know that my motifs grow out of the earth, animals; human beings - in fact, they adhere to every thing that exists." [29] Developing these ideas he described: "These *nápěvky* stick so closely to their motivation, their cause, that, when you pick them up, discover them, your soul perceives as if through a flurry the same joy, same pain. *They are intelligible passwords* [his italics] that allow you to visit directly another soul. They intrude themselves sharply because they are outcries of the soul!" [30]

Moreover, Janáček classified and described his collected *nápěvky* according to the emotions he attributed to them through empathy and according to the situations in which they came to his attention. He had the habit of not only psychologizing and emotionalizing but also dramatizing this motivic material by combining it into larger units as continuous sketching exercises for his composing. In strictly musical terms, his *nápěvky* were highly stylized, completely his own, and he did not use them directly. "*Nápěvky* penetrate deeply into my soul, but I do not put them into my compositions," he clearly explained. [31)]

Janáček discussed the complexity of factors in the relationship between speech and melody in his feuilleton "Nota." [32)] In both he found: 1. An emotional focus that could be empathetically perceived; 2. A content which could be intellectually understood; 3. An effort to articulate, more evident in speech; 4. Something which he described as "sureness of noises and tones," the free inflection and modulation of speech which is schematized into exact intervals when the speech is transcribed as melody.

For Janáček, changing *tempi*, absolute pitches, certain favorite tonalities, intervallic and chordal combinations, instrumental colors, types of voices, various harmonic progressions, complex rhythms, unusual accents and meters, and so forth had specific emotional and dramatic connotations and expressive values, which were very subjective in nature at times. Some of Janáček's *nápěvky* corresponded to musical meter; many were only a free, rhythmic transcription, without any fixed meter. As Janáček worked with them further, he adjusted principal verbal accents and consequently had to recur to unusual or quickly changing meters. He used standard time values rather as absolute units of duration which partly eliminated the necessity of marking tempi. Certain of his *nápěvky* give the impression of experimental attempts to write down non-musical phenomena, but the majority are shaped as conventional melodic fragments. Janáček's fondness for using a wealth of accidentals and his habit of associating certain keys with specific moods have often been noted. High and low tessituras also had a special characterological meaning for him. The use of unexpectedly large intervals and skips clearly falls under the heading of 'music is intensified, dramatized speech.' It is interesting to note that Janáček did not establish any notation of pitch deviations, though he was very aware of subtle rhythmic irregularities. Microtones were later derived from folk music by Alois Hába in Czechoslovakia and by other musicians elsewhere. Bartók, for example, paid much attention to the notation of non-standard pitches. Janáček definitely remained satisfied with the tempered scale in all of his music as well as in his *nápěvky*. His harmony and chord blendings, may somewhat substitute for microtones by creating diffuse dissonances which serve as a background for his melodic lines.

Because of these highly original aesthetic ideas and procedures, he naturally could not work with musical forms in the traditional manner, and thus incurred much wrath from many of his contemporaries. As the musical expression of emotions in specific, life-like situations was his principal goal, he adjusted the form to his dramatic needs, structuring most of his larger compositions as a series of contrasting, even clashing, episodic segments of varying inner tension or using only simple traditional formal schemes for his short pieces. Such statements as: "My tone is like a drizzle. You can't get away from it. It falls on the path, on the field, on the little flower ... My tone is like a mist. It would grow cool on the keyboard. It only seeks life. In it the clouds thicken and storms brew up ..." [33] show the almost sensual pleasure which he derived from sound, and indicate his expressive aims. After the storms, however, many of his works - not only the operas - culminate in a true Aristotelian catharsis in which all of the carefully accumulated "painful emotions are 'purged' and turbulent emotions are transformed into serene or calm ones." [34] Such catharses take the form of public confessions, of baring one's soul. Janáček's most intense 'public confession' catharses are found in *Jenůfa, Katya, Makropulos, The House of the Dead*. The concluding monologue of the forester in the *Vixen* is another sort, a more personal catharsis, which comes to terms with aging and death. In a sense, the string quartet *Intimate Letters* is Janáček's own 'public confession.'

Janáček's dramatic timing was excellent and psychologically very sensitive. He gave his listeners time enough to recognize the prevailing emotion and to react to it through their capacity for empathy. Then he drove on, more often in an abrupt, *non sequitur*, "metaphoric" manner than by working out smoothing, "logical" transitions. Especially in his operas, action happens at different levels at the same time; he paid meticulous attention to the figure-ground relationship and concentrated the action in an almost dream-like manner. [35] He certainly worked by suggestion and symbolization through *pars pro toto* [36] to achieve further acceleration and tightness of his dramatic action. Consequently he could express his concepts with great economy of means and in much less time that other composers such as Wagner, Mahler and Richard Strauss required. In his era, these qualities were disturbing, and were often viewed as a lack of technique or invention. Terms like primitivism, naturism or naturalism were used to describe his style. Comparisons with impressionism and expressionism were made later, but the designation of realism seems to have prevailed, especially in Czechoslovakia.

Janáček did not worry too much about such categorization. He was aware of the process of "man as composer; the more experiences, the better the expression. A composer must live with the whole Nature and society. There are composers who disregard completely the environments and the rhythm of the milieu. They compose sitting at a table. Their works are all alike." [37] In March, 1928 he said to a reporter during an interview: "I penetrate because truth is in my work; truth, to its very limit. Truth does not exclude beauty, on the contrary, there should be more and more truth and beauty. Mainly life, permanent youth. Life is young. It is the spring. I am not afraid of living; I like it terribly." [38]

This last statement, made about five months before his death, is extremely characteristic of Janáček whom we could call a biophile of the highest order - a passionate lover of life - to apply a term introduced by Erich Fromm. [39] Another psychoanalytic concept that fits Janáček's *Weltanschauung* very well is Eros, the life principle that goes way beyond any sexual love and is that "energy that binds all living substance together and is the guarantor of life." [40] Its antithesis, Thanatos, source of human destructiveness, the unconscious drive toward dissolution and death, naturally found expression also, even though Janáček had developed a striking avoidance, most prominent in his later years, of anything having to do with aging and dying. To gain insight into his inner conflicts we shall refer once more to Arieti's exposition of creativity.

Arieti, identifies personal traits, habits and conditions that foster creativity: solitude, periods of inactivity, daydreaming, thinking freely, being in a state of readiness for catching similarities, gullibility, the remembrance and inner replaying of past traumatic conflicts, alertness, and discipline. [41] Janáček enjoyed creative solitude and purposefully arranged occasional periods of inactivity to daydream, brainstorm or simply recharge his energy and improve his physical, not too robust health. We have seen that he was able to think very freely and independently, even if such thoughts made him go against current trends in his field of endeavor. Many examples of his writing show that he was always in a state of readiness to catch similarities between apparently non-related elements, to come up with surprisingly stimulating new ideas or insights. We have demonstrated indirectly how alert Janáček remained into his old age, and how observant he was of his psychic life and the life around him. He was very disciplined and capable of hard and consistent work, even when his efforts went unrewarded.

Arieti uses the term gullibility to describe a willingness to explore anything by suspending critical judgment, and the ability to be open, innocent and naive before rejecting anything. Such a non-critical curiosity or inquisitiveness in Janáček is amply documented.

Janáček's devoted and highly respectful housekeeper commented several times on his lack of practical shrewdness and tact in his contact with others. He tended to be outspoken and quick to offend. "At the same time, he was sensitive to any unfriendly look or word, saw offense where there was none, and changed in a moment from the best friend into an enemy for life." "He liked to be admired and accepted even outright flattery, though he pretended not to notice it or declined it. The problem was that in friendship as well as in praise he could not distinguish between honesty and falsehood, sincerity and pretense, and this way he often was disappointed and on the other hand was unjust to his faithful friends." [42] His remark: "I am a person who trusts too much," in a letter to Gabriela Horvátová proves he was somewhat aware of this trait. [43]

To use a current turn of phrase, he often set himself up for disappointments, but his social naiveté also endeared him to many persons to whom he turned most sincerely for advice or help. For example, his collaboration with Max Brod was based on a firm conviction that everything would go well with him and his music if Brod would translate his operas. "[Janáček] suddenly got it into his head (he said) that Brod was just the man to introduce his work to the world. Fitting action to the thought, he rushed down to the Brno station and jumped on the next train to Prague, where he arrived at six o'clock on a Sunday morning ... 'I've been thinking,' he announced to the half-awake

Brod. 'If you'll take me on, everything will follow; if not - nothing; I'll be exactly where I was before.' No promises, no terms, no contracts – just the cards on the table; the composer was leaving himelf open to the most ruthless exploitation ... It was precisely Janáček's disingenuousness and naiveté that Brod found so disarming. 'In for a penny, in for a pound!' cried Janáček cheerfully. Very well, said Brod, he would think about taking on the job of translating [Jenůfa] ... As it turned out, he was to do a great deal more." [44]

Another glimpse of this quality comes from the reminiscences of the Czech pianist Rudolf Firkušný, who took music lessons from Janáček in his childhood during World War I. In an article published in 1938, he wrote: "It was not an easy task to explain to a five-year old child the principles and truths of music, keep him to his work and make the lessons interesting and enjoyable ... He understood a child's naiveté, but in his contact with the child he could maintain almost the same relationship as with an adult. He taught children with the help of his own childish characteristics." [45]

Janáček's often-reproached lack of sophistication in the choice of some of his literary sources also seems to belong into this category. Who but Janáček would find inspiration in the daily newspaper and create a masterpiece like the opera The Cunning Little Vixen on basis of pictures and humorous comments that represented an equivalent of today's comic strips? The texts for the dramatic song cycle The of One Who Vanished and for the playful Nursery Rhymes came from the same source, Lidové noviny. And what self-respecting and experienced composer of international renown would react with such self-deprecatory humor as Janáček did when his attention was called to the sad fact that he wrote a certain passage in his Vixen for violins below the range of the G-string? He laughed and exclaimed: "For goodness sake, gentlemen, that little spark [of inspiration] just flared up too low and too high, simply too much all around." [46]

In a way, such gullibility appears to be the best safeguard of self-renewing freshness of approach to new tasks, and an excellent barrier against developing blasé cynicism and inflated self-importance. But it could also be a source of painful experiences and social misunderstandings.

Remembrance and inner replaying of traumatic conflicts of the past play an important role in Janáček's creativity. Psychological conflict is generally considered to be a source of motivation for many kinds of action. In a creative person, neurotic conflict would be a hindrance, for it would limit the functions of the psyche. Therefore, replaying refers to resolved or almost resolved conflicts that allow perspective and sublimation of the original drives. In this sense, products of creativity retain a personal significance but are not narrowly autobiographical, because the artist will have transcended his self sufficiently to find a universal meaning for whatever he expresses. The process of creative work can perhaps be seen as a partial analogy to the "working-through" processes of the psychoanalytic technique, but it is a kind of self-treatment and has very specific goals which are different from those of the psychoanalysis.

Many of the traumatic events in Janáček's life which shaped his conscious and unconscious life philosophy and creative work would be of interest to a clinician. For example – a childhood spent in poverty, in a rural environment; leaving home at the age of 11, shortly before his father's death; four years as a resident chorister at the school of Augustinian monks in Brno; extreme poverty during the following years as a music student; the poorly paid career of a music teacher in provincial Brno; marriage at 27 with 16-year old, overprotected and inexperienced Zdenka Schulzová; problems with in-laws and two years of separation after the birth of daughter Olga; the death of his mother; reconciliation with his wife and birth of his son Vladimír, who died at 2 1/2 years of age; death of Olga at 21; the nadir of his life, when Prague continued to reject his opera *Jenůfa* for 12 years; another marital crisis which almost led to divorce when Janáček was 62 (1916) at the time of his first significant successes. As Janáček often repeated, fate was not kind to him and taxed his strength to its utmost limits.

Let us now explore how Janáček interpreted these traumatic memories through his creative work. We find much self-awareness, and a musical connotation as well, in his following early memory: "The inner milieu lived in childhood may have the most decisive influence on the artistic creativity. I remember from my fourth year: They yelled: Fire. It was at night, in summer. They carried us [children] in blankets onto the slopes of the woods; my frightened crying against the fiery screen of the conflagration forms an indivisible memory in my mind even now. And the key of c# sharp minor in *On the Overgrown Path* is its echo." [47)]

Also revealing is his comment that he went to the convent school when his ill father found it would be a good prospect for the boy's schooling and future career - perhaps priesthood, perhaps teaching. Janáček describes it in his lapidary way: "Alone. Unfamiliar people, aloof; strange school, a hard bed, harder bread. No tenderness. - My world, exclusively mine, was commencing. All was falling into that pattern. My father died; an inconceivable cruelty." [48)]

Even though Janáček received an excellent musical training and a good basic education in that school and learned much self-discipline, his need for affection was not met. Some of his negative attitudes toward religion and death were undoubtedly associated with these feelings of the loss of security of a warm home. However, he also commented with certain pride on feelings of independence and expanding horizons toward personal autonomy. Thus he gained satisfaction from this situation, even though it must have been a traumatic experience for which he was not ready. Exactly this sort of simultaneous but contradictory feelings constitutes the inner psychological conflict which persists as long as one cannot tolerate the ambivalence. For decades Janáček reacted almost exclusively to the negative aspect of such personal experiences. For example, Janáček avoided funerals in his later years. He had sung at too many of them as young chorister. Mářa Stejskalová, who was his housekeeper for many years, informs us: "He did not even go to Hukvaldy for the funeral of his mother [who died in November 1884]. He excused himself because of his cough and the cold weather, although he loved her very much and grieved for her for a long time ... He very seldom visited the graves of Vladíček and Oluška [the nicknames of his children] and always alone ... Later he almost never went to the cemetery." [49] It would be interesting to explore Janáček's presumably intense feelings of guilt in connection with Olga's illness and death: he sent his beloved daughter from home to Russia, despite his wife's objections, to 'save' her from dangerous suitors.

After Olga's death in 1903, he "did not attend church, did not pray, as if he were not the same person who spoke so beautifully about God and Heaven when Olga was dying." [50] His niece Věra Janáčková confirms this observation in her article "My uncle and Death." [51] "A church, he told me, is concentrated death. Tombs under the floor, bones on the altar, pictures which are nothing but torture and dying. Rituals, prayers, chants - death and nothing but death. I don't want to have anything to do with it."

He faced these issues in a much more complex and subtler way in his creative work. It is generally accepted that his cantata *Amarus*, composed in 1897 on a poem by Jaroslav Vrchlický, had a very personal meaning for him. In the work the monk Amarus, the Bitter One, an illegitimate foundling born in sin, takes care of the eternal light in the church. He asks an angel when he will die, and received the answer that it will be the day he forgets to put more oil in the lamp. One beautiful spring day, the aging Amarus sees a pair of lovers in the church and then in the monastery garden. Next morning the lamp remains unlighted and Amarus is found dead on the grave of his suicide mother, with his face turned toward the blooming lilac trees - where a bird continues singing. This motif of yearning and heartbreaking longing in search of life and love stayed with Janáček until his death.

Between 1903 and 1907, Janáček composed his fourth opera, *Fate* - his most personal and least performed opera. It was not staged until 1958, and then only with extensive adaptation to make it somewhat feasible. He created the story himself, calling it "Fragments of a Novel from Life." The original stimulus came from an experience of Kamila Urválková, another Kamila whom Janáček met in Luhačovice. Janáček undoubtedly identified with the protagonist, a composer he named Živný, who was writing an autobiographical opera. The hostile mother-in-law who goes insane and destroys herself and her daughter is the instrument of Fate - and *Fatum* was one of his tentative titles. In the last scene Živný is stunned by a lighting during a sudden thunderstorm but survives, somewhat broken in spirit, leaving the conclusion of the third act (both of the real opera and the 'opera within the opera') in the hands of God. Brod pronounced the libretto to be impossible. Janáček apparently was unable to master this complex material, which from all indications must have had very specific meaning for him at the time. It is interesting to compare *Fate* with his *Intimate Letters* from 1928, an even more personal work which was achieved much more successfully.

His search for life and love appears in another guise in his non-liturgical *Eternal Gospel*, again using Vrchlický's poetry as a text. *Evangelium aeternum* refers to the writings of 13th century's Joachim di Fiore who announces the coming of the third Kingdom, the reign of supreme love, personified by St. Francis who extended Christ's loving care also to animals and the nature. Janáček composed this cantata during the end of 1913 and the beginning of 1914, when he was gradually finding a way out of prolonged grieving, despair and doubts about his creative abilities. That he expressed this faith in loving humanity shortly before the beginning of World War I is another irony of his life. His remark from the war years: "The more horrible the times, the faster the flow of ideas for compositions," [52] indicates he never gave up the struggle for creative expression and his hope for eventual recognition. The quotation from St. Francis in Janáček's animal opera-idyll *The Cunning Little Vixen* might also be mentioned.

Janáček's often-noted ability to express compassion toward the protagonists of his compositions, especially in his operas, was probably a consequence of his early emotional deprivation. In a way he always identified with the underdog, with the victims of human cruelty or social injustice. But he also directed this compassion to some of the victimizers who could not act other way than they did, because there is the dark, destructive and violent component in the human makeup. This element, and the associated motive of guilt, add a fateful, tragic-dramatic dimension to his works, especially in the moments of catharsis.

Janáček's identification with his characters is very significant. It is necessary to understand that, on the level of the primary processes similarly as in dreams, every person in his works would symbolize a part of Janáček's personality and every dramatic action would have roots in his unconscious. In case of an inspiration from other sources, his choice of the subject and the changes or arrangements he did would be revealing as to his inner motivation.

It would be tempting to try to figure out some of such multiple identifications in detail. Brod once suggested that Professor Freud should analyze the characters in *Jenůfa* and their relationships. Janáček's French biographer Daniel Muller claims that Laca is a "temperament mélancolique" in the medical sense, displaying the true temperament of many great artists, including Janáček himself. [53] And Mářa Stejskalová states "that hard love of Kostelnička - that is [Janáček], there is much of his disposition in that [role]." [54]

For such an outspoken lover of life and hater of death as Janáček was, we find too many instances of violent death or suicide in his compositions to pass them over only as an external characteristic of the lyrico-dramatic operatic genre. Moreover, the protagonists who perish are exactly those whom Janáček consciously loved most, like: Maryčka Magdónova, the good schoolmaster Halfar, the murdered baby son of mutilated Jenůfa, unworldly sinning-innocent Katya Kabanova, much sinned against Akulka, self-sacrificing young Janek in *Makropulos*, and others – not to forget the vixen Bystrouška who was not only shot to death, but was made into a muff for the foxy lady Terynka. Significantly, his equally-loved villains are often weak males like Števa in *Jenůfa* and Katya's husband, and very strong females such as the stern Kostelnička and Katya's destructive and conventional mother-in-law. The excellent and sympathetic characterization of such roles is proof that Janáček was psychologically in touch with his own "dark" aspect.

He openly treated his personal taboo, the fear-provoking topic of the human mortality only in compositions such as *Sonata 1.X.1905* for piano, whose second movement bears the subtitle "Death" and his last two operas, *The Makropulos Case* and *The House of the Dead*. A comparison between this sonata and the scene of the prison hospital in *The House of the Dead* reveals much about Janáček's stylistic and expressive development. In the movement "Death," dirge-like rhythms are used, as they often are, to express the grief of a funeral procession. In the opera, the sighs and cries of the dying Luka are very naturalistic and dramatically striking. Can we forget that Janáček was capable of sitting next to the bed of his dying daughter Olga and write down the sounds of her mortal struggle as 'nápěvky'?

He may have expressed feelings of being an "abandoned orphan" in his ballad for orchestra *The Fiddler's Child* (1912), which was inspired by a poem by Svatopluk Čech. A poor village fiddler dies, leaving a violin and a baby girl. In the middle of the night he comes back to reclaim both - in the morning the baby is found dead, safe from all earthly suffering, and the fiddler is gone. The parallel between Janáček's poor teacher-musician-father and the fiddler is quite obvious. Janáček came to terms with other early traumata in feuilletons and other compositions.

And in his *Sinfonietta* (1926) he at last made peace with Brno, where he had lived for so many years as "some sort of a lonely Moravian Diogenes," suffering in the stifling, provincial atmosphere of a town too far from the capital, Golden Prague, where, he felt, his creative life would have been easier.

"According to his own words it expresses 'the contemporary free man, his spiritual beauty and joy, his strength, courage, and determination to fight for victory' – to defend the young state and its hard-won independence. This explains the dedication 'To the Czechoslovak Armed Forces' as well as the original title *Military Sinfonietta*. Janáček insisted on this title, and when before the Prague premiere he saw it called in the programme *Sokol Sinfonetta* he protested vigorously 'No Sokol – Military Symphonetta!' He jotted down the following titles for the movements: 1. Fanfares. 2. The Castle. 3. The Queen's Monastery. 4. The Street. 5. The Town Hall ... these is a clue to this typical Janáček mystery at the end of his article of 24 December 1927 called 'My Town.' After recalling the small, inhospitable Brno of the Austo-Hungarian days, Janáček ends with the words: 'And then I saw the town undergo a miraculous change. I lost my dislike of the gloomy Town Hall, my hatred of the hill from whose depths so much pain was screaming, my distaste for the street and its throng. As if my a miracle, liberty was conjured up, glowing over the town – the rebirth of 28 October 1918. I saw myself in it. I belonged to it. And the blare of the victorious trumpets, the holy peace of the Queen's Monastery, the shadows of the night, the breath of the green hill and the vision of the growing greatness of the town, of my Brno, were all giving birth to my Sinfonetta.' "[55]

He was seventy when he composed his good-humored and optimistic sextet *Youth* (1924), relating it to the lighter side of the life of the Blue Boys, the choristers with attractive blue uniforms. Two years later, he produced his

Glagolitic Mass (1926), unorthodox in every sense, using an Old Slavonic text he had sought out as early as 1921 or 1922. It was not a composition for church in his mind. He compared "the fragrance of moist Luhačovice woods" to the incense and imagined how "the cathedral grew out of the giant-like magnitude of the forest and the vault of the sky with its misty distances. The bells were the ringing of a flock of sheep ... the candles - tall firs of the forest lit up with altars." [56] In creating this cathedral according to his taste, his intention was to show how many should talk to God, freely and fearlessly. Janáček's pantheistic leanings sometimes seem to be evident in this work and in *Vixen.*

He talked about the period when he wrote these and other late works as a time when his soul "made peace with the rest of the world." [57] This statement precisely confirms the previously-mentioned need to resolve old traumatic conflicts, to overcome the old hurts, fears, guilt and pain, and allow oneself to live more fully, in a mature and realistic manner.

It was harder, however, to make peace within the intimate setting of his marriage than by means of his old feelings through creative work. He fell in love with his piano pupil Zdenka Schulzová when she was 14, than left Brno for his studies in Leipzig and Vienna. Against the wishes of her parents, their love persisted and they married when she was a few weeks short of 16. At the time, Zdenka described her situation as "better unhappy with Leoš than happy with someone else," [58] and remained loyal to him until her death in 1938. The tragic death of their children was a stunning blow to both spouses; it alienated them further rather than bringing them together. Despite many tensions and alternate quiet periods, it was Janáček's creative work and his late successes that caused the most severe marital disagreements.

In 1916, in the middle of the war, Prague National Theater's opera chef Karel Kovařovic finally changed his opinion of Janáček's *Jenůfa* and decided to produce it. The composer began to make frequent trips to Prague for the rehearsals, the premiere on May 26, 1916, and for subsequent performances. The mezzo soprano who sang the role of Kostelnička was Gabriela (Jelča) Horvátová, the Croatian-born wife of Bedřich Noltsch. Their mutual effort to create a Kostelnička according to Janáček's exact wishes led to close contact, and then to an intimate friendship. Many years later Gabriela summarized their relationship in an interview for the magazine *Divadlo* as follows: "He was my friend, my artistic holy love, and I his. There were times when we were not separated even for a moment." [59]

Janáček's feelings for Gabriela at one time seen to have been very deep. He wrote to Kovařovic: "A composer could have a happy life with her."[60] According to Marie Stejskalová, he was in the midst of a domestic crisis at the time. "Madam's nerves started to fail. Our Master sent for Dr. Papírník to examine her mental state. That drove Madam into complete despair." A passage in her diary explains further: "On July 10, 1916, Madam poisoned herself with morphine, was saved in the hospital," without clearly stating whether it was an accident or a suicide attempt. [61] About the same time, a divorce contract between the Janáčeks was worked out by their lawyers, but it was never put into effect.

Janáček's intense relationship with Gabriela Horvátová lasted for less than two years, although he wrote to her as late as in April 1918: "Yesterday I wrote you a letter full of longing. Do not wonder [about it], and nobody else should wonder either: that's the lot Nature gave us, excitable and high-strung composers. We can't help it." [62] A few months earlier he explained to Gabriela (January 11, 1918): "I have no more thoughts of conquest - that is over. You were my only, my last joyful outcry of delight." [63] This statement, however, was not exactly true.

We come now to Mrs. Kamila Stösslová, who figures so prominently in Janáček's last days. He met her in the summer of 1917 at the Spa Luhačovice and immediately felt much attraction and compassion for her. She was thirty-eight years younger than he. She had just endured serious illnesses of her children; her husband was on the front and his antique business was destroyed. At almost the same time that he wrote a letter full of longing for Gabriela he wrote to Kamila: "You don't have any idea how heavy my mind is. To live this way, so alone, so reserved, without any attachment to the world and environment - I will not be able to stand it for long. Despite my fame and great successes I feel, ironically, like a most unhappy man! I deaden myself through my work; I throw myself into difficult challenges to forget the man who is also in me and who cannot be affectionate as he would like to be. That is my fate ... I love happy people so much!" [64]

This happy person, so different from his wife, whom Helfert called a tragic "mater dolorosa," became the inspiring Muse of the aging composer.

According to information currently available, Kamila never comprehended Janáček's creative personality and his importance; that precisely may have been the reason why he could project all of his his complex emotions upon her, and to see in her his most important female protagonists, from the "black" Gipsy Žefka in *The Diary* to Akulka from *The House of the Dead*. On a personal, human level, he could vicariously experience some of his frustrated fatherly emotions through her two sons. It may be significant that his carefree *Youth* and playful *Nursery Rhymes* (1926) fall into this period of his artistic development. Brod and others call attention to this unfulfilled need, noting that Janáček was a father figure for many of his students, strict but at the same time quite indulgent in many ways. Brod goes further, perceiving Janáček as an omnipotent, compassionate father to all his suffering "children," the *personae* of his operas.

During the last year of his life, Janáček was on the verge of a cathartic public confession concerning Kamila Stösslová. He consulted his younger, but more sophisticated friend and confidant, Max Brod, in a letter on January 18, 1928: "Tell me, is it feasible to disclose in which person my motifs are crystallized? Has any writer ever revealed it? With the painters it is no secret. But a composer? Would it, be misconstrued if such a spiritual relationship, this artistic relationship were made public? ... We both, she and I, have a need to be free from any accusation of another kind of relationship than is ours, a purely spiritual one." [65)]

He also tried to explain this idealized relationship to his wife, without being able to win her approval, or at least such understanding that would, most probably, free him from any self-reproach and inner torments. He commented on it in a letter to Kamila: "After all, the world between the two of us is beautiful, but all that what is permanent - the longings, desires - is imaginary! I told ... that this imaginary world is as important for my life as air and water. I told ... how your appearance [in my life] had freed me ... and how you have been for eleven years, without knowing it, my protector in all aspects. I told ... that it is you, there where warm feelings, sincerity, truth, ardent love permeate my compositions." [66)]

Brod's advice, if any, has not been preserved. Instead of a written confession, Janáček again expressed himself creatively through his music. Between January 29 and February 19, 1928, he composed his *Second String Quartet*. His first intention was to title it *Love Letters*, but discretion prevailed, as he did not want to "have my feelings at the mercy of idiots." [67)] He definitively changed its title to *Intimate Letters*. The content is subtly autobiographical, without specific, musically defined details, demonstrating Janáček's mastery of expression on a highly sublimated level, commensurate with that stage of his creative and personal development. He even gave up his original idea including a viola d'amour, a concrete musical image associated with his sensitivity to feminine voices with a specific loving quality. For example, he described Kamila Urválková as "one of the most beautiful women. Her voice was like the viola d'amore." [68)]

Then, the circumstances of his death became an involuntary public revelation whether we look upon them as a kind of a fateful, poetic justice, or as a culmination of Janáček's somewhat reckless disregard for conventional niceties. Whether he needs an apology depends on the individual point of view of the commentator.

The singer Marie Calma and her husband František Veselý broke with Janáček, primarily because of his behavior at the time of the Horvát affair. Nevertheless, she said: "His artistic contribution is so great that it outweighs the human flaws of his character." [69)] Similar evaluations, taking into account his passionate temperament, usually concede an artist's license of self-actualization to him, although with reservations pertaining to the social and moral climate of his time and his rather conservative milieu. By describing Janáček as a singular mixture of "Jupiter, Tonans and Adonis," Brod places him above the common run of men and even gives him "the right of a creative person to be (unfortunately) unjust" in order to be able to create. [70)]

Janáček once confided to Gabriela: "Long, long ago, about 15 years ago, I thought I would die [1917]. Instead, I unexpectedly revived that year." We do not know why he felt that way, and therefore must rank it with other of his frequent presentiments or beliefs in various omens. It is also possible that he was inaccurate about the dates. Related in mood would be, e.g., his comment to Brod in 1926: "I don't know why I fear so much for myself," and similar statements, sometimes connected with "nerves" or other physical complaints, other times apparently referring to momentary creative blocks. [71] His meeting with Kamila Stösslová in 1917, coinciding with the preparations for the Vienna performance of *Jenůfa*, seem to be the most obvious reason for his "unexpected revival." There were, however, many other factors which we will briefly examine with the aid of the characteristics of the creativogenic society proposed by Arieti.

Arieti describes this society as follows: "One may fairly assume that if a society sponsors the "four freedoms" – freedom from fear and want, freedom of speech and worship – as Franklin D. Roosevelt advocated, more people will strive toward creativity than in a society deprived of these freedoms ...In order to provide a climate propitious to creativity, society must have more specific characteristics ... availablity of cultural (and certain physical means); openness to cultural stimuli; stress on becoming, not just on being; free access to cultural media for all citizens, without discrimination; freedom; exposure to different and even contrasting cultural stimuli; tolerance for an interest in diverging views; interaction of significant persons; promotion of incentives and awards." [72]

Janáček was born into a society in which music had been traditionally encouraged on many levels of proficiency. Let us observe that the Czech term "Kantor" has been for centuries the colloquial equivalent for "schoolmaster," and thus infer the emphasis on music in the rural environment of Janáček's forebears. Musically talented boys, no matter how lowly their socio-economic origin, could gain access to a living cultural tradition with a relative ease.

Janáček's encounters with important personalities and contemporary musical trends began at an early age. In the Brno convent school, Janáček became intimately acquainted with the music then characteristic of the whole Austro-Hungarian monarchy, including the regional elements. It was fortunate that his teacher Pavel Křižkovský (1820-1885), the director of the Augustianian school, was the foremost nationalist Moravian composer of that era. He formed an enduring personal and artistic friendship with Antonín Dvořák while studying in Prague during 1874 and 1875. He said: "Do you know what it is like when somebody takes your words out of your mouth before you say them? That's how I always felt in Dvořák's company." [73] He saw the ailing Bedřich Smetana only once, at an 1875 concert.

We have mentioned Janáček's isolation in Brno. Nevertheless, he was able to meet, at least fleetingly, many famous foreign musicians, and had continuous contact with Czech and Moravian contemporaries. Among other musicians, he met Tchaikovsky in 1888, Lehár in 1908, Richard Strauss in 1916, and Bartók in 1925. With his growing recognition, such contacts increased and became more rewarding. However, he usually hurried back home to Brno or into the recuperative solitude of Hukvaldy after his short trips abroad, which generally had to do with performances of his works; for example the trips to Berlin, to festivals of the International Society for Contemporary Music (ISCM) and to London.

Janáček encountered a cross-cultural atmosphere when he came to Brno; it was torn by nationalistic tensions and conflicts between German and Czech factions. He became an ardent Czech patriot, refusing contact with the Germanic element during certain periods of his life – for example, denying himself attendance at the local German opera, and developing an interest in Russia as an "antidote" when his brother František lived in St. Petersburg. However, we find inconsistencies in this area of interest.

Janáček's Slavophilism found particular expression in his works with Russian subjects. But on a deeper level let us tentatively suggest that this subject may have been painful for him, and that he had ambivalent feelings which were worked out through music. There are many examples: the relentless presence of the eternal Volga river (off-stage chorus wordlessly vocalizing what Vogel calls "the theme of guilt") as a background for the love affair of Katya-Kamila who eventually finds her death in it, perhaps becoming Katya-Olga. *The House of the Dead*, the "black" opera of Janáček which he found very difficult and oppressive to compose, has a Gulag-like atmosphere. Nevertheless, he carried it through although he left projects such as *Anna Karenina* unfinished. And why should he have prophesized the glory of the Slavs by depicting the fratricidal war of Slavic brothers - Poles and Russians - in his rhapsody for orchestra *Taras Bulba* (1915-1918)?

He courted his Zdenka in German, even though his insistence on using the Czech language caused severe conflicts with her parents after they were engaged. [74] And it is interesting to note that Gabriela Horvátová was Croatian, and Kamila Stösslová and Max Brod were Jewish, to mention only a few of his close friends. Once again, we find many contradictions in his attitude; Janáček could be intolerant and intransigent to reinforce his autonomy, or be quite broadminded to satisfy his need to be a part of the ever-so-fascinating larger world.

The creation of the independent Czechoslovak Republic in 1918 was a very important event in Janáček's life, and he wholeheartedly appreciated the new freedom of his nation after the three hundred years of oppression. At last he could represent a society that was fully his and in which he was a first-class citizen. Among the rewards he received were: the celebration of his 70th birthday (1924) nationwide, especially in Prague where he met the President; state prizes for several of his works; the honorary doctorate from the Masaryk University in Brno (1925); the Belgian order of King Leopold; membership of the Prussian Academy of Art (1927), and other proofs of recognition.

He was particularly gratified by the celebration on July 11, 1926 in Hukvaldy, when a memorial plaque was unveiled on the house of his birth with the inscription: "To the genius of Czech music, PhD. Leoš Janáček, born in this house on the 3rd July, 1854." At that occasion he said, among other things: "People say that I have achieved something. An artist's work is seldom praised or even noticed and yet is so important. When I now and again wirte something which I know is enjoyed far away from here, perhaps in South Bohemia in Písek or in the West in Plzeň or in the North in Mladá Boleslav or in the East or in Moravia or Slovakia, then it occurs to me that there is something in the power of art after all; that I have plucked at a string which resounds everywhere, which ties us all together so that we feel as one nation. This is what I value in my own art, and the most important thing is that it binds us all together, that it makes us strong and defiant and proof against everything in the world. Everything else, the notes, that to me is secondary. If I can unite our nation which is so irate, so quarrelsome and disunited, if I have done this, then, I feel, I have not lived in vain." [75] Those are words of a mature and self-confident artist who had reached his peak of creativity in the then receptive and stimulating society, and seem to paraphrase our definition of Eros.

Those who knew him in old age often describe him as "the youngest among the Czechoslovak composers" and stress his energy, enthusiasm and youthful optimism. There is a dissenting voice, the pen of Daniel Muller: "Janáček was a great pessimist. I have read too many articles ... which spoke about optimism: that's because those articles were written by young men who were fooled by his vigorous appearance, by the 'verte vieilless du musicien' [literally: the 'green' old age of the musician]. Everything in him denies optimism: his life, his habits, his love of solitude, his adoration of the nature, his sympathy for the animals, the tone of his diaries, letters, articles ... and, above all, his music does not lie." [76] Muller evidently had Janáček's operas and their special dramatic quality in mind. Michael Ewans describes their character as follows: "Janáček's tragic operas affect their spectators by a unique blend of emotional and intellectual power. By confronting the causes of tragic action directly, Janáček enables us to see his characters - and through them ourselves, mankind at large in moments of suffering - not merely with compassion but as creatures endowed with nobility ... Janáček's tragic operas heal our wounds, make sense of our existence: they have within them much of what it is to live." [77]

This concept of individual nobility and human dignity maintained even under the most adverse and degrading conditions is explicitly expressed by the motto of *The House of the Dead,* "In every creature a spark of God." This concept is an intrinsic component of Janáček's genius.

We have found striking parallels between Arieti's strictly psychiatric, generalized opinions about genius and Janáček's creative personality. Arieti's concluding statement includes relevant quotations from Nathaniel Hirsch:

"... the genius beholds another world ... he has a more profound perception of the world which lies before [others] also, in that it presents in his mind more objectively and consequently in greater purity and distinctness." "The works of genius are produced by an inner or 'instinctive necessity;' genius never proceeds from intention or choice, nor from utility nor gain. For the genius, his works are an *end*, sufficient and necessary in themselves; for others a *means*." [78]

On February 12, 1925 Janáček wrote to the members of the Ostrava musical societies: "In the book of my life you are to read: Grow out of your innermost selves. Never renounce your beliefs. Do not toil for recognition, but always do all you can, so that the field allotted to you may prosper." [79]

During the dress rehearsal of *The Cunning Little Vixen* in 1924, Janáček wept and remarked to director Ota Zítek that he wished to have the forester's monologue which concludes the opera performed at his funeral. [80)]

At his funeral, this music became a most heartfelt farewell - and a self-fulfilling prophecy when the words were heard: "And people will go past with bowed heads and they will know that they are experiencing superhuman bliss." It is heartening to know that today, fifty years after his death and 125 years since his birth, increasing numbers of people - on a worldwide scale - are finding their way to Janáček's music.

Notes

The first section of this study was presented at the Ninth World Congress of the Czechoslovak Society of Arts and Sciences, Cleveland, Ohio, October 26-29, 1978, as part of the Janáček Symposium honoring the 50th anniversary of his death.

The study is not intended to be a psycho-history or a true case story of the composer, even though it suggests some parameters of his personal psychodynamics. Its main purpose is to explore Janáček's creative development systematically within Silvano Arieti's comprehensive exposition of all aspects of creativity forms in a theoretical framework. Janáček's statements are used as primary data to present the man and the artist in as personal a manner as possible. His writing style is very difficult to translate, for it often is somewhat strange in Czech as well. An effort has been made to render his ideas as accurately as possible, in as idiomatic a manner as the material allows.

Editor's note: This text was prepared from drafts in Czech and English. Dr. Fischmann seems to have moved substantial passages of the original Czech article to footnotes in the English article in an attempt to reduce its length after adding the introduction describing Janáček's death. This material has been restored to the main body of the text. Other information from footnotes has been added to the main text to provide clarification; when such information is readily available in English-language biographical dictionaries, it has been omitted to reduce the complexity of this study. Footnotes have been verified where possible and at times amended. At times the English text has been brought into closer correspondence with the Czech text.

Most readers will probably be unfamiliar with theories of creativity which were discussed in America by members of the Freudian school approximately quarter of a century ago. Accordingly, Dr. Fischmann's use of concepts from Silvano Arieti's *Creativity: the magic synthesis* has been clarified by inserting quotations from the passages to which she refers.

Passages from Max Brod's biography of Janáček and Walter Susskind's *Brod and Janáček* have also been added. Introductory material from Dr. Fischmann's unpublished paper *Janáček's nápěvky (Speech Melodies) in Theory and Practice* (which is, for the most part, a straightforward presentation of musical examples which are reprinted in Leoš Janáček, *Fejetony z Lidových Novin*) was added to the passage on *nápěvky*. Some of the original quotations have been expanded as well.

According to Dr. Fischmann's publisher, Dr. Karel Absolon, she did the research for this paper and her edition of the Janáček – Newmarch correspondence in Brno.

Dr. Fischmann relies extensively on the 1962 English edition of Jaroslav Vogel, *Leoš Janáček, His Life and Works*, and on the second edition of Marie Trkanová's *U Janáčků podle vyprávění Marie Stejskalové*. These books have recently been published in revised editions. New information about Janáček's relationships with his wife and other women are documented in *My life with Janáček: the memoirs of Zdenka Janáčková*, edited and translated by John Tyrell (London and Boston: Faber and Faber, 1998) and *Intimate letters: Leoš*

Janáček to Kamila Stösslová, also edited and translated by John Tyrell (Princeton, New Jersey: Princeton University Press, copyright 1994).

1) Marie Trkanová, *U Janáčků podle vyprávění Marie Stejskalové* [At home with the Janáčeks, according to the reminiscences of Marie Stejskalová] (Prague: Panton, 1964) second edition, p. 117. This passage describes an atmosphere of premonitions and omens before and at the moment of Janáček's departure for Hukvaldy. Máňa Stejskalová was housekeeper for the Janáček family for many years.

2) Trkanová, p. 167.

3) Trkanová, p. 169.

4) *Korespondence Leoše Janáčka s Otakarem Ostrčilem* [The correspondence of Leoš Janáček with Otakar Ostrčil], edited by Artuš Rektorys. (Prague: Hudební matice Umělecké besedy, 1948), p. 56. (Janáčkův Archív, vol. 2)

5) Silvano Arieti, *Creativity: the magic synthesis* (New York: Basic Books, 1976).

6) Mortimer Cass, "A note on music," in Arieti, pp. 236-238.

7) Arieti, pp. 12-13. Arieti identifies his theory with those of members of the Freudian school - Ernst Kris, Lawrence Kubie, Phyllis Grenacre, Philip Weissman, and E. H. Erikson – rather than with the concepts of Freud himself, pp. 24-25. "Within the framework of the Freudian school, Ernst Kris was perhaps the most prominent author who did not study creativity exclusively from the point of view of unconscious motivation. To Kris must be given the credit for having stressed the importance of the primary process in the formal mechanisms of creativity. He considered the use of the primary process in creativity as 'a regression in service of the ego.' " In his summary pp. 411-412, he states, "I have not referred to Freud's structural theory, or division of the psyche into id, ego, and superego, because I have found it more fruitful and pertinent to use instead Freud's concept of the primary process, to which I have connected some aspects of the id as well as the archaic ego. In my own frame of reference the participation of the secondary process pertains to the ego, while the unconscious motivation concerns some aspects of the id and superego … I have already referred to Kris's brilliant but partial interpretation of creativity as 'regression in the service of the ego.' "

8) Arieti, pp. 184-185. Editor's note: In the following paragraphs, Dr. Fisehmann uses concepts which are discussed in pp. 185-187 and in Arieti's concluding statement, pp. 405-410.

9) Adolf Veselý, *Leoš Janáček: Pohled do života a díla* [Leoš Janáček: a survey of his life and work] (Prague: F. Borový, 1924), pp. 95-96.

10) *Korespondence Leoše Janáčka s Maxem Brodem* [The correspondence of Leoš Janáček with Max Brod], edited by Jan Racek and Artuš Rektorys (Prague: Státní nakladatelství krásné literatury, hudby a umění, 1953), p.172. Letter of October 31, 1924. (Janáčkův Archív, vol. 9)

11) *Korespondence Leoše Janáčka s F. S. Procházkou* [The correspondence of Leoš Janáček with F. S. Procházka], edited by Artuš Rektorys (Prague: Hudební matice Umělecké besedy, 1949) p. 60. Letter of December 19, 1917. (Janáčkův Archív, vol. 3)

12) Arieti, p. 162.

13) Arieti, p. 167.

14) Jaroslav Vogel, *Leoš Janáček, His Life and Works;* English translation by Geraldine Thomsen-Muchová (London: Paul Hamlyn, 1962), p. 262. Letter to Kamila Stösslová, August. 10, 1917.

15) *Korespondence Leoše Janáčka s Maxem Brodem,* p. 231.

16) Vogel, p. 321.

17) Jaroslav Vogel, p. 375. Letter of November 30, 1927.

18) Cf. Jon Karlsson, M.D., *Inheritance of Creative Intelligence,* Chicago: Nelson-Hall Inc., 1978.

19) Arieti, p. 162.

20) Max Brod, *Leoš Janáček* (Vienna: Universal Edition, 1956) 2nd revised and enlarged edition, p. 28.

21) Leoš Janáček, "úvodní slovo k otevření konzervatoře v Brně" [Introductory remarks for the opening of the Brno Conservatory] *Lidové noviny*, vol. xxvii no. 278, October 7, 1919, reprinted in *Leoš Janáček: Fejetony z Lidových novin se studiemi Jana Racka, Arna Nováka, Vladimíra Helferta a Leoše Firkušného* [Feuilletons from *Lidové noviny* with articles by Jan Racek, Arne Novák, Vladimír Helfert, and Leoš Firkušný], edited by Jan Racek and Radovan Cigler (Brno: Krajské nakladatelství, 1958) second edition, pp. 213-214.

22) Arieti, p. 412.

23) Leoš Janáček, "Ticho" [Silence], *Lidové noviny*, vol. xxvii no. 236, August 26, 1919, reprinted in *Leoš Janáček: Fejetony z Lidových Novin*, pp. 38-39.

24) These statements largely correspond to passages in Mortimer Cass, "A note on music" in Arieti, pp. 236-238.

25) Leoš Janáček, "K čemu se přiznávám" [I confess] in *Lidové noviny*, vol. xxxv no. 78, February 13, 1927. , reprinted in *Leoš Janáček: Fejetony z Lidových Novin*, p. 55

26) Leoš Janáček, interview in *Literární svět*, vol. 1, March 8, 1928, quoted in Zdenka E. Fischmann, *Janáček's nápěvky (Speech Melodies) in Theory and Practice.*, p. 3-4.

27) Leoš Janáček, "Sedm havranů" [Seven ravens] in *Lidové noviny*, vol. xxx no. 600, November 30, 1922, reprinted in *Leoš Janáček: Fejetony z Lidových Novin*, p. 131.

28) Leoš Janáček, "Á la polka" in *Lidové noviny*, vol. xxx no. 292, June 13, 1922, reprinted in *Leoš Janáček: Fejetony z Lidových Novin*, p. 219.

29) *Korespondence Leoše Janáčka s Maxem Brodem*, p. 231. Letter of January 28, 1928.

30) Leoš Janáček, "Jaro" [Spring], *Lidové noviny*, vol. xx supplement no. 14, April 6, 1912, reprinted in *Leoš Janáček: Fejetony z Lidových Novin*, p. 110.

31) Jaroslav Šeda, *Leoš Janáček* (Prague: Státní hudební vydavatelství, 1961) p. 374.

32) Leoš Janáček, "Nota" [A note], *Lidové noviny*, no. 375, July 28, 1926, reprinted in *Leoš Janáček: Fejetony z Lidových Novin*, pp. 223-230.

33) Josef Sudek, *Janáček – Hukvaldy.* With commentary by Jaroslav Šeda. (Prague: Supraphon, 1971) p. 121.

34) Arieti, p. 176.

35) The connection of music and tenets of Gestalt psychology should be at least mentioned here as a possible theoretical paradigm. Another interesting approach might be the exploration of aspects of Janáček's creativity on the basis of Jungian archetypes. Cf. Arieti, pp. 26-27: "Jung believed that the creative process, at least when it pertains to art, occurs in two modes: the psychological and the visionary. In the psychological mode the content of the creative product is drawn from the realm of human consciousness ... The visionary is the mode that concerns Jung more deeply. In this second mode, the content does not originate in the lessons of life but from timeless depth, from what Jung calls "the collective unconscious." The collective unconscious is the depository of the archetypes – primordial experiences that have repeatedly occurred in the course of generations. The archetypes may surpass man's understanding. They may be many-sided, demonic, and grotesque. In the visionary mode the creative person is at the mercy of the re-emerging content. He is, according to Jung, in a passive situation. 'The work brings with it it own form, what he [the author] would add to it is declined; what he does not wish to admit is forced upon him.' In the visionary mode the creative person is more conscious of an 'alien' will or intention beyond his comprehension. Especially in the visionary mode, the emerging product of creativity is an autonomous compoer which, like a neurotic complex, is a detached portion of the psyche that leads an independent life. Its psychic energy has been withdrawn fron conscious control. The creative process thus consists of an unconscious animation of the archetype. The primordial image, connected with the archetype,

compensates for the insufficiency and one-sidedness of the creative person's experience of life, or even of the spirit of the historical time in which the creative person lives. In other words, the great work of art transcends life experiences, personal factors, and the historical perion in which its produced happens to live. By reawakening the wealth of experiences dominant in the collective unconscious, the creative process confers upon the work of art a universal significance. The artist's lack of adaptation to his environment becomes his real advantage: it facilitates the re-emergence of the archetypes; it induces him to enter into a mystical participation with the ancient sources. It is easy to recognize that Jung's concept of the collective unconscious colors his whole theory of creativity, just as the concept of libido colored Freud's. Jung was definitely right in pointing out that the great work of art cannot be seen only as the result of personal life experiences, dependent on the usual cognitive mechanisms. However, Jung also believed that what goes beyond personal experience originates in the collective unconscious Thus, in some ways, the collective unconscious occupies the role in Jungian theory that the primary process has in the Freudian system ... in most of his work Jung conveys the impression that he believes this is so. He finds in the archetype 'an invariable nucleus of meaning.' "

36) Arieti explains this term, p. 287: "Philosophers use the three modes of operations which I have described [of seconary-process cognition which are particularly important in the process of creativity: 1. Facing the primary process; 2. The use of concept; and 3. The concept as an ideal.] However, they use them at a very abstract level. After having collected pertinent data – the mode of contiguity – they often see a similarity between the world and a system of conceptions; that is, they see a correspondence, or parallelism, or coincidence, between the world and their philosophical views. Plato is again the first philosopher to come to mind. His system is founded on the great similarity between the world of particular thngs and the supersensible, superior world of ideas, where the real forms are perfect and unchanging. Particular things as we see them, according to Plato, are like the shadows seen in the cave by the prisoners. Plato had to create, at an abstract level, a system of ideal forms that coincides with (or is similar to) the world of particulars ... he saw a similarity between the world and a philsophical structure he concieved. Once [Plato] had envisioned (or constructed) this coincidence, he embarked upon deducing all the other facts that the system presupposed (the mode of *pars pro toto*)."

37) Jan Racek, "Tvůrčí profil Leoše Janáčka" [Creative Profile of Leoš Janáček] reprinted in Leoš Janáček, *Fejetony z Lidových Novin* n *Feuilletons*, p. 238.

38) Vogel, p. 383.

39) Erich Fromm, *The Anatomy of Human Destructiveness.* (New York: Holt, Rinehart & Winston, 1973), p. 366 ff. Fromm considers Albert Schweitzer a biophile *par excellence.*

40) Fromm, p. 471.

41) Arieti, p. 372 ff.

42) Trkanová, p. 40, 70.

43) *Korespondence Leoše Janáčka s Gabrielou Horvátovou* [The correspondence of Leoš Janáček with Gabriela Horvátová] (Prague: Hudební matice, 1950), p. 81. (Janáčkův Archív, vol. 6) Letter of March 21, 1918.

44) Charles Susskind, *Janáček and Brod* (Yale University Press: New Haven and London, 1985), pp. 40-42.

45) Presumably an article in *Musicologie* vol. 1, 1938.

46) Šeda, p. 376.

47) Arieta, p. 378.

48) Šeda, p. 377.

49) Trkanová, p. 74.

50) Trkanová, p. 98.

51) *Lidové noviny*, August 7, 1940.

52) Leoš Janáček, "Výlety Páně Broučkovy" [The travels of Mr. Broucek], *Lidové noviny*, vol. xxv no. 351, December 23, 1911, reprinted in Leoš Janáček, *Fejetony z Lidových Novin*, p. 53.

53) Daniel Muller, *Janáček* (Paris: Les Éditions Rieder, 1930, p. 43 ff).

54) Trkanová, p. 92. Editor's note: in the Czech draft of this article, there is a handwritten note by Dr. Fischmann, "not motiviation but identification" at this point.

55) Jaroslav Vogel, *Leoš Janáček: a biography*, revised English edition (Prague: Adacemia, 1997), pp. 322-323.

56) Leoš Janáček, "Glagolskaja missa" [Glagolitic Mass], *Lidové noviny*, vol. xxxv no. 598, November 27, 1927, reprinted in *Leoš Janáček: Fejetony z Lidových Novin*, pp. 57-61.

57) Šeda, p. 364.

58) Vogel (1962), p. 74.

59) *Korespondence s Gabrielou. Horvátovou*, p. 9.

60) *Korespondence Leoše Janáčka s Karlem Kovařovicem* [Correspondence of Leoš Janáček with Karel Kovařovic], edited by Artuš Rektorys (Prague: Hudební matice, 1950), p. 36. (Janáčkův Archív, vol. 7)

61) Trkanová, p. 80, p. 154.

62) *Korespondence s Gabrielou Horvátovou*, p. 88. Letter of April 23, 1918.

63) *Korespondence s Gabrielou Horvátovou*, p. 56. Letter of January 11, 1918.

64) Šeda, p. 368. Letter of April 15, 1918.

65) *Korespondence Leoše Janáčka s Maxem Brodem*, p. 232.

66) Trkanová, p. 167. Letter of June 8, 1927.

67) Otakar Šourek, introduction to the pocket score of *Intimate Letters* (Prague: Hudební matice Umělecké besedy, 1949).

68) Vogel (1962), p. 168.

69) *Korespondence of Leoše Janáčka s Marii Calmou a MUDr. Frant.Veselým* [Correspondence of Leoš Janáček with Marie Calma and Dr. František Veselý], (Prague: Orbis, 1951), pp. 69-70. (Janáčkův Archív, vol. 8)

70) Max Brod, *Leoš Janáček: Život a dilo.* [Leoš Janáček: life and work] (Prague: Hudební matice Umělecké besedy, 1924), p. 5.

71) *Korespondence s Gabrielou. Horvátovou*, p. 51, letter of January 1, 1918; *Korespondence Leoše Janáčka s Maxem Brodem*, p. 209, letter of November 17, 1926.

72) Arieti, p. 313 ff., summary p. 324.

73) "Znáte to, když někdo Vám z úst slovo bere, dřív než jste je vyslovil? Tak mi bylo vždy ve společnosti Dvořákově. Mohu osobu jeho zaměnit s jeho dílem. Tak ze srdce mi bral svoje melodie. Takový svazek nic na světě neroztrhá." Leoš Janáček, "Za Antonínem Dvořákem" [For Antonín Dvořák] in *Hudební revue*, vol. IV, nos. 8-9, pp. 432-433.

74) Leoš Janáček, *Dopisy Zdeňce* [Letters to Zdeňka], edited by František Hrabal, translated from German by Otakar Fiala (Prague: Supraphon, 1968).

75) Vogel (1962), p. 346.

76) Muller, pp. 10-11.

77) Ewans, pp. 13, 236.

78) Arieti, p. 341, quoted from Nathaniel Hirsch, *Genius and Creative Intelligence* (Cambridge: Sci-Art Publishers, 1931), pp. 288-289, 291-292.

79) Štědroň, p. 174.

80) Reminiscence of Mářa Stejskalová quoted in Robert T. Jones, "Afterword" in Rudolf Těsnohlídek, *The Cunning Little Vixen*, translated by Tatania Firkušný, Martiza Morgan and Robert T. Jones. (New York: Farrar, Straus and Giroux, 1985), pp. 183-184.

THE VIXEN BYSTROUŠKA AND HER CHAMPIONS

Leoš Janáček was not at all secretive about the sources of his inspiration and the reasons why and how certain people and places influenced his creative work. He caught the vixen Bystrouška "for the sake of the forest and for the sadness of old age." Death was a source of anxiety for Janáček during his adult life (he was over sixty-five in 1920), and it was the theme of his next opera, *The Makropulos Case*. However, he placed Bystrouška in his beloved Hukvaldy forests and meadows, a setting governed by the eternal natural process of death and renewal. If the vixen and the majority of forest creatures represent the vitality of the youth, the domesticated dog, the "capitalist" badger, the forester, and the other human males are aware of their own aging. Janáček manipulated this polarity with deep feeling but without mawkish sentimentality. The sarcastic, boisterous humor of the original tale he modulated and refined by introducing into his libretto elements of compassion, empathy, and allembracing love. The existence of two versions of the opera has at times created practical problems. For example, in preparing for the memorable East Berlin production of 1956, Walter Felsenstein consulted with Brod (then living in Tel Aviv) and with Janáček's biographer Jaroslav Vogel in Czechoslovakia; he studied the literature on the opera and finally decided to use the Brod version, with a few modifications. [1] However, this version has now fallen into disfavor, and the opera is usually produced in a form as close to Janáček's original intentions as possible.

The history of Bystrouška's transition from tale to opera was outlined in an article, "The Vixen Bystrouška in the Theater" which appeared in *Lidové noviny* on November 1, 1924, shortly before the Brno world premiere on November 6. The editor Dr. Bohumil Markalous had suggested to the journalist and writer Rudolf Těsnohlídek that he write a humorous verse narrative to accompany a set of original drawings by Stanislav Lolek illustrating the tale. Těsnohlídek provided a prose narrative instead. The resultant book, published in 1921, provided the material that Janáček put into a form suitable for the stage, particularly the behavior of the unruly foundling Bystrouška. The scenery and costume designs for this first production were designed by Eduard Milen. Some of the dignified opera stars were initially put off in rehearsal when they were asked by director Ota Zítek to move about on "four paws" or to mimic the movements of insects, but they were reconciled to such necessities as the enchantment of Janáček's vision and music took possession of them. It was to this singular power of Janáček's art that Max Brod referred in in 1928; for him the first truth about Janáček was his ability to carry his audience away to a "sea of beauty and order," to which "slow, careful access [was] absolutely illegitimate and impossible." [2]

Brod was another of Bystrouška's early champions, and he translated Janáček's opera into German. But he also elaborated the parallels between humans and animals, and added the explanatory story of the foxy lady Terynka. His changes were then introduced into the Czech text.

Of particular interest to admirers of Janáček's music is the recent appearance of an English translation by Tatiana Firkušný, Maritza Morgan, and Robert T. Jones of Těsnohlídek's Czech rendition of the tale, *The Cunning Little Vixen* (Farrar, Strauss & Giroux, 1985). This volume includes an informative afterword by Mr. Jones and illustrations by Maurice Sendak which were originally made for the New York City Opera production in 1981. Among those consulted to assure the book's authenticity was the internationally recognized Czech musicologist Alena Němcová.

The authenticity of subject matter and the choice of illustrator probably explain why the book trade generally considered this version of *Vixen* to be "children's literature." However, when it reached the desks of newspaper reviewers, their praise ran high. For example, the reviewer for the *Los Angeles Times* found the translation to have "an eloquent and natural simplicity, despite the difficulties (which Jones mentions) of working from the Brno dialect." He adds: "Why the book has never before been translated into English and published here is one of those mysteries of the trade. But, better late than never ... " [3] The book also provides a great deal of interesting information: a biography of Těsnohlídek; the essential details of the story's publication in *Lidové noviny* between April 7 and June 23 1920; a discussion of allusions in *Vixen* to various topical issues that were being debated in the young Czechoslovak Republic; the history of Janáček's introduction to Bystrouška; a summary of the differences between the book and his libretto; and comments on problems of translation.

Much has been written about the name Bystrouška and the connotations it brings to the title of Janáček's opera. The adjective *bystrý* means quick, mentally sharp, keen, shrewd, bright, cunning, or wise; its feminine diminutive form *bystrouška* has an affectionate, slightly ironic coloration. By analogy, use of the diminutive form *chytroušek* from the adjective *chytrý* [clever] does not constitute undiluted praise.

The afterword to the translation provides further information about the title. "Těsnohlídek named both his heroine and his book *Liška Bystronožka* [Vixen Fleet-Foot], but at the last moment a typesetter misread the word, and *Bystronožka* came out *Bystrouška* – 'Sharp–Ears.' Těsnohlídek thought the new name just as good as the old and let it stand. (The more evocative *Cunning Little Vixen* is from the German title (*Das Schlaue Fuchslein*) of Janáček's opera, a name supplied by Max Brod, creator of the German version for Janáček's Viennese publishers." [4]

Particularly interesting are the passages in Těsnohlídek's book that suggest music. For example, Catcher (the dog), after "singing at night melancholy songs he himself composed," is "beaten by the forester who did not understand such artistry." [5] The sounds of forest insects remind Těsnohlídek of "the village feast in Ricmanice" [6] when two competing bands play; the schoolmaster (*kantor*) hears music during the sunflower episode and indicates its instrumentation; the mosquito dances after getting drunk from biting the intoxicated forester's nose; and so on.

Especially striking is the description of the woodpecker, sexton of the woodland community, in the passage referring to Bystrouška's wedding: the woodpecker "knew how to climb the green vault of the forest cathedral, how to straighten the candles of the fir trees and the lamps of horse chestnut blossoms; how to ring the tips of pine trees like bells, better than any human sexton could. Twilight was spreading through the forest, and the moment seemed holy enough to stop one's breath." [7] Janáček scholars will be reminded of the composer's 1927 article about his *Glagolitic Mass*. Janáček speaks there of the moist and fragrant Luhačovice forests, where "a cathedral grew up in the giant vastness of the mountains," where "tall fir trees were the candles kindled by the stars" and "a flock of sheep rang the bells in that natural temple." [7]

A genuine friendship developed between Janáček and Těsnohlídek. The writer described his first meeting with the formidable composer, which took place among the blooming shrubs of Janáček's garden, by comparing the musician's white-haired head to another large, bright flower.

Těsnohlídek's book also throws some light on the story of Terynka, Max Brod's *femme fatale*, the elusive Gypsy orphan who becomes in his version of Janáček's opera a symbol of wildness and freedom analogous to the untamed vixen. In Těsnohlídek's original, *only* the schoolmaster loves Terynka, and he does so for twenty-five years and from afar while she manages with her brother a prosperous sweetshop inherited from their parents. She finally marries someone else, and the schoolmaster sadly resigns himself to his lonely life of a bachelor. Consequently, the back-to-Janáček version of the opera discards Brod's enchanting Terynka.

Těsnohlídek was a talented story-teller, a rather sardonic commentator on the human condition, and a stylist whose language was at times quite uninhibited-like his animal personages. For the people of Czechoslovak background, the new translation of his book, done with such love and skill, is a treasure. Perhaps it will contribute in the English-speaking world to that goal which Janáček cherished for his music when he said, if his music could bring people together, he would not have lived in vain.

Notes

1) See Walter Felsenstein, "Vier Briefe zum 'Schlauen Füchslein' " in *Leoš Janáček Materialen*, edited by Jakob Knaus (Zurich, 1975); Walter Felsenstrin, "On Janáček's dramatic works" in *The Music Theater of Walter Felsenstein*, edited and translated by Peter Paul Fuchs (New York: W. W. Norton, 1975), pp. 79-82.

2) Max Brod, obituary of Leoš Janáček, *Musikblätter des Anbruch*, X, 7 [1928] p. 235)

3) Charles Champlin, book review in the *Los Angeles Times*, January 26, 1986.

4) Robert T. Jones, "Afterword" in Rudolf Těsnohlídek, *The Cunning Little Vixen*, translated by Tatania Firkušný, Maritza Morgan and Robert T. Jones, illustrated by Maurice Sendak (New York: Farrar, Straus and Giroux, 1985), pp. 178-179.

5) Těsnohlídek, p. 25.

6) Těsnohlídek, p. 13.

7)   Těsnohlídek. p. 157.
8)   Leoš Janáček. "Glagolskaja missa" [Glagolitic Mass]. *Lidové noviny.* vol. XXXV. No.
     598. November 27. 1927. quoted in Leoš Janáček. *Feuilletons from Lidové noviny,* ed.
     Jan Racek. (Brno: Krajské nakladatelství. 1958) second edition. pp. 57-61.

MAX BROD'S LIFE IN MUSIC

On April 15, 1969, the Czechoslovak Society of Arts and Sciences in America (SVU) held a meeting to pay homage to the memory of its honorary member, Max Brod, who had died in Tel Aviv on December 20, 1968, five months before his eighty-fifth birthday. On that occasion, the writer Johannes Urzidil [1] spoke of his personal friendship with Brod, describing it as "the last manifestation of the Prague-German cultural mutuality and of deep love for the literature and poetry of our native city and the Czech land, once called by Goethe a continent in the center of the [European] continent." [2]

At the time, Urzidil was the last surviving member of the Prague Circle, one of the first to have experienced the flourishing of German-language literature in Bohemia before and during the auspicious rise and tragic fall of the Czechoslovak Republic. Almost forty-five years earlier, in 1924, Urzidil and Brod had spoken at Franz Kafka's funeral. Now, Urzidil felt very much alone as he bade farewell to Max Brod.

Brod, said Urzidil, was "one of the last universalists, who had not only created his own world of literary works and characters but also was the author of an extensive oeuvre comprising theoretical, literary-historical, musical, theatrical and religious topics." [3]

An extensive article by this writer was published in the 1985 volume of *Cross Currents* to commemorate the one hundredth anniversary of Brod's birth. [4] It concentrated on Brod's life and work in Palestine (later Israel), where he settled in March 1939. The present companion essay seeks to focus in greater depth on Max Brod the musician.

There have been many musicians who studied law, as Brod did at his father's wish, but who dedicated their lives to their art. We also encounter many-sided individuals who were talented in music as well as literature, and put both gifts to good use. Max Brod's music studies began in his early childhood and so systematic and intensive that he seriously contemplated a career as a concert pianist at one point. The piano remained a faithful friend throughout Brod's life. It offered him personal solace, gave him much satisfaction in playing with chamber music ensembles or accompanying soloists, and served him well as a means of illustrating his frequent lectures on musical topics. He wrote to Leoš Janáček in 1917, "Your *V mlhách* [In the Mists] are beautiful pieces. I play them every day." [5] Elsewhere he mentions the unique occasion when he performed a Mozart sonata with violinist Albert Einstein, whom he met at the home of friends during the physicist's stay in Prague. [6] And he recalled with pleasure, at a much later date, how he lectured on Gustav Mahler and played examples of Mahler's songs at various Israeli kibbutzim. [7]

In his autobiography, Brod reminisced nostalgically about playing piano pieces for four hands with his younger brother Otto, [8] accompanying his sister Sophie, who sang, regularly performing violin sonatas with Felix Weltsch [9] and forming trios, quartets - and occasionally even a quintet - with a group of friends. He said that "to visit a friend who plays the violin beautifully, to sit down at the piano after brief greetings and then, together, spellbound, make wonderful melodies shine brightly like the sun-all that can sometimes mean more happiness than to attend a concert of great virtuosi." [10)]

Brod's piano studies were complemented by the instruction he received from his friend Adolf Schreiber (1883-1920), a violinist as well as a composition student of Antonín Dvořák. One year Brod's senior, Schreiber taught him harmony, counterpoint and other theoretical aspects of music. They played much music together; Brod's plays were premiered in Berlin with incidental music by Schreiber.

After Schreiber committed suicide by drowning himself in the Wannsee, Brod published a monograph in tribute to that little-known musician. [11)] He also published a selection of ten of Schreiber's songs. Leoš Janáček discussed this publication in a feuilleton entitled "Adolf Šrajbr" in which he mused upon the tragic fate of this "delicate but truthful composer" and compared him to "a firefly that gave a strangely intimate and fascinating light, but came to a sad end because of a supposed weakness and worthlessness." By this, Janáček meant to say that the composer had been driven to despair and premature death by his complexes, self doubts and frustrations. Janáček added that many Czechoslovak composers had ended similarly, either in insanity or in drunkenness, because "our country has a way of subjecting composers to suffering and torture." [12)]   Janáček's fame was in the ascendant, but only after many years of struggle; consequently, he could easily empathize with Schreiber's fate. Brod's monograph and Janáček's feuilleton provide the principal documentation of Schreiber's artistic activities. Although Brod openly strove for recognition as an author, poet and playwright, he was always hesitant to discuss his own musical creativity. Whenever he was asked about this aspect of his activities, he would give an evasive answer or make statements like the one noted by Rosemarie Alstaedter, a physician and writer in Cologne, to whom Brod the musician came as a surprise since she had known him mainly as the discoverer and biographer of Franz Kafka. Alstaedter quotes Brod as saying, "I am an unnatural father. I have never tried to put my compositions into the proper light. Many of them have never even been performed to date. But that's all going to change. I will give more thought to the care of my musical progeny [Musik-Kinder]." [13)]

However, it seems that Brod did not keep records of his compositional activity. Apparently the first comprehensive worklist of his compositions was compiled and published by Yehuda Cohen in Max Brod: Ein Gendenkbuch, 1884-1968. [14)] It is based on Brod's own reconstruction of his musical output and includes thirty-eight opuses, mostly without dates of composition. Only a few of Brod's compositions have been published: Opus 10, Vier Lieder published by Universal Edition, Vienna, in 1927; Opus 14, incidental music to Brod's drama, Die Höhe des Gefühls [The Height of Emotion], which appeared in 1912 without the music publisher's name; and Opus 31, Zwei jemenitische Lieder [Two Yemenite Songs] for the Israeli singer Beracha Zefira, published in Israel by Merkaz LeTarbut.

There seem to have been two periods in Brod's life when he was very productive as a composer. Most of his songs date from the beginning of the twentieth century, when he was establishing himself as a writer and before he became absorbed by other activities, including organized politics, during the 1920s and 1930s. His second period of musical activity was during his early years in Palestine, which were marked by World War II, the Holocaust, the death of his wife in 1942, and the problems of mastering modern Hebrew and adjusting to life in the old-new Jewish homeland.

There was a hiatus of almost a decade in his literary output between the concise *Das Diesseitswunder oder die jüdische Idee und ihre Verwirklichung* [The Miracle of This World, or The Jewish Idea and Its Realization], published in Tel Aviv in 1939 (92 pages), and the first volume of his *Diesseits und Jenseits* [This World and Beyond], published in Switzerland in 1947. From 1951 until his death, Brod wrote and published at least one important book each year but composed almost no music.

In 1953 Brod revised and partially rewrote some of his old songs from the period of 1900 to about 1920. Among them was Opus 2, *Tagebuch in Liedern* [A Diary in Song]. Of this cycle of nineteen songs, thirteen had texts by Brod himself; three used poems by Hugo Salus [15] and three others, one poem each by Lessing, Bierbaum and Heine. A revised version of *Psalm CXXVI* (1921) from Opus 10 was republished in 1953 by IsraMusic Corporation in New York City, thus making it Brod's only composition available in the United States. The text of the song was printed in Hebrew letters along with a transliteration and an English translation was fitted to the music. Though the accompaniment is written for the piano, Brod made the following specification for one phrase: "In these two bars the pitch should be raised by almost a half step; sing freely, like an Oriental singer!" This statement corresponds to Brod's concept of a Mediterranean style as a basis for Israeli music. [16]

As Brod was a poet and a connoisseur of poetry, it is interesting to look closely at his choice of texts for the nearly ninety songs he composed. Goethe leads with twenty-two poems; there are fifteen by Brod himself, seven by Heine, four by Shakespeare, four by Salus, three by Kafka, three by George, two by Baudelaire, and one each by a number of other poets. He did not set any poems by Franz Werfel, even though the story of Brod's friendship with Werfel and his promotion of Werfel's poetry is well known. [17]

Brod's first attempt in the early twentieth century to use Oriental subjects was his Opus 6, *Lieder aus Asien* [Songs from Asia]; his Opus 32 (undated) was entitled *Acht Lieder aus Goethes 'Chinesisch-Deutschen Jahresund Tageszeiten'* [Eight Songs from Goethe's 'Chinese-German Seasons of the Year and Times of Day'] and was dedicated to his long-time secretary and collaborator Ilse Ester Hoffe. Opus 22, *Shir Nekamah* [Song of Retribution] was written for the piano and a recited text by David Zahavi.

For Opus 35, *Tod und Paradies* [Death and Paradise], Brod arranged passages from Kafka's diaries into two poems and invented a title appropriate for the work. The original version, with piano accompaniment, is dated 1951;

an orchestral version followed in 1952. Another poem by Kafka, *Schöpferisch schreite!* [Creatively Stride!], was set to music by Brod in 1956 and was included in the unpublished Opus 37, *Fünf Lieder*. This opus includes also the last song composed by Brod, in 1964 on a text by Goethe, *Nachts, wenn gute Geister streifen* [At Night, When Kindly Spirits Roam].

Despite his familiarity with the piano, Brod created relatively fewer works for that instrument than he did songs. Several unfinished fragments (Opuses 3 and 9) were followed by Opus 12, *Schlägt vom Hradschin die Uhr*, variations on a Czech folk song, 'Hradčanské hodiny' [The Clock of Hradčany Castle], 1916; Opus 13, *Elegie aus den Tod eines Freundes* [Elegy on the Death of a Friend], 1908; Opus 17, *Aphorismen* [Aphorisms], 1938-1939; and Opus 18, *Klavier-Sonatine*, undated. However, none of these works were ever published. Brod did not follow a strict chronological order in assigning opus numbers to his "musical progeny." Thus, the *Kleiner Walzer für E.T.* [Little Waltz for E.T.], dedicated to Else Taussig, Brod's future wife, and dated 1911, is included among the *Aphorismen*.

After settling in Palestine, Brod composed the following works for the piano: Opus 23, *Zweite Klaviersonate*; (his first sonata for the piano was one of his earliest unfinished works composed during his Prague period); Opus 25, *Fantasie* [Fantasy]; Opus 28, *Mittelmeersuite* [Mediterranean Suite]; Opus 29, *Unseren Toten* [To Our Dead]; Opus 34, piano suite *HaVishuv: Das Volk in Seinem Lande* [The People in Their Land] and Opus 38, *Invokation* [Invocation and other piano pieces, unfinished]. However, all these compositions remained unpublished: His Opus 30, *Zwei Israelische Bauerntänze* [Two Israeli Rustic Dances], composed in 1943, are extant in a piano and an orchestral version.

Brod's contribution to chamber music consists of Opus 7, *Trio*, "L'éducation sentimentale" (unfinished) and two finished works: Opus 11, *Sonate für Violine und Klavier* and Opus 33, *Klavierquintett*, subtitled "Élégie dramatique." He also wrote unpublished incidental music to his play *Der Fülscher* [The Forger], first performed in 1922, and to his drama *Eine Königin Ester* [A Queen Esther], premiered in 1918 (Opuses 15a and 15b, respectively).

There are also two very special compositions which Brod created in the early 1940s and dedicated to the memory of his wife: Opus 20, *Requiem Hebraicum* on a text by the poet Shin Shalom, Brod's largest work, for a baritone and piano or orchestral accompaniment), and Opus 21, *Yizkor* [In Memoriam], with Hebrew texts by Rachel, Mordechai Langer, Shin Shalom and Jehuda Halevi.

In summary, Cohen's catalog of Brod's compositions includes thirty-eight opus numbers, most of which are groups of short pieces or songs. Brod uses two distinct terms to describe the state of his works: *unvollendet* (unfinished) and *unfertig* (not ready, but he does not explain whether he means not ready for publication; or for performance).

Information on the performances of Brod's compositions is quite sketchy. His *Two Israeli Rustic Dances* were premiered by the Israel Philhar-

monic Orchestra under the baton of Charles Munch; they were repeated in
Israel and performed also in Berlin. The *Requiem Hebraicum* was played in
concerts and broadcasts in Israel and other countries. Brod's two settings of
Kafka's poems were premiered by Martha Mödl in Germany in 1967. His
Klavierquintett, reportedly composed in 1943, was broadcast by Radio Jerusalem in 1962. *Psalm* CXXVI was performed on the Berlin Free Radio. More
research in Israel and other countries may yield information. on other, more
recent performances.

Rosemarie Alstaeder of Cologne, who became Brod's friend after they
had made contact concerning articles on Salus and on Kafka's illness, recalls
how she had first become interested in Brod's music. In 1966, at her request,
Brod sent her a clean copy of the manuscript of his *Klavierquintett*. She and
some friends, among them the pianist Hans Priegnitz, planned a public performance of this quintet for March 1968. However, the recital was postponed
and rescheduled several times due to the illnesses of various performers. In the
end, Brod died before it could take place, but at least he had the satisfaction of
knowing the interest aroused by his music. [18]

Another reminiscence from one of Brod's numerous post-World War II
friends from Europe illustrates his need to create his music in a very private
ambience. When the journalist and writer Gertrud Isolani visited Brod in Tel
Aviv in 1961, she did not see a piano in his modest living room or in his library. When she asked Brod where he kept his instrument, he explained that it
was in his bedroom, next to his bed. He got his best musical ideas during the
night and would immediately play them very, very softly, in order to capture
them before he went back to sleep. [19]

Brod once said that, in playing certain passages from the works of
great masters he loved, he would "sense the perfection emanating from those
pure tones. And I sense the creative force which speaks through them." [20]
However, it seems that the thought of putting himself into the position of a
creative composer somehow made him uncomfortable. Perhaps he wanted to
improve or revise his compositions before exposing them to a critical audience. Shortly before his death he reportedly informed his friends that he
"needed at least another five years to finish all [of his] projects." [21] If these
projects included his unfinished musical compositions, it seems that he never
had the chance to accomplish what he felt was necessary.

However, there is a strange lack of information about his musical
works, even from his Prague period. One rather unexpected reference occurs
in the diary of Franz Kafka (entry on March 17, 1912): "Max's concert Sunday. My almost unconscious listening. From now on I can no longer be bored
by music." [22] Was Brod by chance playing his own works to impress his supposedly unmusical friend to such an extent? Was he in the habit of sharing his
songs and other compositions with his musical siblings and his friends?

We know that Brod occasionally mentioned his novels or plays in his
letters to Janáček, but he was silent about his own musical works. In fact, the
preface to *Korespondence Leoše Janáčka s Maxem Brodem* [Correspondence
of Leoš Janáček with Max Brod], which summarizes Brod's career as an au-

thor and music critic in Czechoslovakia in detail and fully acknowledges his role in promoting Czech music on the international scene, has only this terse footnote about Brod's musical activities: "Brod was also active as a composer. He devoted himself to minor chamber music, especially to the writing of songs. His *Vier Lieder für Gesang und Klavier* was published in 1927 by Universal Edition in Vienna." [23)] Since Brod was corresponding with the editors of the *Correspondence* and was his usual cooperative self, it would have been easy for them to obtain more information about his compositions, old and new, but the idea of Brod as a composer, then as now, may have seemed somewhat incompatible with the image of his other activities. It is only fair to note that few of Brod's compositions were available to the editors.

All his personal experiences as a performer and composer naturally enhanced Brod's skills as an original and knowledgeable music critic for the Prague dailies *Prager Abendblatt* and *Prager Tagblatt* and later, in Israel, for the German-language *Yediot Hadashot*. In the latter newspaper, his reviews appeared under the title "Klang und Schatten, Musiktagebuch von Max Brod" [Sound and Shadow: The Musical Diary of Max Brod]. [24)] To understand his style of criticism, we must take into account his general aesthetic attitude toward international music and the pointedly polemical tendency in many of his critical and analytical essays whenever he made a musical discovery for whose recognition he was willing to fight.

What kind of music did Brod like best? He tells us in detail in his autobiography. Of the old masters, he adored Scarlatti and Bach; among the early Romantics, he favored Schubert, Schumann and Berlioz. He accepted, without any aesthetic prejudices, both Brahms and Wagner. He upheld Wagner as the ideal of exalted drama and a bone of contention in heated discussions with Franz Werfel, who consistently preferred Verdi and mocked Wagner. Among his more modern contemporaries, Brod had a high regard for Reger, whose work is rarely performed today, as well as for Debussy, Stravinsky and Bartók, who were only beginning to emerge during his lifetime. Surprisingly, he was also attracted to Offenbach, perhaps because of Offenbach's satiric texts and witty music. Finally, Brod developed a very special feeling for Mahler, noting what he regarded as Jewish characteristics in Mahler's songs.

Some of these composers were not as popular during the first decades of the present century as they are today. It is a proof of Brod's broadminded and intelligent assessment that he appreciated and publicized them at an early date. "I have an incurable weakness for anything that is willful and urgent," he said in his autobiography. [25)] His independent judgment and enthusiastic bias toward many artists who were not appreciated at the time, but of whose greatness he was convinced, frequently brought him into conflicts with other critics. However, in music as well as in literature, subsequent developments mostly proved him right. The enormous popularity of Baroque music in our time, the recent re-evaluation of Berlioz, and the appreciation accorded to the music of Mahler, who was famous primarily as a conductor during his lifetime, are only a few examples of changes in musical taste which Brod intuitively predicted.

When he sought to promote a composer, Brod mostly did not stop with writing a polemical, theoretical article but went into action. In the case of several musicians, he made every effort to have their works performed and published. Sometimes Brod succeeded in these endeavors because he had connections with several artistic centers in Europe. One case in point was that of the Danish composer Carl Nielsen (1865-1931), whom Brod equated with Sibelius in significance. Letters shows that Brod tried to persuade Janáček to perform a Nielsen symphony and simultaneously called Nielsen's attention to Janáček's operas. This method of international cultural exchange can be very effective if it succeeds, and Brod knew well how to use it. Though it failed in Nielsen's case at the time, Brod's opinion was eventually vindicated. In 1965, Nielsen was posthumously discovered and widely performed during the centennial celebration of his birth. Brod must have been pleased by this belated success of his favorite Scandinavian.

"Among the Czechs, he tried to win understanding for the Germans; among the Germans, for the Czechs; among Christians, for the Jews; among Jews, for Christians, and among us-the modern barbarians-he pleaded the case of Cicero, Plato and Catullus, whose love poems had been masterfully translated by Max Brod," Hermann Kesten writes in describing Brod's multiple activities. [26] Gitta Pazi, who wrote a dissertation on Brod, viewed his rich European cultural experience as preparation for taking up the role of cultural mediator again in Israel. She stated: "Max Brod brings Western literature and musical history and the Western attitude toward the arts, into the kibbutzim he loved so much." [27] In Tel Aviv, Brod translated works of Israeli writers into German, wrote articles and books on Israeli musicians and promoted Israeli music in the homeland and on the international musical scene through his journalistic criticism.

Brod's most important artistic discoveries were Franz Kafka in literature and Leoš Janáček in music, as their current popularity confirms. These two artists, so different in their ethnic origins, lifestyle and specialty, and so unlikely to be mentioned together, came into prominence largely though Brod's helpful actions. Had Brod not preserved Kafka's manuscripts, there would have been little of Kafka's work left to publish today. And if Brod had not undertaken the translation of *Jenůfa* into German, Janáček would not have been performed in Vienna as early as 1918.

As a result, we can also indirectly add the two operas based on Kafka's books to Brod's credit. It is reported that Brod heard *The Trial* by Gottfried von Einem (premiered in Salzburg on August 17, 1953) and dryly commented, "There have been times when I laughed more." [28] Another opera based on Kafka is *Amerika* by Roman Haubenstock-Ramati; [29] its world premiere was held in Berlin on October 8, 1966.

The story of the collaboration between Janáček and Brod has been told so many times that it seems redundant to repeat it here again. We will therefore touch upon only a few facts which were either previously less known or are not so often repeated. In connection with the first contact between Janáček and Brod, mention should be made of the role of Jan Löwenbach, a lawyer who wrote widely on music and was Brod's and Janáček's legal copyright advisor. [30] Immediately after the first performance of Jenůfa in Prague in 1916, Löwenbach repeatedly tried to interest Brod in translating the libretto into German, but Brod consistently refused. Löwenbach thereupon sought the help of the composer Josef Suk, knowing that Brod respected Suk's artistic judgment. Suk thus became the disinterested, friendly link between Brod and Janáček, who arranged their first personal meeting, which resulted in Brod's decision to do the translation after all. However, it must be acknowledged that the original initiative came from Jan Löwenbach.

To translate the text of any vocal composition and adapt the translation to the music is a most difficult task. Janáček's unique vocal style and his unusual declamatory requirements stemming from the use of a Moravian dialect must have made the translation into German particularly difficult. In translating Jenůfa, Brod sought to avoid the German language of opera libretti and Austrian dialect. Since Janáček's operas were thought to be unsingable at the time, the fact that Brod's translations of Janáček's works are still in use today is proof of Brod's great literary skill and musical sensitivity. Recent research suggests that Brod may have asked the opinion of Kafka, who spoke Czech fluently and commented on Brod's translation of Jenůfa.

Janáček kept Brod informed about his artistic plans and also of his moments of indecision when he did not know what to compose next. Brod often suggested literary works which he considered suitable for operatic libretti. Janáček conscientiously read and discussed the books recommended by Brod but, except for a few unfinished sketches, he did not act on Brod's advice. In view of the friendship between the two men and the fact that Janáček accepted Brod as a sort of dramatic-literary mentor, it seems strange that there is no indication of Brod's ever having attempted to create an original libretto for Janáček. He wrote libretti for Gurlitt and Krása, and later, in Israel, for Marc Lavry's opera Dan HaShomer (Dan, the Guard), which is considered the first (or, by some, the second) original Israeli opera. [31] One of Brod's unusual experiences was his collaboration with Paul Dessau on a modernized version of the Passover Haggadah for presentation at a secular kibbutz. He tells the story in his autobiography, concluding his account with the resolve never again to play the role of a religious reformer. [32]

In any event, neither Brod nor Janáček ever mentions the idea of a libretto by Brod which could have been a culmination of their artistic collaboration and an answer to Janáček's continuous search for operatic subjects. Perhaps the idea did not occur to them, or perhaps neither one was sufficiently outspoken to suggest it to the other. All the known Janáček literature remains silent on this point. Consequently, while Brod translated and often reformulated the dramatic structure of Janáček's operas, Janáček made arrangements for his libretti on his own, not always with the most felicitous results. Brod proceeded in the same way with the translations of Křička's opera Bílý pán [The Gentleman in White] and Weinberger's Švanda dudák [Schwanda the Bagpiper], for which he rewrote the whole first act. [33]

During the Nazi era, the Janáček-Brod team became a subject of official attention when the Dresden Theater, in an inquiry dated June 22, 1933,
asked the Berlin State Commission for the Arts, Sciences and Public Instruction whether it would be in order to produce *Jenůfa*: "We would like to know
whether there are any objections against the performance of the opera *Jenůfa*
by Janazcek [sic]. The opera as such is an excellent work of art, for it stems
from Czech folklore and is based on folk music. The composer supposedly is
not a Jew ..." The answer from Berlin, dated June 26, 1933, stated: "There are
no objections against the performance of the opera *Jenůfa* as such, but it
would be advisable to show respect only for those foreign countries that be-
have in a friendly manner toward Germany, which unfortunately cannot be
said at this time about Czechoslovakia [*die Tschechei*]." [34)]

Brod's translation apparently was not considered sufficient reason for
prohibiting *Jenůfa* in Germany in 1933. However, after Bohemia and Moravia
became a Nazi protectorate, works on Russian themes were prohibited by Nazi
censorship. This ban affected such operas as Janáček's *Katya Kabanova* and
From the House of the Dead along with works by Jewish or emigré composers. Weinberger, whose *Švanda dudák* and popular operettas gained him an
international reputation, was not only a Jew but also an emigré, having settled
in the United States, and therefore a non-person from the Nazi perspective. By
that time Brod was in Palestine getting acquainted with the music of his new
homeland, and Janáček was no longer alive.

From the 1950s until shortly before his sudden death in 1968, Max
Brod regularly traveled to Europe with his Israeli passport. He visited Czechoslovakia only once, but made many trips to Switzerland, Austria and Germany
to lecture or in connection with the publication of his books. In the present
study we will mention only those of Brod's writings that deal with music.

Brod's earliest collection of essays and music criticism, *Sternenhimmel, Musik-und Theatererlebnis* [Starry Skies: Musical and Theatrical Ex-
periences] (Prague: Orbis, 1923), was republished after the war under the title
Prager Sternenhimmel [The Starry Skies of Prague] (Hamburg, 1966).

Brod wrote the first biography of Janáček on the occasion of the latter's
seventieth birthday in 1924. *Leoš Janáček, Leben und Werk* appeared in Czech
translation in Prague that same year and in the German original in Vienna the
following year (1925). A second German edition was published in 1956 by
Universal Edition in Vienna, with an epilogue written by Brod in 1953 about
the last four years of Janáček's life.

We have already mentioned Brod's correspondence with Janáček, beginning with a letter from Brod dated November 28, 1916 and ending with a
cable from Max and Else Brod, dated August 13, 1928, to Mrs. Zdenka
Janáček, expressing the Brods' sympathy and shock on Janáček's sudden
death.

In 1962 Brod turned his attention once again to a Czech composer
about whom he had written repeatedly with great understanding and affection:
Bedřich Smetana. In his early *Über die Schönheit hässlicher Bilder: Ein
Vademecum für Romantiker unserer Zeit* [On the Beauty of Ugly Pictures: A

Vademecum for Romantics in our Age] (Leipzig: Wolff Verlag, 1913); (Vienna: Zsolnay Verlag, 1967), Brod had analyzed Smetana's style as well as his significance for his nation and for the development of world music. At the age of seventy-eight, Brod returned to this theme in his book *Die verkaufte Braut: Der abenteuerliche Lebensroman des Textdichters Karel Sabina* [The Bartered Bride: The Adventurous Life of the Librettist Karel Sabina] (Munich: Bechtle, 1962). Brod had always felt that Sabina had been unjustly deprived of credit for the success achieved by *The Bartered Bride* in that only his initials, K.S., not his full name, were allowed to appear in advertisements of the opera's premiere. He also believed that it was too harsh a judgment to label Sabina as a traitor to his country. Thus, the book explored the weaknesses of Sabina's character and the handicaps under which he lived and worked.

"You are building the road to success [for my music]," Janáček wrote to Brod in 1921. [35] And he summarized his feelings of gratitude toward Brod in the oft-quoted passage: "[Brod] came at the right moment as a messenger from above. A poet himself ..." This statement is a genuine appreciation of Brod's countless unselfish efforts to promote the causes of music and literature during his long and productive life. Brod simply considered his actions as being in character with his very simple maxims of "Be good!" and "It is better to give than to receive."

On this note we rest the case of Brod's life in music.

Notes

1) Johannes Urzidil (b. Prague, 1896; d. New York, 1970) studied philosophy, the history of art, and German and Slavic studies in Prague. He left Czechoslovakia in 1938 and, after a stay in England, arrived in the United States in 1941. He wrote stories and essays, and was active as a translator and lecturer. Among his books are *Goethe in Böhmen* [Goethe in Bohemia], *Da geht Kafka* [There Goes Kafka] and *Prager Triptychon* [Triptych of Prague]. He was an honorary member of the Czechoslovak Society of Arts and Sciences. His tribute to Brod was published in two parts in the Society's Czech-language quarterly *Proměny* [Metamorphoses], Vol. 6 1969, No. 3, under the titles "Za Maxem Brodem" [To Max Brod] and No. 4, "Německý spisovatel v českém prostředí" [A German Writer in the Czech Environment].

2) Johannes Urzidil , "Za Maxem Brodem" [To Max Brod] *Proměny*; Vol. 6, No: 3, p. 35.

3) Urzidil, "Za Maxem Brodem," p. 32.

4) Zdenka E. Fischmann, "The Max Brod Centennial," in *Cross Currents 4. A Yearbook of Central European Culture*. L. Matějka and B. Stolz, eds. (Ann Axbor: University of Michigan, 1985), pp. 299-307. Another evaluation of Brod's musical achievements in Czechoslovakia, "Brod a hudba" [Brod and Music], *Proměny*, Vol. 7, No. 2, 1970, pp. 26-31, reprinted in this volume.

5) *Korespondence Leoše Janáčka s Maxem Brodem* [Correspondence of Leoš Janáček with Max Brod], edited by Jan Racek and Artuš Rektorys (Prague: SNKLHU, 1953), p. 40. Letter of November 28, 1917.

6) Max Brod, *Streitbares Leben* [A Contentious Life; Munich: Kindler Verlag, 1960]. The Czech translation by Bedřich Fučík, entitled *Život plný bojů* (Prague: Mladá Fronta, 1966), was used as a source for this article. This work will henceforth be referred to as *Autobiography*. The reference to Einstein appears on p. 53 of the Czech version.

7) Gustav Mahler (b. Kaliště, Bohemia, 1860; d. Vienna, 1911) studied music in Vienna. From 1880 he was active as a conductor in several European cities, including Olomouc and Prague. His position with the Opera in Hamburg (1891-97) led to appointments in Vienna and New York City. His renown as a prominent conductor of operas eclipsed his activities as a composer during his lifetime. He promoted Czech music, especially Smetana's operas. Though his father was a practicing Jew, Gustav Mahler converted to Catholicism. Brod wrote a book on Mahler, *Gustav Mahler: Beispiel einer deutsch-jüdischen Symbiose* [Gustav Mahler: Example of a German-Jewish Symbiosis] (Frankfort am Main, Ner Tamid, 1961). Brod held that there was a deep relationship between Hasidic songs and songs composed by Mahler, the similarity being especially notable in Mahler's rhythms. Brod lectured on this aspect of Mahler's music in Israel.

Brod came to know Hebrew well enough to deliver his lectures in that language but at first he wrote out his notes in transliteration for easier reading. There is a well-known Israeli anecdote that Brod's eyes moved in the "wrong" direction as he delivered his lectures; i.e., from left to right instead of from right to left, but his Hebrew sounded "right."

8) Otto Brod (b. Prague, 1888; d. Auschwitz, 1944) is frequently mentioned in Max Brod's *Autobiography*, in *Der Prager Kreis* [The Prague Circle] and other writings. Otto was the author of *Die Berauschten* [The Intoxicated, 1934] and of an unfinished biography of Voltaire, entitled *Es siegte das Recht* [Justice Prevailed]. In collaboration with Max, Otto Brod also wrote a novel entitled *Abenteuer in Japan* [Adventure in Japan; Amsterdam: de Lang, 1938]. Otto Brod is mentioned in H.G. Adler, *Theresienstadt* 1941-1945. *Das Antlitz einer Zwangsgemeinschaft,*, published in English as *The Face of an Enforced Community* (Tübingen; Mohr, 2nd ed. 1960), pp. 443, 590, as a member of the Terezín ghetto administration and as the author of a play, *Der Erfolg des Kolumbus* [The Success of Columbus], which was performed in Terezín. Max Brod referred to this play as *Das Ei des Kolumbus* [The Egg of Columbus], a comedy. Otto Brod and his wife were sent to Auschwitz with the last transport from Terezín in October, 1944. Their daughter, Marianne, who perished in Bergen-Belsen, sang in the choir in a performance of Verdi's *Requiem* conducted in Terezín by Rafael Schächter.

Unlike Otto, Sophie, the youngest Brod sibling, is mentioned only as an intermediary in the conflicts between Franz Kafka and his fiancée Felice Bauer in 1912. In 1961, Max noted that Sophie was living in America and had visited him in Israel, bringing him two letters that he later published in his *Max Brod über Franz Kafka* [Max Brod on Franz Kafka] (Hamburg: Fischer Taschenbuch, 1974), pp. 123 ff.

9) Felix Weltsch (b. Prague, 1884; d. Jerusalem, 1964) was one of Brod's oldest school friends from Prague. Their friendship and literary collaboration continued in Israel until Weltsch's death. Weltsch was a librarian at the University of Prague and, after 1938, at the Hebrew University in Jerusalem. Beginning with 1913, he wrote works on philosophy. In collaboration with Brod he wrote *Anschauung und Begriff* [Intuition and Comprehension] (Leipzig: Wolff Verlag, 1913), *Zionismus als Weltanschauung* [Zionism as a Philosophy of Life] (Moravská Ostrava: Färber, 1925) and several shorter essays.

10) Max Brod, *Autobiography*, p. 237.

11) Max Brod, *Adolf Schreiber. Ein Musikschicksal* [Adolf Schreiber: The Fate of a Musician] (Berlin: Welt Verlag, 1921).

12) Leoš Janáček, "Adolf Šrajbr," *Lidové noviny*, Vol. xxix no. 480, 1921, reprinted in in *Leoš Janáček: Fejetony z Lidových Novin se studiemi Jana Racka, Arna Nováka, Vladimíra Helferta a Leoše Firkušného* [Feuilletons from *Lidové noviny* with articles by Jan Racek, Arne Novák, Vladimír Helfert, and Leoš Firkušný], edited by Jan Racek and Radovan Cigler (Brno: Krajské nakladatelství, 1958), pp. 216-17. It seems significant that Janáček uses a Czech spelling for Schreiber's name. Janáček also gave a lecture on Schreiber in Prague in 1921.

13) Rosemarie Alstaedter, née Bock (b. Premnitz, Germany, 1924) studied pharmacology and German studies at Göttingen and later medicine in Bonn, earning her doctorate of medicine in 1951. She has lived in Cologne since 1953. Her "Begegnungen mit Max Brod"

[Encounters with Max Brod] appears in *Max Brod: Ein Gedenkbuch*, 1884-1968 *Gedenkbuch* [A Memorial Volume, 1884-1968] (Tel Aviv: Olamenu, 1969) (hereafter referred to as *Gedenkbuch*), pp. 203-12.

14) This book was originally intended as a Festschrift honoring Brod on his eighty-fifth birthday. The editor of the book, Hugo Gold, was born in Vienna in 1895. He was active in Brno from 1924 to 1939, and settled in Israel in 1940. The editor of the *Zeitschrift für Geschichte der Juden in der Tschechoslowakei* [Journal for the History of the Jews of Czechoslovakia] from 1929 to 1938, Gold published several works on the history of Jewish communities in pre-1938 Czechoslovakia. Brod knew about Gold's plans for the *Festschrift* and read some of the articles but did not live to see the book published. In view of Brod's death, the title was changed to *Max Brod: Ein Gedenkbuch 1884-1968* and the contents modified accordingly.
This volume includes two articles by Yehuda Cohen: "Max Brod, der Musiker" [Max Brod the Musician], pp. 277-83, und "Das musikalische Oeuvre von Max Brod" [The Musical Oeuvre of Max Brod], pp. 284-87. Cohen (b. Prague; 1910) studied music in his native city and settled in Israel in 1936. He became a music critic for the newspaper *Yediot Hadashot* and director of the Israeli broadcasting system. He was also active as a composer.

15) Hugo Salus (b. Česká Lípa; 1866; d. Prague, 1929), a well-known Prague gynecologist, was also active as a poet and writer. Arnold Schoenberg supposedly used one of Salus' poems for a song he composed in 1901, but current music dictionaries make no mention of such a song. See Ernst Pawel, *The Nightmare of Reason: A Life of Franz Kafka*. (New York: Farrar; Straus & Giroux, 1984), p. 153.

16) Max Brod, *Die Musik Israels* [The Music of Israel] (Tel Aviv: Sefer, 1951) is a rather brief but thorough study presenting an analysis of Israeli music and of such Israeli composers as Paul Ben-Haim, Marc Lavry and Alexander Uriah Boscovich. So-called Oriental melodic patterns combined with all contemporary styles of composition form the basis of what Brod calls the Mediterranean style.

17) Franz Werfel (b. Prague, 1890; d. Hollywood, California, 1945) became world-famous as a prolific novelist, dramatist; essayist and poet. Brod helped Werfel publish his first anthology of poems, *Der Weltfreund* [Friend to the World]. Brod describes his friendship and conflicts with Werfel in his *Autobiography* and elsewhere.

18) *Gedenkbuch*, pp. 209-10.

19) Gertrud Isolani (b. Dresden, 1899) left Germany in 1933 for Paris, where she was interned in 1942 and became active in the French underground before escaping to Switzerland. She published a number of novels. She met with Brod many times, when he visited Switzerland. Her contribution to the *Gedenkbuch* is entitled "Ein Genie der Freundschaft" [A Genius for Friendship], pp: 268-70.

20) Quoted in "Vertrauen zum Unzerstörbaren" [Faith in the Indestructible], by Berndt Wessling in *Gedenkbuch*, p. 123. Wessling (b. Bremen, 1939) was a musicologist, music critic and writer in Hamburg. He was also active for in the German diplomatic service in Brussels. In 1969 he became music director of the Deutsche Welle broadcasting system in Cologne.

21) Quoted by Josef Mühlberger, "Meine letzte Begegnung mit Max Brod" [My Last Meeting with Max Brod] in *Gedenkbuch*, p: 303. Mühlberger (b. Trautenau, Bohemia, 1903) studied in Prague and Uppsala. He is the author of many novels, poems and plays. He translated Jan Neruda's *Malostranské povídky*, Božena Němcová's *Babička* and Wolker's poetry from Czech to German. He has lived in Württemberg since 1946.

22) *The Diaries of Franz Kafka 1910-1913*, edited by Max Brod (New York: Schocken Books; 1965), p. 256.

23) *Korespondence Leoše Janáčka s Maxem Brodem*, p. 9.

24) Iwan Lilienfeld, "Mitbürger und Mitarbeiter" [Fellow Citizen and CoWorker] in *Gedenkbuch*, p. 265. Lilienfeld (b. Upper Silesia, 1910) Studied law in Berlin and

Freiburg. He left Germany in 1933 and lived in Italy and Holland before settling in Israel in 1935. In 1938 he became the editor of the Israeli newspaper *Yediot Hadashot*.

25) *Autobiography*, p. 238.

26) Hermann Kesten, "Max Brod" in *Gedenkbuch*, p. 231. Kesten (b. Germany, 1900), a writer, publicist and editor, went to the United States after the outbreak of World War II. He lived in Rome after the war.

27) "Max Brod aus Israelischer Sicht" [Max Brod Seen from the Israeli Viewpoint], in *Gedenkbuch*, p. 168. Pazi, a native of southern Bohemia, was interned on Mauritius before reaching Israel in 1945. She studied philosophy and Gertnan, English and French literature in Paris and London, earning her doctorate at the Julius-Maximilian University in Würzburg.

28) Quoted by Rosemarie Alstaedter in "Begegnnungen mit Max Brod" in *Gedenkbuch*, p. 207.

29) Roman Haubenstock-Ramati (b. Krakow, 1919), a composer, was music director of Radio Krakow from 1947 to 1950 and a director of the State Music Library in Tel Aviv from 1950 to 1956. He then lived in Austria. He is an exponent of experimental avant-garde music. The premiere of his opera *Amerika* caused "an uproar" in the musical world.

30) Jan Löwenbach (b. Rychnov nad Kněžnou, 1880; d. New York City, 1972) was an attorney specializing in copyright law and a writer on music. He knew Brod, Janáček, Suk, Martinů and most of the Czech musicians of his time. After spending the years of World War II in New York, he returned to Prague but subsequently resettled in the United States. He promoted Czechoslovak music in other countries and wrote on American music for the Czech reading public. The author of libretti for Martinů and Křička, he translated operatic libretti from Czech into German, and / vice versa. Cf. *Jan Löwenbach a Leoš Janáček. Vzájemná korespondence* [Jan Löwenbach and Leoš Janáček. Mutual Correspondence], Ivo Stolařík, ed. (Opava: Slezský studijní ústav, 1958).

31) Manfred Gurlitt (b. Berlin, 1890; d. Tokyo, 1972), a conductor and composer, was dismissed from his position in Germany by the Nazis after 1933 and settled in Japan in 1939. Brod wrote the libretto for Gurlitt's opera *Nana* (1933). Hans Krasa (b. Prague, 1899; d. Auschwitz, 1944) studied with Zemlinsky. He was chorus director at the German Theater in Prague, then became conductor at the Kroll Opera in Berlin. In 1928 he settled in Prague; in 1942 he was deported to Terezín and from there to Auschwitz. His opera *Brundibár* was performed approximately fifty times in Terezín with child inmates as performers. He planned to compose an opera entitled *Lysistrata* on a libretto by Brod, but was unable to carry out this plan. Marc Lavry (b: Riga; 1903; d. Haífa, 1967) studied in Leipzig and was active as a conductor in Germany and Sweden. In 1935 he settled in Israel, where he headed the music section of Kol Zion leGolah, the World Zionist Organization's broadcasts to the Diaspora, from 1949. His opera *Dan HaShomer* was premiered on February 17, 1945 in Tel Aviv.

32) Brod tells the story of this modernized Haggadah in his *Autobiography*, pp. 280-81. Paul Dessau (b. Hamburg, 1894; d. East Berlin, 1979) was active as an opera conductor in several German cities. After 1933 he lived variously in Europe, Palestine and the United States, leading a rather unsettled existence. After 1948 he worked in East Germany, writing and producing works with political themes.

33) Jaroslav Křička (b. Kelč, Moravia, 1882; d. Prague, 1969) was a highly respected Czech composer and teacher of music. Jaromír Weinberger (b. Prague, 1896; d. St. Petersburg, Florida, 1967) studied with Křička and Hofmeister in Prague and with Max Reger in Leipzig. He first visited the United States in 1922 but returned to Europe. In 1939 he settled permanently in St. Petersburg, Florida. His opera *Švanda dudák* [Schwanda the Bagpiper], premiered on April 27, 1927, brought him international renown.

34) Joseph Wulf, *Musik im Dritten Reich* [Music in the Third Reich] Gütersloh: Sigbert Mohn Verlag, 1963; Rororo Taschenbuch edition, 1966), pp. 95-96. Wulf (b. Krakow, 1912), initially a theological student, is a survivor of Auschwitz. After the war he worked for Jewish historical organizations in Poland and subsequently in Paris. He eventually settled

in West Berlin where he engaged in research on the arts, music, literature, communications media and other aspects of culture during the period of the Third Reich.

35) *Korespondence Leoše Janáčka s Maxem Brodem*, letter of April 30, 1921.

THE MAX BROD CENTENNIAL

In June 1984, the prominent German weekly *Die Zeit* (no. 24) announced the results of an international opinion poll it had organized jointly with analogous French, Spanish, Italian, and British newspapers. The readers in all five countries were asked to vote in a "Literary Parliament," to choose the ten most significant writers from the lists proposed by the other four countries, and thus to find out whether there was a common West European literary tradition. Among the ten winners, Franz Kafka placed fifth – after Shakespeare, Goethe, Cervantes and Dante. That was a rather unexpected outcome and another indirect confirmation of Max Brod's unerring aesthetic judgement.

This paper, however, does not intend to retell the well-known story of Kafka's manuscripts. The fact remains that without Brod there simply would be no Kafka chapter in twentieth-century literature. Nor will we review Brod's important contributions to the popularization of Janáček and other musicians, besides young Werfel, Hašek and many more of his talented contemporaries whom he discovered and devotedly promoted. All these accomplishments belong to the time Max Brod spent in his native Prague. In Czech sources his story usually seems to fade out with his train journey through Moravská Ostrava during the night the Nazis invaded Czechoslovakia. Yet for the fifty-five-year-old Brod it was only a new beginning, and he lived until age 84. In retrospect he wrote: "But today I am of the opinion that the improbable intervention of Lady Luck in the night of March 14 [1939] compensates for anything bad that Fate has ever dealt to me." [1]

By his choice, and "obeying the genius of my life" he went to Palestine instead of accepting the professorship in the United States that Thomas Mann had arranged for him. [2] He never regretted this decision. Yet, according to Ernst Pawel, " ... one comes to suspect that Brod was at home nowhere but in Prague. When he had to flee, in 1939, he took his hometown with him to Tel Aviv, along with his Kafka manuscripts ..." [3]

Brod used to say: "One must always start again at the beginning" [4] and did so in his chosen new fatherland. The reception of the new *oleh* was very cordial, to the point that his wife Elsa commented: "It's rather nice, after all, to be a kind of a prominent [person]." [5] the offer of a job as the dramaturgist of the Habimah Theater soon followed.

The Brods settled in Tel Aviv, but he described the initial period as follows: "Overall, I lived in confusion ... I was deeply happy and, at the same time, deeply unhappy." [6] The biggest worry was the fate of those family members and friends who did not escape from Nazi-occupied Czechoslovakia. However, despite the nearby WWII operations, only during the War of Independence did Brod witness the "shelling of our Tel Aviv ... the first gunfire I ever heard ... the lacuna in my education was filled," [7] as seemed proper for a representative of this turbulent century. Despite this, and the Six Day War of

1967, Brod remained a convinced antimilitarist and pacifist, hoping until his death for reconciliation between the Jews and the Arabs. After all, he had experienced life in the "triple ghetto of Prague" [8] and the precarious coexistence of minorities in Masaryk's republic.

The language was another serious problem, deeply felt by the writer. Brod did not consider himself particularly skilled in foreign languages, except for Hebrew, "in which I have progressed far enough. I can spar in it in a debate, especially if it concerns abstract concepts or arts. But it is more difficult when [I am] buying vegetables." 'In any case, there were old and new friends and colleagues willing to help, teach, or translate into Hebrew. For his part, Brod translated Israeli literary works into German under the title "Klang und schatten, Musiktagebuch von Max Brod." (Sound and Shadow, Musical Diary of Max Brod) He lectured in Hebrew, "yet remained a German author, attached to German culture and the Western tradition," though he became a good Israeli patriot "who raised the flag out of his window on holidays." [9]

Brod found in Tel Aviv a neighborhood Café Roma in which he could be a *Stammgast*, but it did not exactly come up to the informal but institutionalized artists' meetings of the "Arconauts" at Café Arco or Café Louvre in Prague, with their lively debates, hot arguments and friendships going back to school days – as Brod remembered and Johannes Urzidil described them in his *Prager Triptychon*. Nor could the exotic strand of the Mediterranean Sea compare with the frequent strolls across the Charles Bridge up to Hradčany or along the Vltava quais.

Brod saw his native city once more, in 1964, when he was officially invited by the Union of Czechoslovak composers and "was received in a very friendly, one could say triumphal, manner." [10] František Kafka, who talked with him at that time, perceived Brod "as an elf, the way they appear in a book of dream interpretations – a benign, white and luminous being." [11] Before that, Brod actively cooperated by mail with Jan Racek and Artuš Rektorys, the editors of his correspondence with Leoš Janáček. In his 1951 preface to the correspondence, Racek called Brod a progressive, democratic Prague German writer who came close to socialistic humanism and had a strong sense of a dialectic interpretation of life. [12]

Descriptions of Brod's unique personality abound, such as: the mediator, discoverer, Columbus of the arts, Haluts of the spirit, the great lover, great reconciliator, a genius of friendship, unselfish, always ready to help, very modest and even secretive about his own accomplishments. [13] His friends and admirers have also categorized him as "a man who does not know hate." However, he could be critical, outspoken, sharp and militant when his principles were tested or his passions were aroused. Pawel comments on Brod in a penetrating way in his recent biography of Kafka: "Brod's most critical talent, if fact, lay in an almost unprecedented combination of critical acumen and generosity of spirit;" referring to his early childhood curvature of the spine (Kyphosis), he describes his "permanently deformed physique, whose apparent frailty seemed accentuated by the strikingly massive head ... his subsequent promiscuous generosity as a lover was inspired by the need to reaffirm

his wholeness." Yet, still in Pawel's words, "Brod's perennial optimism was
... an outgrowth of that passionate enjoyment of life," and he "seemed to pos-
sess the secret not only of how to survive but of how to celebrate survival
..."[14] Some of these features apparently caused problems in Brod's marriage,
and Pawel may stress them more than prior biographers had done, to contrast
Kafka's "quest for purity" with the guilt-free sexuality of young Brod and his
other contemporaries.

One the other hand, Stefan Schwarz recognizes that "in him the joy of
eroticism ... is mixed with the urge of a brooding philosopher toward meta-
physics." Brod puts it differently: "But in my innermost conviction these two
areas [poetry and philosophy] are not at all separated, as they might seem to be
under a strict analysis of concepts. Underground paths lead from one field to
the other, underground currents rush through their foundations in a unitary
flow." Here we clearly grasp why the quality of "bridge building and of
unifying the opposites" has been so often stressed as "the true and permanent
characteristic" of all Brod's activities. The Britannica briefly sums it up:
"Brod's many novels blend fantasy, mysticism, and eroticism," which is a
statement that would fit most writers of the Prague Circle, whose "public
character" Brod became. [15] But that would be another story.

We have to return to Brod's life in Palestine-Israel, about which he
wrote: "Except for *Saul* (a drama translated into Hebrew by Shin Shalom) I
wrote very little in the early years of the war. At first I indulged in the joyful
excitement, then I was suddenly dragged down into an abyss – the war, the
ugliness of the disrupted world, the constant threat – the death (in 1942) of my
gifted wife, with her sense of humor and her understanding of the finest spiritual values ..." [16] This relative literary hiatus lasted almost ten years, though
he worked on Kafka's diaries which were published in 1948 and 1949, to be
followed by the edition of Kafka's letters in the fifties. The two volumes of
Diesseits and Jenseits, published in 1947 and 1948, broke the creative stand-
still.

It is interesting to notice that Brod composed more during that period
of novelistic silence. Among his composition, mostly unpublished, were the
Requiem Hebraicum op. 20, and *Jiskor* op. 21 - a cycle of four songs on Hebrew poetry – both works created in memory of his late wife. He confessed
that "many of those things for which I cannot find the words anymore, I can
express only in tones ..." [17] In the fifties, when he started to produce the
first of a considerable number of books, his composing again declined.

It would be tedious to enumerate all the title of this late period. A
complete bibliography by Zeev Barth can be consulted in *Max Brod: ein
Gedenkbuch.* [18] *Galilei in Gefangenschaft* (1948), which received the Bialik
Prize and *Johannes Reuchlin and sein Kampf* (1966), "written to show one
German who stepped in valiantly at a dangerous time for Judaism" [19] are his-
torical biographical novels; *Mira* (1958) is a novel about Hoffmansthal; *Der
Meister* (1951) concerns Jesus; *Unambo* (1949) narrates the Jewish-Arab war;
Streitbares Leben (1960) is Brod's autobiography; *Die Verkaufte Braut* (1962)
is an apology to Sabina and a salute to Smetana, whose music Brod highly

appreciated; *Diesseits und Jenseits* and *Das Unzerst Örbare* (volume I, 1968; Volume II was printed posthumously) are compendia of Brod's ethical, philosophical and religious thoughts; *Der Prager Kreis* (1966) and *Prager Tagblatt* are memoirs, actual and semi-fictional. Besides all this, Brod, produced more studies on Kafka, Mahler, the music of Israel, collections of stories and novellas, one volume of poetry, a modernized *Haggadah* presentation, dramatizations of *The Castle* and *Reubeni*, a libretto for Lavry's opera Dan Hashomer, an other works. These new books and some reprints of his prewar novels appeared, mostly in Germany, Austria and Switzerland.

Little of his complete work is available in English: *Tycho de Brahes Weg zur Gott* (1916) was published as the *Redemption of Tycho Brahe* in 1928; the novel that was so popular as to be filmed, *Die Frau nach der man sich sehnt (1927)*, became *Three Loves* a year later; *Heidentum, Christentum, Judentum (1921)* appeared as *Paganism, Christianity, Judaism: A Confession* in 1970; the Heine biography (1934) which gained Brod a Heine Plakette in Düsseldorf (1954) was translated into English in 1956; the book on Jesus was the only one that appeared in the German original and an English version, *The Master,* in 1951. And there are also Brod's Kafka studies, which cover the span from the first biography of 1937 to the sixties in new printings up to the present – and are an intrinsic basis of international Kafka scholarship.

Beginning in 1942, Brod was assisted in all of his literary work by Ilsa Ester Hoffe, born in Opava, about whom he gratefully wrote: "[she] continues, much too modestly, to call herself my secretary; but she has been more: a creative collaborator, my strictest critic, helper, ally, friend." He dedicated *Der Meister* to her. [19]

Brod kept busy in other ways as well. He reportedly acquired his first Israeli passport in 1954 and began lecture tours through Germany. His *Distanzliebe* (love at a distance) and the feeling of being only culturally, never politically close to German allowed him to look at the new, young generation of Germans as innocent of Nazi crimes, and to maintain a hope for a better future among all countries. Jörg Mager recalls that Brod came to Düsseldorf "as a messenger of peace, yet ready to fight. In the times of officialdom and of guided delegations, he appeared as an individual standing outside any power apparatus." [20] During his European visits he renewed some old friendships, made new friends and acquaintances, and was officially honored on several occasions. A rumored trip to the United States in 1964 / 65 unfortunately did not materialize, and Brod did not get the opportunity to directly revise whatever image of America he had acquired through his reading and Kafka's novel of that name, which he had edited.

We mentioned earlier that Brod believed in the combination of creative writing and philosophy, of poetic invention and realistic observation. This trait is manifested in his novels, whose protagonists, fictional and historical, often tend to philosophize about the meaning of life and to discuss religion, politics, music and other arts in a very intellectual manner. Brod the teacher shows through in such places. One interesting example is how Brod managed to get even President Masaryk into his *Die Frau nach der man sich sehnt,* or

Three Loves. The narrator-protagonist introduces his second love, Aneschka Omcirkova, that is, Agnes, in a paragraph starting with the question: "Can there be a higher duty than humanity? she said hoarsely, in a simple and straightforward way. – Agnes was very intelligent. She was educated, as the larger part of the young Czech generation was, in the spirit of the ideas of the President Masaryk, whom she considered the greatest philosopher of that time. She had studied his works – his totally untragic conception of the world, in which everything made sense and which showed to every individual, as well as to every nation, a way toward realistic progress; true, a progress that was difficult to achieve, but was an unquestionable right for all. A quiet optimism filled her, so to say, to her fingertips, and all her living expression radiated it."[21]

In his novels and stories, Brod consciously mixed autobiographical features with those of real people he met. Thus he said that his Kepler was in some details modeled after "my friend Werfel rather than after Einstein," [22] as some reviewers assumed, and that a part of his description of the "sanguine, hot-tempered nature of Brahe" [23] was derived from a stormy encounter with the composer Max Reger. His wife's qualities characterize, according to him, Gallilei's daughter and are also found in the figure of Edith in *Rebellische Herzen.* (1957) [24] His university professor of sociology and economics, Alfred Weber, became a partial model for some scenes in *Jugend im Nebel;* (1959) [25] then we have his friend from the Prague Bar Kochba student club, Viktor Mathias Freud, whose life is reflected in *Beinahe ein Vorzugsschüler.* (1952) [26] Bruno Kafka, Franz's baptized second cousin, figures as a prototype in another book, and so on. We leave it to other experts to identify further instances of such a blend of fantasy and reality in Brod's oeuvre.

Some of Brod's ethico-religious philosophical theses are the core-ideas of his works *à clef.* With his usual self-awareness he specifies one such moment of truth, in the climax of his *Brahe* and again in his *Saul,* when "the teacher gets on his knees before his own pupil" [27] recognizing that the pupil's genius surpasses his own. This seems to apply as well to Brod's real life position whenever he faced his more talented "discoveries," Kafka in particular. His lack of empty competitiveness speaks well of his self-confidence. He explains this as having never observed in himself the proverbial "Jewish self-hate" or any Jewish inferiority complex. [28] To expect thanks meant for him self-comdemnation and a complete depreciation of the good deed. [29] On the contrary, to serve any recognized greatness and do no harm to anybody was the highest value of Brod's life.

Another idea that emerged as early as *Brahe* (1916) and was further developed in *Stefan Rott* (1931) and *Heidentum, Christentum, Judentum,* is that God wants to suffer because even this kind of existence ought and must find expression in His infinite sphere. The man and the animal; those are God's provinces where he suffers." [30] As a consequence, God who suffers needs the finite humans, their trusting love and faithful hope. In Brod's explanation "the confrontation of the absolute with the relative ... marks man's tragic lot." [31] Brod then proposes his theory of the "noble and ignoble adversity." Noble adversity belongs to the category usually defined as "an act of God," to be accepted and humbly suffered, while ignoble or ordinary adversity can be overcome, as it refers to such evils and "war, hate among the nations, social oppression" and similar human conditions. One must strongly combat such unnecessary evils, "so to say, as God's delegate." [32]

Brod sees fundamental Jewish ethics in the active fight against these ignoble adversities, because Judaism means for him a "mission of the deed," as compared with the Christian "mission of the word." [33] Moreover, for a Jew it is the individual action and the individual form of grace that count.

After the book *Diesseits und Jenseits*, where these ideas were treated more fully, came Brod's last finished work, his literary "last will," *Das Unzerstörbare*. We might interpret this title as "That Which Is Indestructible and Eternal," rather than simply use the noun Indestructibility. This concept refers to an ultimate, very rare deed, accomplished in a moment when the actor becomes detached and free from the law of causality and performs and action that is above time, above all egoism, above any power struggle, but makes a great impact and in some particular way permanently changes the course of the world. Willy Haas considers Brod's saving Kafka's manuscripts as such a timeless deed. [34]

The goal of reaching and experiencing this indestructibility of human spirit seems to have been for Brod another step in his continuous effort to transcend himself, a step in his personal "Weg zu Gott." He did not try to create a complete theological system but gradually elaborated his thoughts about how man can preserve his integrity and how he can improve the human condition in this very real, imperfect world. Brod made his last European trip in the fall of 1968 and reportedly informed his friends that he "needed at least another five years to finish all his projects." [35] He then suddenly died on December 20. "He was buried at the Pantheon cemetery in Tel Aviv, next to the graves of the founders of Hebrew literature, Achad Haam, Bialik and Tschernickowski," accompanied by many mourners and several official representatives.[36] The writer Schalom Ben-Chorin and the poet Shin Shalom, among others, gave funeral speeches. "The sun broke through the stormy clouds for a few minutes, then it started to rain," remembers Alice Schwarz in her contribution to the *Gedenkbuch*, which offers further touching details about the funeral. [37]

The topic Brod had planned to write about at the time of his death was immortality. Depending on our personal beliefs, we could use our fantasy to imagine Brod eagerly exploring the hereafter. But, in purely human terms, we can ensure his immortality by not forgetting his many merits and good deeds and his lasting contributions to Czechoslovak and world culture.

Pawel offers the following general evaluation: "There was a dark side to Brod, to his frenzied activity, his relentless exuberance and compulsive sociability. Precocious, brilliant, and facile, he spread himself thin, forced the growth of his many talents and gave none of them a chance to ever fully mature." [38] This seems to contradict the opinions of those who knew Brod in the last years of his life from close contact. Yet, there is some truth in it, though the concept of the "Renaissance man" allows for such multiple interests as were his. Moreover, Brod's description of the generation "trotz Allem" (in spite of everything) in his autobiography puts this issue into a larger perspective: "It was a generation of fearless humanists, naturally originating not only from Prague but dispersed all over Europe; a very diversified generation as to denominations, faith and nationality, varied as to professions ... We considered a simple and quiet unselfishness our basic tenet, or solution for many problems which people like to consider unsolvable, because they, under the strangest pretexts, avoid the simplest solution: 'Be good!' " [39] Is this sentimental nostalgia old-fashioned idealism, or a viable model to emulate: Can this ethical model still be followed today, when the historically unique Prague amalgam of Jewish, German and Czech cultural roots definitively belongs to the irretrievable past?

About the Sources

The doctoral dissertation (Julius-Maximilian Universität Würzburg), *Max Brod* (Bonn, 1970) by Czechoslovakian-born Margarita(Gitta) Pazi was not available. Her contribution to the *Gedenkbuch*, pp. 167-173, "Max Brod aus Israelischer Sicht," was written while she had direct contact with Brod in Israel, where she had lived since 1945.

References

Brod, Max. *Život plný bojů* (Praha: Mladá Fronta, 1966). Translated into Czech by Bedřich Fučik from Brod's *Streitbares Leben* (München: Kindler, 1960). The page numbers in this article refer to the Czech edition. This work is referred to in the footnotes as *ŽB*.

Max Brod. *Ein Gedenkbuch*, edited by Hugo Gold (Tel Aviv: Olamenu, 1969). Vienna-born Gold was active in Brno between 1924 and 1939, and went to Israel in 1940. He published works on the history of Jewish communities in pre-war Czechoslovakia and edited *Zeitschrift für die Geschichte der Juden in der Tschechoslovakei* (1928-1938). Gold planned this book as a *Festschrift* for Brod's eighty-fifth birthday. Brod knew about it but did not live to see the book published. The title was changed and the contents modified to include Brod's death. This work is referred to in the footnotes as *GB*.

Pawel, Ernst, *The Nightmare of Reason. A Life of Franz Kafka* (New York: Farrar-Strauss-Giroux, 1984). This newest Kafka biography dedicated to the memory of Ottla Kafka and Milena Jesenská promises to provoke controversy. The book received the "1984 Los Angeles Times Book Prize" in the category of biography. This work is referred to in the footnotes as *NR*.

Specific Background Bibliography

The Jews of Czechoslovakia (New York: The Jewish Publication Society of America, Philadelphia, and The Society for the History of Czechoslovak Jews) Vol. I, 1968; Vol. II, 1971; Vol. III, 1984. In volume I, see Harry Zohn, "Participation in German Literature," pp. 468-522, and Paul Nettl, "Music," pp. 539-558, for specific data. Volume II contains information about the history of Czechoslovak Zionism, the Jewish National Council, the Jewish Party of Czechoslovakia, and related topics.

Brod, Max. *Tychos Weg zu Gott*. Vorwort von Stefan Zweig (Frankfurt am Main: Suhrkamp Taschenbuch Verlag, 1978).

_____ *Der Prager Kreis*. Nachwort von Peter Demetz (Frankfurt am Main: Suhrkamp Taschenbuch Verlag, 1979).

_____ *Über Franz Kafka*. (Frankfurt am Main: Suhrkamp Taschenbuch Verlag, 4th printing April 1980).

_____ *die Frau nach der man sehnt* (Reinbeck bei Hamburg: Rohwolt Verlag, 3rd printing, December 1962).

Lessing, Theodore. *Der jüdische Selbsthass* (Berlin: Zionistischer Bücher-Bund, 1930.

Engreth, Ruediger, *Im Schatten des Hradschin* (Graz – Wien – Köln: Stiasny Verlag, 1965). Short biographies and samples of the writings by members of the Prague Circle; Brod's fragment from *Tycho* is included.

Urzidil, Johannes, *Prager Triptychon* (München: Heyne Verlag, 1980).

Alt-Prager Geschichten, Peter Demetz, ed. (Frankfurt am Main: Insel Verlag, 1982). Brod's "Giulietta" is included, as well as selections from other Prague Circle authors.

Notes

1) *ŽB*, p. 267.
2) Ibid., p. 233.
3) *NR*, p. 201.
4) *GB*, p. 17.
5) *ŽB*, p. 270.
6) Ibid., p. 276.
7) *GB*, p. 264.
8) Ibid., p. 233.
9) Ibid., pp. 277, 265, 137.
10) Ibid., p. 155.
11) Ibid., p. 194.
12) Jan Racek and Artuš Rektorys, editors, *Korespondence Leoše Janáčka s Maxem Brodem* (Praha: SNKHLU, 1953).
13) Ibid., pp. 44, 249, 268, 289, and elsewhere in the literature.
14) *NR*, pp. 111, 113, 112, 126.
15) *GB*, pp. 272, 38, 167.
16) *ŽB*, p. 295.

17) *GB*, p. 277.
18) *GB*, pp. …
19) *ŽB*, p. 279.
20) *GB*, p. 185.
21) Max Brod, *Die Frau nach der man sich sehnt*, p. 62.
22) *ŽB*, p. 187.
23) *ŽB*, p. 235.
24) *ŽB*, p. 295.
25) *ŽB*, p. 190.
26) *ŽB*, p. 48.
27) *ŽB*, p. 13.
28) *ŽB*, p. 205.
29) *ŽB*, p. 35.
30) *ŽB*, p. 298.
31) *GB*, pp. 39.
32) *ŽB*, p. 309.
33) *GB*, pp. 40.
34) *GB*, pp. 217.
35) *GB*, pp. 303.
36) *GB*, pp. 132.
37) *Gedenkbuch*, pp. 249-258.
38) *NR*, p. 126.

MUSIC IN TEREZÍN 1941-1945

Let us just remember Terezín, whose German name places it in a terrible litany: Auschwitz, Mauthausen, Dachau, Buchenwald, Bergen-Belsen, *Theresienstadt* ... Located an hour's drive north of Prague, it was one of the nightmarish hostelries scattered along the Nazi hellway to their "final solution" of the Jewish problem. Originally it was intended as a transit camp for Jews from Bohemia and Moravia; from there they would be moved as rapidly as possible to the death camps in the East. Later large numbers of Jews from Germany and Austria also passed through Terezín, and near the end of the war it became a dumping place for Jews displaced from camps located elsewhere in the shrinking Reich. At the peak of overcrowding around the end of 1942, the number of prisoners in Terezín approached 60,000; by the spring of 1945, this figure had fallen to around 17,400, of which a substantial number were *Mischlinge* and Christians (36.6%). At different times, different age, sex, and nationality groups bore the brunt of the transports, but the goal was always the systematic, total destruction of everyone when their turn came. As they awaited their fate, the internees were forced to live in a typical ghetto of Nazi design; rigorously isolated from the local population, they were systematically deprived of basic necessities so that the sick, the weak, and the elderly would die quickly, reducing the pressure on the transports. At the end of 1942, Terezín had become a merciless "old folk's home;" the average age of the prisoners had risen to 51.3 years, and the number of non-working inmates was almost 39,000. Ultimately, of the almost 140,000 people who passed through Terezín's gates, 33,419 died there, only 16 of which were actually executed for trivial offenses. The victims included 15,000 children under the age of 15. Such were the foundations laid by the Nazis for what they envisaged in the future, a "model" German settlement in Terezín.

But something else was built on these foundations in Terezín, not only a monument to cruelty and suffering and courage, but to the power of art to comfort, sustain, and strengthen human beings in the last extremities of adversity. A moving record of this confluence of horror and beauty is to be found in a recent book by Joza Karas (Beaufort Books, 1985), the title of which I have borrowed for this overview of his work. The origins of the richly diversified and well-organized cultural activities described by Mr. Karas are not fully known, but once established they were constantly and vitally present during almost the entirety of the ghetto's brief, gloomy existence. Singing was the first, spontaneous form of musical expression, and recitals of classical songs and arias were given without accompaniment or with the accompaniment of an accordion until a wreck of a piano was found and fixed. Operas and oratorios were then performed with piano or reed organ accompaniment; in time, more instruments, perhaps even a harpsichord, were acquired, and small orchestras and bands were formed. Incarcerated concert artists depended initially on their memorized repertoire until a supply of sheet music and some scores were smuggled in. New arrangements for the available vocal and instrumental combinations were made from the very beginning, and original compositions were written on any scrap of paper and performed.

Mr. Karas has reconstructed the extensive musical repertoire performed in Terezín, adding many details previously unknown to specialists on the Holocaust. Czechoslovak internees staged operas such as Smetana's *The Bartered Bride* and *The Kiss*, Krása's *Brundibár*, and Blodek's *In the Well*. Rafael Schachter conducted Mozart's *The Marriage of Figaro* and *The Magic Flute, Bastien and Bastienne* for the children, and Pergolesi's *La Serva Padrona*. The Viennese Franz Eugene Klein conducted the concert versions of *Rigoletto* and *Tosca*, and a fully staged Carmen. Concert versions of *Cavalleria Rusticana* and *Aida*, as well as Haydn's *The Creation* and Mendelssohn's *Elijah*, were conducted by Karl Fischer.

Seasoned, professional opera and stage singers from Austria, Czechoslovakia, Holland and elsewhere performed together, and at times sang in their mother tongues, making some large vocal works multilingual performances. Among these singers, were the Viennese coloratura Ada Hecht, the alto Hedda Grab-Kernmayer, the mezzo-soprano Hilda Aronson, the Dutch lyric tenor Machial Gobets, Walter Windholz, a bass-baritone from Brno, Karel Berman, a bass from Prague, and many others. Leading instrumentalists from several major European orchestras also found themselves in Terezín, and they formed many chamber ensembles. One of the early arrivals was Egon Ledeč, associate concertmaster of the Czech Philharmonic. He participated in the Doctors' Quartet, Ledeč Quartet, and the Terezín Quartet, as well as performing as a soloist; he also composed. Armin Tiroler from Vienna was an excellent and much sought-after woodwind player, who performed as soloist in, for example, Haydn's oboe concerto. They were among the numerous artists who perished at Auschwitz in 1944, as the collapsing Third Reich raced against time to meet its genocidal obligations.

Chamber music concerts and solo recitals featured works by Beethoven, Bach, Mozart, Chopin, Schubert, Brahms, Dvořák, and other composers, primarily Classical and Romantic. Beethoven seems to have been the most popular composer. Interestingly, the music of Mahler received only a few performances, while Offenbach's opera *The Tales of Hoffmann* was performed upon a direct order from the SS commander. On the other hand, Wagner was completely ignored; indeed, because he was considered "*the* true German composer," his music could not be played by the Jewish musicians. It is worth remembering that in Nazi Germany all Jewish artists were barred from public performances and dismissed from their teaching and other positions as early as the spring of 1933, a policy later extended to all occupied areas. This policy included a prohibition upon works by composers of Jewish descent and by "enemy" composers (i.e., from the Allied countries). The *Entjudung* (de-Judaization) of music made even *Carmen* suspect because of its Gypsy elements; Handel was somehow "cleansed" of his Old Testament features; many beloved German Romantic songs on texts by the "Jew Heine" fell into question, and so on. It was from this world that Jewish musicians brought their music to Terezín.

Compositions that might promote patriotism or resistance in occupied countries were of course prohibited, along with those associated with avant-garde or experimental ("degenerate") currents in music. Former students of Arnold Schoenberg and Alois Hába (of the quarter-tone system) were certainly prisoners at Terezín, together with numerous representatives of other avant-garde and "enemy" tendencies. But Nazi purity was not systematically and vigorously enforced there and "degenerate, *kultur-bolschevist*, Zionist, pluto-cratic," and other forms of "non-music," including "Americanizing" jazz, flourished under the noses (or ears) of the SS. When Schachter presented Smetana's *Czech Song*, it carried a message. When the actor-composer-comedian Karel Švenk ended the first Terezín cabaret with his "Terezín March," the last line of which declares, "And on the ruins of the ghetto we shall laugh," he echoed the antifascism and optimism found in the prewar Pra-gue, Liberated Theater of Voskovec and Werich. When Kaff played Mussorg-sky'ss *Pictures from an Exhibition* in 1944, it was a conscious act of defiance, which was well understood by his listeners. When Robert Brock from Prague was ordered by the SS in March 1945 to produce a children's opera (to im-press representatives of the Red Cross), he composed in three days a medley of Czech folksongs as incidental music for *Broučci* (*Fireflies*). But he en-hanced his production by concealing the melody of the Czech national anthem in the middle voices. The work was a smash and was performed some fifteen times before the liberation. Nevertheless, for safety's sake, applause was pro-hibited at all performances.

Music in Terezín did much more than provide a means to express resis-tance and defiance; among its spiritual comforts was the sense of personal and cultural continuity with the past that it awakened. Traditional music in Hebrew or Yiddish and Zionist songs were popular, and choirs were available for reli-gious services and special occasions (for example, a celebration of Herzl's anniversary in 1944). Zeev Shek made extensive use of such music in his work with the children in Terezín (he died in Rome in 1978, during his tenure as the Israeli Ambassador). However, the majority of the Terezín internees were in-clined to secularism and had assimilated the culture of their native countries. Consequently, to achieve a brief illusion of pre-Hitler "normality," the musi-cians continued to prefer standard works, created in the styles they were schooled in and accustomed to hearing and performing. Only a few perform-ances provoked controversies among the prisoners. The operetta *Die Fleder-maus* was deemed inappropriate by some, and the light, entertaining music played by ensembles like the Ghetto Swingers or a "town band" met with mixed reactions. And Verdi's *Requiem*, produced by Rafael Schachter and movingly performed some fifteen times, did not escape criticism as "a bad choice" for Terezín (especially when it was included in a gala performance for the Red Cross in 1944). In such disagreements one can still hear the tragic echoes of human voices reacting, each in its own way, to an arbitrary, terrible, senseless fate.

Mr. Karas describes in his introduction ("How This Book Came into Existence") the very long international path he traversed in collecting his materials, beginning in 1970. Along the way he collected a considerable number of original compositions by prisoners in Terezín, some of which he had to transcribe painstakingly from faded, often damaged manuscripts. In 1965 the Council of Jewish Religious Communities in the Czech Lands published a memorial volume entitled *Terezín* and enclosed a small recording of four songs and a fragment of a sonata for piano; by comparison Mr. Karas' list of compositions written in Terezín (p. 201) identifies fifty preserved works. Some are individual songs, but most are groups of up to four songs utilizing Czech, German, Hebrew, or Yiddish texts. Some are for a single voice, others are chamber vocal settings or choruses. For piano solo there are three sonatas by Viktor Ullmann, the *Suite Terezín* by Karel Berman, and a sonata by Gideon Klein. String quartets and several compositions for other quartets, trios, and duets indicate the popularity of chamber music, which was relatively easy to perform in Terezín conditions. No compositions for full orchestra have been found, although a symphony by Ullmann has been reported by former prisoners, and Taube's lost *Terezín Symphony* premiered there. The two largest works are the children's opera *Brundibár* by Hans Krása and the opera *Der Kaiser von Atlantis* by Viktor Ullmann, for which vocal and scores written for small orchestral ensembles exist. In a tribute to this music from Terezín and to stimulate interest in it, Mr. Karas has performed the chamber works in various places, with the string quartet he formed and which bears his name. [1]

The most productive of the Terezín composers was Viktor Ullmann, whose opera *Der Kaiser von Atlantis*, rehearsed in Terezín but then apparently lost after Ullmann and most of his cast were abruptly shipped to Auschwitz in October 1944, was found in 1973 and finally premiered in Amsterdam in 1975 under the baton of Kerry Woodward. It has also been performed in Brussels and Spoleto, and a television version in West Germany received the Prix Italia. In 1977, the San Francisco Opera gave the work its American premiere, with a favorable critical response. The opera's libretto (by the prisoner poet Petr Kien) is first of all a transparent allegory on the hollowness and fatuity of human pride in the face of universal death: When the corrupt and arrogant King of Atlantis orders Death to lead his army into a war, the goal of which is his own glory, Death demurs and goes on strike. No one can die, chaos ensues, and the King comes to his senses. But Death drives his usual hard bargain: he will resume his labors only if the King is his first victim. If this sounds deeply pessimistic and resigned in Terezín conditions, this is not truly the case. Defiance is obvious in the refractions of Hitler and his collapsing Reich in the King and his sinking Atlantis. And if: Ullmann mocks the Nazis by incorporating in a minor key their anthem *Deutschland, Deutschland über Alles*, he moves to a much broader vision in suggesting they embody only the nether regions of the human heart: he concludes his opera with an adaptation of a glorious hymn by another, great German spirit, Martin Luther - *A Mighty Fortress is Our God*. Even here there is a kind of mystical defiance: Terezín is an old fortress town.

The complete title of Krása's children's opera is *Flašinetář Brundibár* [Brundibar the Organ Grinder]; it is a special work for Mr. Karas, who brought about its American premiere, performed in Czech, in 1975 and introduced it in an English translation prepared with the assistance of his late wife (to whom his book on Terezín is dedicated) in Ottawa in 1977. [2] This opera was composed around a libretto by Adolf Hoffmeister shortly before the occupation of Czechoslovakia, and was premiered in a Prague Jewish orphanage about the time the deportations to Terezín began. The conductor of that performance, Rudolf Freudenfeld-Franek, later conducted all the performances in Terezín. There Krása had to rewrite the orchestration, because he had brought only the piano score from Prague. *Brundibár* then became the most performed and best remembered work in the history of the ghetto, having some fifty-five performances. The child actors and singers were replaced as they were sent East, but in the opera itself they are victorious over the evil old Brundibar, who can easily be seen as a stand-in for Hitler. The buoyant, melodic, memorable music, the charming performances of the children, and the inevitable victory of goodness over evil in this opera acted powerfully upon the imprisoned Terezín audiences, who enjoyed briefly here an enchanted interlude of humanity in an apparently dehumanized world.

Mr. Karas' book is rich in detail, both as a record of cultural activities and a chronicle of talented, now largely forgotten, human lives, and of the life they led in Terezín. Musical activities are systematically presented by genre-choral works, opera, chamber music, recitals, orchestras, the "Light Muse," education through music-with each chapter providing detailed information about the works performed. The immediacy of this experience is heightened not only by copious biographical information on many of the participants but by realia preserved by survivors and loaned to Mr. Karas to illustrate his book-sketches, posters, pages of musical manuscripts, photographs, recital and concert programs. Particularly striking are personal reminiscences from both the living and the dead, which are used extensively and with great effect. They persistently recall the terrible dissonance, almost eerie in its ironies, created by these manifestations of civilized beauty in the midst of barbarism. The continuing and vigorous existence of such beauty can be attributed in large measure to the efforts of the so-called Leisure Department (*Freizeitgestaltung*), a committee of the Council of Jewish Elders, who administered daily life in the ghetto but were answerable to the SS in all things. Within narrow limits, these leaders could act as a buffer between the prisoners and the German authorities, often doing so at considerable personal risk. In the end almost all of them perished by special action. Yet to belong to this officially sanctioned Department meant temporary protection from the transports and the possibility, for musicians, of practicing and using their talents rather than performing hard manual labor or slowly dying of hunger, illness or despair. Interestingly, Karl Ancerl, probably the most famous survivor of Terezín, continued his conducting career there but never agreed to becoming a member of the Leisure Department; he worked in the kitchens instead. He assembled a string orchestra and conducted standard works, such as Mozart's *Eine kleine Nachtmusik*, Bach's violin and piano concertos, Suk's *Meditation on an Ancient Czech Chorale*, Dvořák's *Serenade*, and compositions written in Terezín, among them Haas' *Study for Strings*.

It will come as no surprise to hear that the Nazis used Terezín as "material" for their renderings of the universal art form of totalitarian propaganda–what normal human beings call lying. The first instance was born of necessity. When a transport of 450 Danish Jews arrived in Terezín in October 1943, their government insisted on an inspection of the camp by the Danish and International Red Cross. A thorough "beautification" was immediately ordered by the SS overlords. The initially perplexed inmates were not fooled for long, and the Red Cross inspectors who visited in June 1944 remained suspicious, but the myth of the "Terezín Spa," or the "model ghetto Terezín," was established. Another "beautification" occurred in August-September 1944 in order to shoot the film *The Führer Gave a Town to the Jews*. It was intended as anti-Semitic propaganda, a crude contrast between Terezín, untouched by bombs, and war conditions found elsewhere in the Reich. The film was never shown but was found after the war. Musical and other cultural activities were showcased during Red Cross visits, as they are in this film. Understandably many prisoners balked at participating in the construction of Potemkin villages, but the desire to survive generally proved stronger than such scruples when the SS threatened to produce their most convincing arguments.

Joza Karas' book is organized rather like a tragic pilgrimage, beginning with the "Road to Terezín" and the establishment of the ghetto, moving in its middle chapters through a detailed description of the life, music, and people in the prison town, and concluding with the journey east, to Auschwitz. One is persistently aware of the approach of arbitrary annihilation. Yet the effect of the book is not overwhelmingly depressing, and not only because it concludes with a summary description of the postwar careers of notable survivors. The brutal realities are there, but Mr. Karas does not dwell upon them, wisely depending upon the reader's prior knowledge of the Holocaust. The tension between affirmation and anguish is maintained to the end, and one never loses sight of the book's primary goal: to pay tribute to the spirit and art of people who would not abandon what is best in Western European culture even as that culture was apparently dying beneath Nazi jackboots.

Hudba Terezínského ghetta [Music of the Terezín Ghetto] by Ludmila Vrkočová is an interesting supplement to Joza Karas' book. It was published recently (no date is indicated) by the Jazz Section of the Czechoslovak Musicians' Union (the seven-man Executive Committee of the Jazz Section has been imprisoned since September 1986 and will soon be tried as a consequence of such publication activity-activity, by the way, not legally proscribed in Czechoslovakia). *Music of the Terezín Ghetto* is much shorter than Karas' book; it condenses the history of the musical life in Terezín to a mere thirty pages. Karas met Vrkočová in Prague in August 1970 while he was doing research there, and she gave him a copy of the chapter on Terezín from her doctoral dissertation, *Hudební místopis Čech* [A Musical Topography of Bohemia]. Like Karas' book, it is richly documented with pictorial material preserved from Terezín, much of it from the collection originally amassed by the late Karel Herman.

There is basic agreement between the lists of Terezín composers found in the two books. However, Heinz Alt, Rudolf Brock, Karel Reiner, Karel Svenk, and Bedřich Weiss do not appear in Karas' compilation of composers of "Existing Compositions Written in Terezín" - although he mentions them elsewhere - since Vrkočová also includes works known to have been performed at Terezín and specifies as available those kept in the collections of the State Jewish Museum in Prague. Vrkočová increases our knowledge of the names of Terezín artists, because she pays more attention than Karas to popular musicians, actors, and theater directors. Also important is her short list of postwar musical works inspired by some aspect of the life in the Terezín ghetto (she lists here the composers Reiner, Mácha, Srnka, and Křivinka). At least two works created outside Czechoslovakia should be added to this list. On 22 May 1965 the Cincinnati Symphony Orchestra, conducted by Stanislaw Skrowaczewski, performed the world premiere of *The Song of Terezín* by Franz Waxman (English and German texts from the book ... *I Never Saw Another Butterfly*); the work was commissioned by the Cincinnati Festival Association for its forty-fifth May Music Festival. Written for mezzo-soprano, mixed and children's choruses and orchestra, *The Song of Terezín* uses eight of the Terezín children's poems, ending with "Fear" by Eva Picková and the words "We Want to Live." The other composition is Edoardo Brizio's symphony *Al bambini di Terezín* [To the Children of Terezín], first performed in Rome and then in Prague under the aegis of the Council of Jewish Religious Communities in Bohemia and Moravia and the Prague Jewish community for the 1981 (fortieth) anniversary of the establishment of the Terezín ghetto. The symphony is written for soprano and reader with orchestra.

Notes

1) A Panton record issued in Czechoslovakia in 1985 commenorating the anniversary of the end of the war features Gideon Klein's complete *Sonata for piano* and his *Trio for Violin, Viola, and Cello*, Viktor Ullmann's *Piano Sonata No. 6*, Hans Krása's *Dance* (for violin, viola, and cello), and Pavel Haas' *Four Songs on Chinese Verse* (Nos. 2 and 4 only).

2) The opera was performed in Los Angeles in 1982 and has also been presented several times in Israel since the 1960's. A German-Czech film version of the opera exists; it includes interviews with artists connected with it (Adolf Hoffmeister, Jaromír Bor, Rudolf Franěk), seen against the filmed background of Terezín.

JEWISH MUSICIANS
WITH ROOTS IN CZECHOSLOVAKIA
Part I

INTRODUCTION

Volume I of the trilogy *The Jews of Czechoslovakia* [1] includes an article entitled "Music" by the late Paul Nettl, a well-known musicologist from Prague, who came to the United States shortly after the outbreak of World War II. Nettl started his essay with a brief historical introduction, listing some of the earlier Jewish musicians in Bohemia. He then wrote in greater detail about the recognized Jewish composers, singers, conductors, instrumentalists, musicologists, broadcasters and music teachers who were active in Czechoslovakia prior to World War II. He was personally acquainted with many of them, in Europe or, later, abroad. Nettl also allotted some space to the musicians who had perished in the Nazi death camps or had survived the Holocaust in Nazi-dominated Europe. Since the publication of Nettl's essay more than two decades ago, additional information has accumulated. Some of the musicians he mentions have died, and new personalities have come to attention. For these reasons an update would seem in order to trace the subsequent careers of the musicians discussed in Nettl's essay. This update will also survey data on musicians whom Nettl did not include or whom he only mentioned in passing.

I believe it is only fitting that we begin our new survey with Paul Nettl himself, and his son, the distinguished American ethnomusicologist Bruno Nettl. Paul Nettl was presented in *The Jews of Czechoslovakia* only with the customary biographical mini-sketch as a contributing author. The principal data about his professional career were gathered from standard dictionaries of music. However, a few more personal details are given in a private biographical memoir prepared by Bruno Nettl, who kindly permitted me to read his work.

Paul Nettl was born in Vrchlabí, Bohemia, on January 10, 1889. He earned two doctorates, one in law (1913) and one in musicology (1915). In the latter discipline, he was a student of Heinrich Rietsch [2] at the German University in Prague. After completing his studies, he taught as a *Privatdozent* (unsalaried lecturer) at the university. His hopes of becoming a full professor evaporated when the musicologist Gustav Becking [3] was brought to Prague from Germany in 1931. Nettl continued as an unpaid lecturer; in addition, he lectured for a number of cultural institutions such as Urania, wrote music reviews for the *Prager Tagblatt*, and worked in the paper business owned by his family. From 1933 to 1938 he was the music director of the independent German-language radio station Mělník, and of Praha II.

As a Freemason, democrat and anti-Nazi - and, of course, a Jew - Nettl began to contemplate emigration as early as 1937. He made contacts with various individuals and institutions abroad and sent parts of his library to Palestine (now Israel) and to the United States, not yet knowing where he would be admitted. During the months following the end of Czechoslovak independence on March 15, 1939, Nettl was interrogated by the Gestapo and at one point went into hiding. On September 21, 1939, he was finally able to join his family at the railroad station on their way to freedom via Holland, where, after some delays, they boarded a boat for the United States. He had received a firm employment offer from the Westminster Choir College at Princeton, New Jersey, which made it possible for him and his immediate family to settle in the United States. Other relatives went to Australia and Israel.

Paul Nettl first taught at the Westminster Choir College. He subsequently was a professor of musicology at Indiana University in Bloomington, Indiana, from 1946 to 1959, and continued teaching part-time after his retirement, until 1963. From 1948, he was also a visiting professor at the University of Vienna, Austria. He died in Bloomington on January 8, 1972.

Nettl's principal works in English, which are numerous, were written and published after 1948. [4] However, his European writings, in German, are even more important. The following interesting comment comes from Karl Michael Komma writing about musicology in Bohemia: [5]

> [Guido Adler's] follower in Prague, Heinrich Rietsch of Cheb, trained two indigenous musicologists, Robert Haas and Paul Nettl ... Thanks are due, above all, to the indefatigable efforts by which Nettl, since 1920, has kept acquainting German musicological research with some of the inexhaustible treasures of the Bohemian archives, written up in his individual studies.

Komma then proceeds to list a good bibliography of Nettl's German books and essays from the year 1920 on. A more recent, quite complete bibliography was published by Thomas Atcherson in a privately printed volume, *Ein Musikwissenschaftler in zwei Welten: die musikwissenschaftlichen und literarischen Arbeiten von Paul Nettl* (A Musicologist in Two Worlds: The Musicological and Literary Works of Paul Nettl; Vienna, Schoenborn-Verlag, 1962).

Of special interest for the present study is Nettl's early book, *Alte jüdische Spielleute und Musiker* (Jewish Minstrels and Musicians of Olden Times; Prague, 1923), and the chapter "Die Prager Juden Spielleutenzunft" (The Minstrels' Guild of the Jews in Prague) in his *Musik-Barock in Böhmen und Mähren*. In that chapter, Nettl quotes several seventeenth-century documents about some unusual aspects of synagogue music in Prague: [6]

> Both Jewish and anti-Semitic sources report on the important place accorded to instrumental music in the synagogues of Prague *from time immemorial* [italics added]. In the Maisel synagogue, the Sabbath was ushered in with instrumental music ... [and] the Old-New Synagogue [Altneuschul] in Prague has an organ, which is something quite unusual for Jews; it is played on Friday evening, shortly before the beginning of the Sabbath.

Nettl then documents the protests of the Christian musicians in Prague during the second half of the seventeenth century against "unfair" competition from Jewish musicians. All the correspondence from both parties, addressed to the highest authorities, is reprinted. These were pioneering, original studies, as was Nettl's exploratory research in the music holdings of the monastery in Osek, the library in Roudnice, and many other localities in Bohemia and Moravia.

As one reviews Paul Nettl's career, one can understand the statement of his only child that much had been expected from him, Bruno, as "the son of a great scholar and a fine musician." The musician was Bruno's mother, Gertrud Nettl-Hutter, who had studied piano with Conrad Ansorge. [7] She had never developed a professional concert career of her own but taught music, accompanied other performers or played the piano in chamber music ensembles, specializing in contemporary composers, Czech and others. In addition to the piano, she played the harpsichord and was interested in modern dance (eurhythmics).

Bruno Nettl, who was born in Prague on March 14, 1930, attended a German-language school but, thanks to the influence of several well-remembered nannies and tutors, "was bilingual and had become a Czech patriot." When he was nine years old, Bruno left Europe, feeling, as he put it, "like a boy from nowhere" in America, where almost nobody around him even knew the location of Prague, that wonderful city of his birth. In spite of having been prepared for the New World merely with some "five English lessons," which resulted in "a British pronunciation with a German accent," he did very well. He earned a Ph.D from Indiana University in 1953 and an M.A. in librarianship from the University of Michigan in 1960.

Bruno Nettl has taught at Wayne University and the faculty of the University of Illinois at Urbana-Champaign. He has held visiting lectureships in musicology at Kiel, Germany (1956-58) and at many other institutions. He served as chairman of the musicology department for several years, as president of the Society for Ethnomusicology from 1969 to 1971, and has been the recipient of numerous awards, fellowships, honors and distinctions. In addition to other editorial and consulting activities, he edited the periodical *Ethnomusicology* from 1961 to 1965 and has edited its Special Series since 1985.

Bruno Nettl's research has centered on the music of the North American Indians, and Middle Eastern, European and American folk music. He is a pioneering modern ethnomusicologist and his books have become classics in the field. He has been publishing steadily since the mid-1950s. [8]

Bruno Nettl wrote his private memoir, *Prague*: 1930-1939, in 1976 for his daughters Rebecca (Becky) Nettl-Fiol (a faculty member in the Department of Dance at the University of Illinois) and Gloria.

In this memoir, Bruno Nettl introduces his wife Wanda and such family friends as Viktor Ullmann, Leo and Alice Sommer, the baritone Rudolf Bandler and Walter Kaufmann. We learn that the first opera Bruno heard as a child was *Hänsel und Gretel*, but that he loves best *Prodaná nevěsta* (The Bartered Bride), the Czech national anthem *Kde domov můj* (Where Is My Home) and the city of Prague, even though he had a successful life in the United States.

THE HOLOCAUST

Terezín and the Death Camps

Paul Nettl and his immediate family were among the Czechoslovak Jews who escaped the *furor teutonicus* in time. However, both his parents, who were in their seventies, perished in Terezín. His wife's mother survived the Holocaust and, after the war, came to live with the Nettls in Bloomington, where she died in 1948. In his article, Paul Nettl devotes two long footnotes to musicians in the Terezín ghetto. He quotes a review of Krása's children's opera *Brundibár* which was written by an inmate of Terezín, Dr. Kurt Singer.

Nettl also quotes the reminiscences and testimony of the pianist Edith Steiner Kraus. Born in Vienna in 1913, Kraus lived in Karlovy Vary (Karlsbad) before she was deported to Terezín. She survived the war, settled in Israel and quite recently (late in 1988) played music from Terezín at the first convention of Hitachdut Yozei Czechoslovakia (Association of Former Czechoslovak Jews) in Tel Aviv, celebrating "Forty Years of the State of Israel and the Contribution of Czech Jewry."

Some of the Jewish musicians from Czechoslovakia, or rather the Nazi Protectorate of Bohemia and Moravia, who did not go through the Terezín ghetto, are described as "victims of racial persecution" in *Československý hudební slovník osob a institucí*, (*The Czechoslovak Music Dictionary of Persons and Institutions)* two volumes; Prague, Státní hudební nakladatelství, 1963 and 1965, hereafter referred to as *ČSHS*. [9]

Let us begin with some of those who did not survive the Holocaust. One musician whose death date seems to be unknown, with no details beyond the statement that he perished in a concentration camp for "racial reasons," was Moritz Kaufmann. Born in Karlovy Vary on February 16, 1871, he studied violin at the Prague Conservatory from 1885 to 1891, but did not graduate. From 1896 until the time of the Munich agreement he directed a music school he had established in his native town. He wrote topical articles such as "A. Dvořák in Karlsbad" (1912) and about Brahms, Liszt, Bülow, Beethoven and other composers who had frequented the famous spa. Kaufmann's essays were published in such leading music journals as *Der Merker, Neue Zeitschrift für Musik* and *Der Auftakt*. Kaufmann's bibliography is included in Michael Komma's book, which was quoted earlier.

Moritz Kaufmann's books are histories of the Karlovy Vary region (1927), of the local theater (1932) and of old customs connected with music (1933). According to Nettl, he was Walter Kaufmann's uncle.

The artistic career and personal life of Ervín (or Erwin) Schulhof took a different turn. He was born in Prague on June 8, 1894, and died at the Bavarian concentration camp of Wülzburg on August 18, 1942. His ancestors included the pianist and composer Julius Schulhoff (1825-99), a native of Prague, and, on his mother's side, the violinist Heinrich Wolff (1813-98). Ervín Schulhof studied composition and piano at the Prague Conservatory and subsequently in Vienna, Leipzig and Cologne. During the latter part of World War I, he joined (in Italy) the Czechoslovak Legion that fought on the side of the Allies, to obtain independence for his homeland. He received the Mendelssohn Prize for piano in 1913 and for composition in 1918. Schulhof belonged to the avant-garde group that gathered around Alois Hába, the leader of the quarter-tone school of composition. He experimented with jazz, impressionism and expressionism, and his works were performed at several festivals of the International Society for Contemporary Music (ISCM). He adopted the Communist ideology and, in 1932, was the first composer to set the *Communist Manifesto* to music in the form of a cantata. His cantata was first performed in 1962 by the Czech Philharmonic Orchestra under the baton of Karel Ančerl.

Schulhof visited the Soviet Union in 1933, and in 1939 was granted honorary Soviet citizenship. This special status afforded him temporary protection from the Nazi overlords' persecution, until the German invasion of Russia in 1941. After the outbreak of war between Germany and the Soviet Union, Schulhof was deported for racial and political reasons to the Wülzburg concentration camp, where he died a year later. Many of his compositions for piano, chamber ensembles and orchestra, numerous songs and incidental and ballet music have been published, mostly in Czechoslovakia.

In contrast to the case of Moritz Kaufmann, the transport in which the music critic, librarian and editor Erich Steinhard went to his death is known: it was the third transport (C 533) which left Prague for Lodź on October 26, 1941, and from which only 52 out of a total of 1,000 deportees survived.

Steinhard was born in Prague on May 23, 1886, and died in Lodź probably some time in 1942. He studied piano and music theory with Karel Knittl and Vítězslav Novák. Later he studied law, the history of art and musicology in Prague, working at the University Library and teaching the history of music at the Prague German Academy of Music. With Vladimír Helfert, he co-authored the book *Hudba v Československé republice* (Music in the Czechoslovak Republic; 1938). He wrote many articles on trends of new music, and was editor of the music journal *Der Auftakt* from 1921 to 1938. He was one of the founders of the International Society for Contemporary Music (ISCM), which had a section in Prague.

Another musician who perished in the Holocaust but did not pass through Terezín was Jan Schwarz, Doctor of Law, pianist and composer of songs and choral works. Born in České Budějovice on May 18, 1904, he went into hiding in Southern Bohemia following the Nazi occupation. He was discovered and sent to Mauthausen, where he died on August 25, 1942.

According to *ČSHS*, Sigmund Auspitzer, a teacher of voice, was deported and died under "unknown circumstances." Jana Renée Friesová, in her article "Jews and Music in Bohemia" (*Review of the Society for the History of Czechoslovak Jews*, Vol. 1, 1987, pp. 29-41), states that Auspitzer (she calls

him Auspitz) arrived in Terezín with the first transport from Brno and immediately started to train the promising voice of the young inmate Alexander
(Shonny) Singer. Friesová says nothing about Auspitzer's subsequent fate.
    Professor Auspitzer was born in Brno on November 17, 1861. He stud-
ied at the Vienna Conservatory of Music and sang as a tenor in operettas during the 1880's. After 1888 he taught voice in Brno, first privately and then,
during the 1910's and 1920's, at the Musikverein. The soprano Marie Jeritza
and the tenor Leo Slezak were among his world-famous students. [10] His voice
method, *Winke für die Gesangskunst* (Hints for the Art of Singing) was published in Brno in 1901. He was eighty years old when he was deported.

    Extensive documentary literature exists regarding Czech musicians
who were interned in Terezín. Specific sources include Joža Karas' *Music in
Terezín* 1941-1945 and Ludmila Vrkočová's *Hudba terezínského ghetta* (Music of the Terezín Ghetto). [11]
    Karas and Vrkočová, along with other authors of books on Terezín,
provide much information about the group of leading musicians who were
deported together from Terezín to Auschwitz. The same death date, October
17, 1944, is usually given for them all. [12] They were the violinist Egon Ledeč
(b. Kostelec nad Orlicí, 1889), the pianist Bernard Kaff (b. Brno, 1905), and
the composers Hans Krása (b. Prague, 1899), Pavel Haas (b. Brno, 1899) and
Viktor Ullmann (b. Těšín, 1898). The conductor Rafael Schächter, who was
also in that group, was born (1905) in Rumania, but from childhood lived and
studied in Brno and Prague, where he was active before his deportation to
Terezín. Another outstanding pianist and composer, Gideon Klein (b. Přerov,
1919), also went to Auschwitz with one of the last "November transports"
from Terezín and died shortly thereafter at Fürstengrube, near Katowice, about
January 27, 1945.
    Thanks to diligent research, especially by Karas, additional works
composed and in some cases premiered in Terezín have been discovered and
recorded. [13] Joža Karas, who has copies of most of these works, has performed some of them with a string quartet on various occasions. He has also
arranged and conducted the premiéres of Krása's children's opera *Brundibár*
in the United States and Canada.
    Interesting new information has come to light about Viktor Ullmann's
opera *The Emperor of Atlantis*. Ullmann composed it in 1943 on a libretto by
Peter Kien (1919-44), but no performance of it was allowed in Terezín because its anti-war, anti-Nazi allegories were too obvious. Not until 1975 was
there a posthumous world premiere of the opera in Amsterdam; thereafter, it
was staged elsewhere in Europe, England and the United States. By a coincidence, it was performed in London twice in the spring of 1988, first at the
Bloomsbury Festival by the touring Vienna Chamber Opera Company, and
then by the Mecklenburgh Opera. The latter performance was an original production by a new London company that had derived its name from Mecklenburgh Square. This new company's performance took place within the frame-

work of the London International Opera Festival Season of Twentieth-Century Opera, May 2 - June 11, 1988. [14]

Anne Manson, the Mecklenburgh Opera's music director and conductor; John Abulafia, the director of production, and Diana Hirst, the administrator, researched all available information about Ullmann and his music. They discovered that all the material on Ullmann, originally in the collection of the late Dr. Hans Günther (H.G.) Adler, is now in the Archives of the Anthroposophical Society at Dornach, Switzerland. They were also able to trace Ullmann's *Second String Quartet*, which had been missing until then, to the Schoenberg Institute in Los Angeles; it was performed at a later date at the ISCM Festival held in London.

To acquaint the public with the composer and his style, a prologue was compiled from his list of favorite poems and comments he had made in Terezín. The prologue was titled *The Strange Passenger: A Diary in Verse and Prose*. A few of his surviving early songs and a movement from his *First Piano Sonata*, "Andante quasi marcia funebre: In Memoriam Gustav Mahler," were interspersed with recitations of several selected poems. An intermission followed, after which the one-act opera in four scenes was performed in a new English translation by Sonja Lyndon. Most of London's major newspapers published favorable reviews of this production of *The Emperor* and found the Terezín opera intriguing and vital.

Thus there have been professional performances of at least some of the musical works created in Terezín, and the world has become aware of the important role of music in the ghetto.

Among the pianists interned in Terezín was Juliette Arányi, who was born in Brezno, Slovakia, on December 19, 1912, and reportedly died in 1944.[15] She studied in Bratislava and Vienna and performed under the professional name of Baba Arányi, starting her career at the age of six. She later lived in Prague, from where she was deported to Terezín. It would be interesting to find out if there was any connection between her and the d'Arányi sisters, famous violinists who lived in England. The d'Arányi sisters had a Jewish grandmother, Johanna, sister of the violinist Joseph Joachim. Joachim was born near Bratislava in 1831 and died in Berlin in 1907. Though Adila, Hortense and Jelly d'Arányi were born in Budapest, they spent their summer vacations, perhaps with some members of their extended family, in Slovakia.

Another Terezín musician mentioned only by name in Nettl's essay, Konrad Wallerstein, is introduced in Karas' book (p. 6) as a leading music teacher in Prague. [16] A private performance of Ullmann's songs and piano works took place at Wallerstein's Prague apartment on Sunday, March 3, 1940, at five o'clock in the afternoon. By this time, all public performances by Jewish artists had already been banned, and an early curfew was in effect, but instruments still had not been confiscated, and homes had not yet been requisitioned by the occupation authorities. The singers were Konrad Wallerstein's daughter Margot, Robert Stein and Marion Podolier, with Ullmann at the piano. Ullmann's piano compositions were performed by Alice Herz-Sommer and Arnošt Latzko. Most of these artists and their audiences were to meet again in Terezín.

Konrad Wallerstein (b. Prague, October 30, 1879; d. Auschwitz, some time after October 28, 1944) and his father, Moritz Wallerstein (b. Prague, April 19, 1847; d. there, November 7, 1906) were outstanding voice teachers in Prague and trained many Czech opera singers during their fruitful careers. The elder Wallerstein served as cantor and choir director at the Maisel synagogue. His son (and pupil) graduated from the organ department of the Prague Conservatory of Music, was active in Nuremberg from 1901 to 1903, and then succeeded his father at the Maisel synagogue. Konrad also worked as an assistant at his father's singing school, becoming its director in 1906, in addition to teaching voice at Prague's German Music Academy. Konrad's daughter Margot, who also perished in the Holocaust, was a promising coloratura soprano. Another renowned member of the family was Lothar Wallerstein (b. Prague, November 6, 1882), Konrad's brother. He was a pianist, conductor, opera accompanist and stage director. Lothar Wallerstein immigrated to the United States in 1941 and died in New Orleans on November 13, 1949.

Moritz Wallerstein's most outstanding pupil was the tenor Karel Burian (1870-1924). Wallerstein taught him free of charge and even got him paid singing assignments at the Maisel synagogue. Other students of Moritz Wallerstein's school included the baritone Emil Burian (1876-1926); Karel Burian's brother, the basses Václav Kliment (1863-1910) and Emil Pollert (1877-1935); the Metropolitan Opera baritone Milo de Luca, whose original Czech surname had been Luka, and who died in the United States in 1955; Jan Ouředník (1877-1950); the brothers Antonín and Gustav Svojsík, and the original members of the internationally known České pěvecké kvarteto (Czech Vocal Quartet), founded in 1899, which made a world tour in 1906. Konrad Wallerstein trained a younger generation of singers who later became active at the Prague National Theater. Among them were Božena Petanová (1888-1958), Ada Nordenová (1891-?), Marta Krásová (1901-?), Naďa Kejřová (1902-?), Zdeněk Otava (1902-?) and Otakar Kraus (1909-80).

Moritz and Konrad Wallerstein both published exercises for voice building and methods of singing. The January, 1987, issue of *Věstník židovských náboženských obcí v ČSSR* (Bulletin of the Jewish Communities in the Czechoslovak Socialist Republic) included an article by František Kafka entitled "Remembering the Cantor and Composer Moritz Wallerstein and His Son Konrad." Kafka focused on the high standard of synagogue music that had prevailed during Moritz Wallerstein's tenure at the Maisel synagogue and deplored the fact that Wallerstein's musical material had probably been lost during the Nazi occupation. The State Jewish Museum in Prague has only a few copies of isolated compositions, but a bound copy of some sheet music published by Konrad Wallerstein has been preserved at the Music Department of the Czechoslovak State Library. Another published work of Konrad Wallerstein's is *Kol Nidre und noch andere traditionelle bekannte hebräischen Melodien für Clavier* (Kol Nidrei and Other Known Traditional Hebrew Melodies for Piano). This anthology includes a melody for *Ki hinei ha-homer*, a liturgical hymn for Yom Kippur which portrays God as molding man and his destiny even as a potter shapes a piece of clay. Kafka concluded his article with the hope that, someday, synagogue music might once again reach the standards set by Moritz and Konrad Wallerstein.

SURVIVORS

Czechoslovakia

The following three musicians mentioned in Nettl's study were inmates of Terezín but survived the Holocaust, returned to Czechoslovakia and resumed their musical activities. All three have died since the publication of Nettl's essay.

Robert Brock was born in Rakovník on May 27, 1905. After 1945 he conducted operas in Brno and Prague and taught conducting at the Academy of Music (AMU). In 1948 Brock became deputy director of the Prague National Theater. In 1961 he was awarded the title of "Artist of Merit:" He died in Prague on December 2, 1979. His son Petr, born in 1932, a flutist, teaches and works for Czechoslovak Radio.

The composer and pianist Karel Reiner, son of Cantor Josef Reiner (1872-1942), was born in Žatec on June 25, 1910. In May, 1947, Karel Reiner produced in Prague Alois Hába's quarter-tone opera titled *Mother*. A writer on musical subjects, Reiner was active in such organizations as the Union of Czech Composers. In 1964 he became director of the Czech Music Foundation. He died in Prague on October 17, 1979.

Karel Ančerl, whose son was born in Terezín in February, 1943, was active as a conductor in Prague after the liberation. [17] In 1968 he became conductor of the Toronto Symphony Orchestra. He died in Toronto, Canada, on July 3, 1973, at the age of 65.

A survivor of the Holocaust who devoted his scholarly talents to studies of all aspects of the Terezín ghetto, including music, was Hans Günther (H.G.) Adler, who began his extensive documentation of Nazi genocide immediately after World War II. [18] Born in Prague in 1910 as the son of a bookbinder, Adler was a very versatile individual whose interests included history, sociology, psychology, literature and musicology. He earned his doctorate from the German University of Prague in 1935 with a dissertation, *Klopstock und Musik,* and taught at Urania in Prague.

Following the rise of Nazism, Dr. Adler wanted to emigrate to Brazil but could not carry out his plan. In 1941 he was arrested by the Nazis and spent several months at forced labor. He returned to Prague and was deported to Terezín. From there he went to Auschwitz, Buchenwald, Niederorschel and Langenstein, returning to his native city at the age of 35 as the sole survivor of his family. His wife, Gertrud Klepetar, M.D., had perished in Auschwitz. In postwar Prague He taught children who had survived the Holocaust and worked with organizers of the Jewish Museum in Prague. In 1947 Dr. Adler settled in London, where he married a sculptor, Bettina Gross. He died in London on August 21, 1988.

Joža Karas, author of *Music in Terezín 1941-1945*, recalls visiting Dr. Adler in London after the war. Adler brought with him to London numerous important musical works created in Terezín, including the supposedly lost opera, *The Emperor of Atlantis.* Dr. Adler very kindly and helpfully permitted Karas to study the compositions and other documents from his collection.

Adler tended to be rather critical of writers who overemphasized the uplifting effect of the lighter music performed in Terezín. Based on his first-hand knowledge of the sociological and psychological aspects of the "enforced community" in Terezín, he felt that, rather than serving to boost morale, such music was too "escapist" and actually reinforced the impression the Germans sought to convey to foreign media, especially visiting representatives of the International Red Cross: that Terezín was a "model ghetto" and a "spa."

THE EMIGRÉ MUSICIANS

The United States and Canada

A number of Jewish musicians born in Czechoslovakia left the country in time to escape the Holocaust. Nettl mentions several of those who were still alive at the time his essay went to press. Among the conductors, Fritz Zweig, born in Olomouc in 1893, was active in Prague until 1938 and in the United States after 1940. He died in Los Angeles, California, in 1984. George Schick, who was born in Prague in 1908, settled in the U.S. in 1939 and died in New York in 1985. Walter Susskind, who was born in Prague on May 1, 1913, left Czechoslovakia for England in 1939. He died in Berkeley, California, on March 26, 1980. His son, Peter Susskind, of St. Louis, Missouri, is a musician and occasional conductor. Her received a scholarship in Czechoslovakia to study the Czech and Slovak music which his father had promoted.

Franz Allers, born in Karlovy Vary in 1905, conducted *Strauss' Die Fledermaus* in Orange County, California, as recently as February, 1988. In an interview for the *Los Angeles Times* (February 24, 1988) he commented that, strictly speaking, he should not be identified as a Czechoslovak musician because Czechoslovakia was not yet in existence at the time of his birth. Allers had lived and worked in Germany for some time, and, recalling his return to Czechoslovakia in the early 1930's, he said: "After the Reichstag fire, I knew what was going to happen. In *Mein Kampf,* Hitler had announced his timetable, to which he adhered. The book was so revolting I could not finish it... Being from Czechoslovakia, it was easier for me to leave [Germany]. I took the train and went home." Mr. Allers then conducted opera in Prague until his departure for London in 1938. He subsequently settled in the United States, where he developed a very successful career.

The conductor, musicologist and composer Walter Kaufmann, who had been Nettl's student in Prague and a friend of the Nettl family, was born in Karlový Vary on April l, 1907. From 1938 to 1946 he directed European music for Radio Bombay, India. After his immigration to the United States he became Paul Nettl's colleague at Indiana University. He died in Bloomington on September 9, 1984. According to Nettl, who gives many more interesting details about Kaufmann's musical activities, his wife was distantly related to Franz Kafka.

Among the composers, Oskar Morawetz is generally known as a Canadian composer. Born in Světlá nad Sázavou in 1917, he went to Toronto as a refugee in 1940 at the age of 23 and has lived in Canada ever since. For a detailed biography of Morawetz, see my article "Oskar Morawetz: Humanitarian Composer," published in the *Review of the Society for the History of Czechoslovak Jews*, Vol. II, 1988 J89, pp. 141-54, as a belated tribute to honor his seventieth birthday. [19]

Jan Löwenbach was born in Rychnov nad Kněžnou on April 29, 1880.[20] He studied law, but music was his strong avocation. Combining both these interests, he specialized in copyright law and was active as a writer on music. Prior to World War II, he represented most of Czechoslovakia's prominent composers, founded the Club of Czechoslovak Composers and participated in the activities of such music organizations as Umělecká beseda, Hudební matice and ISCM (The International Society for Contemporary Music). He translated a number of Czech vocal works into German and created Czech librettos for the operas of Bohuslav Martinů and Jaroslav Křička. His pen name was J. L. Budín. He was ably assisted in his translation activities by his wife Vilma Löwenbach, née Zucker, who was born in Strakonice on May 16, 1891.

The Löwenbach family left Czechoslovakia before the Nazi occupation. In 1941, after brief sojourns in Switzerland, England and Cuba, they arrived in New York, where Jan Löwenbach worked as a press attaché at the Czechoslovak consulate in exile during the war. The Löwenbachs went back to Prague in 1946, but returned to the United States two years later, residing in New York City in semiretirement. Jan died on August 13, 1971, and his widow, Vilma, on April 26, 1975.

Unlike Jan, his much younger brother Josef Löwenbach returned to Prague from London to stay after the war, living and working there until his death on March 12, 1962. Born in Prague on June 5, 1900, Josef Löwenbach studied music privately with Jaroslav Křička, Otakar Šín and Václav Štěpán and musicology with Zdeněk Nejedlý and Otakar Zich. He was active in some of the same organizations as his brother Jan and was one of the founders of Devětsil, a cultural association of progressive, leftist-oriented writers, poets and other artists who was active in Czechoslovakia during the 1920's. He spent the years of World War II in England, working for the British Broadcasting Corporation (BBC). After his return to Prague he worked at the Czechoslovak Ministry of Foreign Affairs beginning in 1945 and at the Gramophone House beginning in 1951. He wrote music reviews, articles on Suk, Prokofiev, Mussorgsky's *Boris Godunov* and other topics for various newspapers, writing under the pseudonym of J. L. Lukáš.

Nettl emphasized in his study that both Löwenbach brothers were strongly Czech-oriented and had done much work abroad to promote Czechoslovak music, old and new.

England

Otakar Kraus, one of the bass-baritones trained by Konrad Wallerstein, found a haven in England in 1939 and became a popular singer and actor at opera houses in Britain and elsewhere. Born in Prague on December 10, 1909, Kraus debuted in Brno in 1935 as Amonasro and was engaged in Bratislava from 1936 until 1939. His London debut was in Mussorgsky's *The Fair of Sorochinsk* at the Savoy Theater in 1940. He was then engaged by the Carl Rosa Opera (1943), the English Opera Group (1946), the Covent Garden Opera (1951-68) and the Royal Opera. He left his personal imprint on many roles in the premieres of contemporary English operas and in new productions of the standard repertory from Mozart and Verdi to Wagner. He also performed in Holland, Italy, Bayreuth, Milan (at La Scala), Latin America and elsewhere. In 1973 he retired from the stage but continued teaching. He died in London on July 28, 1980. A brief obituary was published in the January 23, 1982, issue of *Opera News*. His biography is included in *New Grove* (1980).[21]

Italy

One of the less well known composers mentioned in Nettl's study is Riccardo Pick-Mangiagalli, who was born in Strakonice on July 10, 1882, and died in Milan on July 8, 1949. He spent most of his life in Italy. He studied piano and composition at the Giuseppe Verdi Conservatory in Milan and became a concert pianist. However, he preferred composition. In 1936 he was chosen to succeed Ildebrando Pizzeti, director of the conservatory, a position he held until his death. Apparently he was not persecuted by the Mussolini regime. His compositions are listed in *Baker's Dictionary*. He wrote operas which were performed at La Scala, and his major orchestral works, chamber and piano pieces, songs and ballet music made him popular in Europe prior to World War II. His short opera *Il Carillon Magico*, based on *commedia dell' arte* elements, was performed at the Metropolitan Opera on December 2, 1920, in combination with other one-act operas.

Israel

Several Jewish musicians from Czechoslovakia emigrated early and went to Palestine, now the State of Israel. Some of these emigrés, though recognized in Israel, are less known abroad and are neither mentioned in the

ČSHS nor in Nettl's study. One source of information about them was Max Brod, who mentions several in his short monograph *Musik in Israel* (1951; 67 pages in the current reprint). [22] Yehuda Walter Cohen, also a native of Prague who settled in Israel, revised and expanded Brod's essays,[23] adding nearly 100 pages of text, with indexes, bibliography and informative lists. Cohen entitled his contribution "Werden und Entwicklung der Musik in Israel" (The Beginnings and Development of Music in Israel). The new book was published under the title *Die Musik Israels* (1976) by Bärenreiter, Cassel. Brod and Cohen are both named as authors.

Brod ended his slim book with a *caveat*: "Heaven save us from a national *kitsch!* ... Only masterful, highly inspired music has the home-born right to educate the masses of our people and to elicit the best that is in them, in order that they may become a part of, and add new strains to, the universal sound of music common to all humanity." (p. 67)

The following musicians from Czechoslovakia contributed their knowledge, talents and a Brodian type of idealism to the development of music in Israel.

We will begin with Frank Pelleg (originally Frank Pollak), who was born in Prague on November 24, 1910. He studied music theory and composition with Alexander Zemlinsky and Vítězslav Novák. His teacher in piano was Karel Hoffmeister. He also developed an interest in cembalo, which was unusual at the time, and in old music. After graduating from the Prague Conservatory, Pelleg was active as an opera conductor and concert pianist. In 1936 he left Czechoslovakia for pre-Israel Palestine, where he soon became one of the country's most outstanding musicians.

In his piano and cembalo recitals Pelleg performed music from all eras, from Bach to modern Israeli composers. From 1950 to 1953 he served as chairman of the Music Council of Israel's Ministry of Education and Culture. He founded the Central Music Library in Tel Aviv and the Phonogram Archive for Jewish and Oriental Music. He wrote educational materials on music, composed incidental music for the theaters of Tel Aviv and Haifa, and was music director of the Haifa Symphony Orchestra, a position he held until his death.

In addition to music for the theater, Pelleg composed a piano concerto, two quartets, songs and other smaller works. He often performed new works of Israeli composers in world premiéres and repeated them on his tours abroad. Among such first performances were the compositions of Paul Ben-Haim, Sergio Natra, Ödön Partos, Itzhak Sadai, Verdina Shlomsky, Zeev Steinberg and Josef Tal. Sometimes he conducted these works, but more often he himself performed them as the soloist on the piano or cembalo. Certain compositions were written especially for Pelleg. His activities that promoted Israeli music won him the prestigious Millo Prize. A book of Pelleg's radio talks and articles, *Gespräche über Musik*, was compiled by Michal Smoira-Cohn after his death and published in Israel by Merkaz le-Tarbut in 1973.

Yehuda Cohen later recalled what he had written when Pelleg died in Haifa on December 20, 1968, the same day as Max Brod. "I, too, am from

Prague, had been his contemporary and was fortunate to have had a close friendship with both of them [i.e., Brod and Pelleg]. Shortly before their deaths, I had the opportunity... to tape Frank Pelleg playing Brod's piano music, as well as the soprano Friedl Teller-Blum singing Brod's Kafka Lieder *Death and Paradise*, accompanied by Pelleg on the piano." (*Die Musik Israels*, p. 9).

Yehuda Walter Cohen was born in Prague on March 14, 1910. Since his parents did not consider music a stable profession, he earned a degree in engineering at the Technical University of Prague. At the same time, however, he studied violin with František Vohánka and composition with Theodor Veidl. In Prague, he founded and conducted a Jewish Symphonic Orchestra and composed several plays that were not unlike musicals.

Following his arrival in Tel Aviv in 1936, Cohen worked as music program editor for the Israel Broadcasting Service, wrote music reviews for *Yediot Hadashot* (the German-language newspaper for which Brod also wrote), was music correspondent for foreign media, lectured in Israel and other countries, and composed more music. In 1964 he gave a course on Israeli music in Bayreuth. Cohen was awarded various honors by West Germany and Italy.

Yehuda Cohen's compositional output included an opera on the theme of the Maccabees and *Ballad of Lieutenant Trumpeldor* (the Israeli national hero Joseph Trumpeldor), which was performed frequently. In Cohen's own book, *Die Musik Israels*, in which he so carefully documented all his additions to Brod's text and gave credit to many persons for their accomplishments, he did not reveal anything about himself or his own creative work. He died in 1988.

George Singer (1909-83), another Prague-born musician and a student of Zemlinsky, was a conductor under whose baton Frank Pelleg sometimes played. He was also a fine pianist, who easily sightread the most difficult orchestral scores. Arriving in Palestine illegally in 1939, he became the conductor of the Palestine Symphonic Orchestra (later the Israel Philharmonic). He also frequently conducted the Israel Opera Orchestra and the Israel Broadcasting Orchestra and made guest appearances with many orchestras in Europe and the United States. He specialized in music of Czechoslovak and Israeli composers. In 1947 he conducted two movements of Paul BenHaim's *Second Symphony* (1943-45), dedicated to Max Brod, at the Prague Spring Festival. One of his peak achievements was conducting the world premiére, in Jerusalem, of Darius Milhaud's *King David*, an opera in five acts and twelve scenes with the libretto by Armand Lunel. The premiere took place during the King David Festival, on June 1, 1954, celebrating King David's establishment of Jerusalem as the capital of Judea.

One of the older Bohemian-born composers who settled in Israel was Baruch (Berthold) Kobias. Born in Český Krumlov in 1895, he studied in Vienna with Guido Adler and in Prague with Fidelio Finke. In Israel he played the viola in a string quartet, and from 1941 on was the violist in the orchestra of the Palestine Opera. His compositions include ten string quartets, some 100 songs, a *Serenade* for five wind instruments (performed at the Israel Music Festival of 1950); two *Israel Suites; Suite 1948*, consisting of movements "Pastorale" and "A Call to Battle;" *Seventeen Variations on the Israeli Folk Song 'On the Shores of Lake Kinneret,'* premiered by George Singer, and *Violin Concerto* (1956). Kobias died in Tel Aviv in 1964.

Three musicians went to Israel from Slovakia. Jacob Gilboa was born in Košice on May 2; 1920. He has lived in Israel since 1938. Among his teachers were Paul Ben-Haim, Josef Tal and Karlheinz Stockhausen (he studied with the latter in Germany). Gilboa has composed a number of piano miniatures for children (1955); *The Twelve Chagall Windows in Jerusalem* (1966) and *Tau* for harp, and a children's voice-band, with words by his wife Shoshana Gilboa (1968). The latter work was awarded the ACUM Prize bestowed by the Society for Authors' Rights of Writers, Composers and Music Publishers. The ballet scenes *Horizons in Blue and Violet* (1970), *Bilder zur Bibel* (1972; premiered by Zubin Mehta with the Israel Philharmonic Orchestra in 1973) and many more works followed. His style is described as neo-impressionistic.

Yehoshua Lakner was born in Bratislava on April 24, 1924, and settled in Palestine in 1941. He studied music in Israel, in the United States at the Berkshire Center with Aaron Copland, and in Darmstadt and Cologne (electronic music). Since 1965 he has been teaching in Switzerland. Among his compositions are a *Sonata for Flute and Piano* (1948), *Sextet for Woodwinds and Piano* (1951) and *a Toccata for Orchestra* (1958), for which he was awarded the [Joel] Engel Prize. His *Kaninchen* (1973) uses a speaker, percussion and tape; *Umläufe* (1976) is written for flute, bass clarinet, piano and two tapes. The City of Zurich cultural award was bestowed on him recently for his contributions to music and theater in Switzerland, to "test application of the computer to compositions, improvisations and incidental music with special regard to the interaction of visual and aural elements" (*ICJC Newsletter*, Vol. XIX, No. 88 / 89, 1988).

Another interesting musician from Slovakia was the pianist and music educator Leo Kestenberg, who was born in Ružomberok on November 27, 1882, and died in Tel Aviv on January 14, 1962. *Baker's* refers to him as a Hungarian, but his biography is included in *ČSHS*. His father, a cantor, gave him a German education. Kestenberg worked in Berlin during the 1920's, fleeing to Prague from the Hitler regime in 1933. In Czechoslovakia he published articles in *Der Auftakt*, for example one in No. 14 (1934) dedicated to the founding of a music education society in Prague. In 1939 he settled in Tel Aviv, where he lived until his death. From 1939 to 1945 he was music director of the Palestine Symphonic Orchestra and subsequently was chairman of the Music Council of the Israeli Ministry of Education and Culture. He helped organize the International Society for Musical Education. It is reported that he spoke Czech very well.

This essay on the "Jewish Musicians with Roots in Czechoslovakia" is intended to update and complement the article by Paul Nettl. While the present work was in progress, however, numerous other individuals were discovered who it was felt should be included: Some are presented in this article; other musicians of equal importance will appear in Part III, which is now being written.

An intimate memoir of the composer Jaromír Weinberger (1896-1967) was recently prepared by his nephew Jehuda (Julius) Poláček of Jerusalem. Mr. Poláček, a clarinetist, inherited all of the musical and personal documents of his uncle and established the Weinberger Archive in Jerusalem. It is a private archive recognized by the State of Israel.[24] Mr. Poláček's contribution, based on heretofore unknown material from his archive, will appear in Part II, along with data gathered or being researched.

Editor's note: Part II of "Jewish Musicians in Czechoslovakia"is a valuable contribution to Weinberger studies. Since it was written by Yehuda Poláček rather than Zdenka Fischmann, it could not be included in the present volume. It appears in the *Review for the Society for the History of Czechoslovak Jews* part II, vol. 4 (1991-1992), pp. 179-204.

Part III

In the first two installments of this study certain criteria of inclusion were established to achieve consistency; i.e., those Jewish musicians have been presented who were born in the area that became modern Czechoslovakia, without going too far back in history or duplicating the material of specialized books by authors such as Joža Karas, Vrkočová, and others. There has been no bias as to their mother tongue, career, educational background, political beliefs or esthetic orientations. This installment will also strive to provide information about these musicians rather than assessments of their work. Comparison of sources has emerged as a valid and interesting aspect of the search for these musicians. Various editions of standard music dictionaries (*Grove's*, *Baker's*, *Československý hudební slovník osob a institucí*, two volumes; Prague, Státní hudební nakladatelství, 1963 and 1965, hereafter referred to as *ČSHS*, *Thompson's Cyclopedia*, etc.) were consulted and compared, as were encyclopedias (*Britannica*, *Judaica*; particular biographies; *Who's Who in Music;* specific general books on Jewish musicians (Brod-Cohen, Holde, Saleski, Lyman); articles in music journals; personal communications; collected current news in several languages, and so on, as available (cf. references in Parts I and II).

As a result of these comparisons, two facts came across clearly: that the biographers', editors' or compilers' nationality or ethnicity played a role in the selection of who was included in specific sources; and that more research on the Jewish musicians of Czechoslovakia is needed and should preferably be done by scholars with Czechoslovak roots, for the political and multicultural history of Central Europe can be rather confusing for many musicologists and music historians of different backgrounds. Non-Czech sources often provide information not accessible in Czechoslovakia, but often do not identify a Czech or Slovak connection.

Because of the turbulent history of the Czech Lands and Slovakia during the twentieth century, many Jewish musicians are missing from *ČSHS* despite their interesting achievements and a marked allegiance to their homeland and its music. We must ask why that should be so. Was it because of their "wrong" mother tongue, their Jewishess, their political views, their creative orientation which the modern dictators disliked, or perhaps some family skeletons, personal antagonisms, their status as emigrants / exiles, or simply because Mr. or Mrs. Censor said so? It seems inconceivable that, for example, Hans Krása, who received the Czechoslovak State Prize in 1933 for his opera *Betrothal in Dreams* and composed the music for a comedy *Mládí ve hře* (1932) and for *Brundibár*, or Viktor Ullmann (both of whom perished in Auschwitz) should not have been included. Ullmann was briefly mentioned in the fifth edition of *Grove's* (as early as 1954), when his opera *The Emperor of Atlantis* was still considered as lost, and in the books on Terezín by G.H. Adler. Only after the Velvet Revolution could these persons be freely discussed in their own country. This study, originally initiated as an update of Paul Nettl's seminal essay in *The Jews of Czechoslovakia*. Vol. I (1968), provides information also on those musicians who should be included in future editions of *ČSHS*.

We will start with Hugo D(avid) Weisgall of New York, who celebrated his eightieth birthday in 1992. In March 1992 he visited Prague, not as a musician but as president of the prestigious American Academy and Institute of Arts and Letters, founded in 1889. His mission was to deliver a certificate of honorary foreign membership to President Václav Havel for his literary achievements as a playwright in a ceremony at the Castle. This, of course, was not a first in Weisgall's diplomatic career, for he had served in Prague as cultural attaché in 1946-47. But I am not sure whether Weisgall's music was ever heard there.

Hugo Weisgall was born in Ivančice, Moravia, on October 13, 1912, into a musical family. His father, Abba Joseph (Adolph J. Weisgal [sic] b. Kikol, Poland, 1885; d. Baltimore, 1981) was an opera singer before he trained as a cantor and composer of synagogue music. Hugo's uncle, Meyer Wolf Weisgal, who settled in the United States in 1905, was the national secretary of the Zionist Organization of America, a close co-worker of Chaim Weizmann in the 1940's and later, in Israel, director and chancellor of the Weizmann Institute of Science. Journalism, literature, music, playwriting and other arts had been Meyer Weisgal's special interests since the 1920's.

Adolph Weisgal, his wife and his two sons (the younger, Fred E. Weisgal, who divided his interests between music and law, died in 1992) settled in Baltimore in 1920. Hugo studied music at the Peabody Conservatory and, privately, composition with Roger Sessions; he earned diplomas in composition and conducting from the Curtis Institute and his Ph.D. degree in 1940 from the Johns Hopkins University. Military service during World War II interrupted his studies but also brought him to England and Europe. His experiences in the U.S. diplomatic service and, above all, opportunities to compose and guest-conduct during the postwar years in several countries served to enhance his career.

Returning to Baltimore in 1947, he continued to promote and create American music. As a conductor, he founded the Chamber Music Society of Baltimore and the Hilltop Opera Company. He taught at Johns Hopkins, at Queens College and at the Juilliard School, and was composer-in-residence at the American Academy in Rome. He also was chairman of the Cantors' Institute at the Jewish Theological Seminary of America in New York (starting in 1952).

Dr. Weisgall composed ten operas that were premièred soon after their completion, mostly in New York. He used librettos adapted after well-known literary and dramatic works: *Tenor* (Wedekind, 1952); *The Stronger* (Strindberg, 1955); *Six Characters in Search of an Author* (Pirandello, 1959); *Purgatory* (Yeats, 1961); *The Garden of Adonis* (Shakespeare and Obey, 1959); *Athalia* (Racine, 1964); *Nine Rivers from Jordan* (Johnston, 1968); and *Jennie, or The Hundred Nights* (Mishima, 1976). Four ballets, instrumental and orchestral compositions, and many songs constitute the body of his lifelong creative work. He also wrote many liturgical choral settings, arrangements of Hebraic and Yiddish folksongs. Hugo Weisgall composed *Tekiatot* for orchestra in 1985.

One strange detail in the *American Grove* concerns the date of March 19, 1942, on which an arrangement of the Fugue and Romance from Weisgall's ballet *One Thing Is Certain* (1939, premièred in Baltimore) allegedly was performed by the Prague Chamber Orchestra. At that time no works of Jewish or "enemy" composers (i.e., composers living abroad) were allowed to be played - and Hugo Weisgall, of course, would fit both categories, unless the censor did not know his background, or the pieces were programmed under some pseudonym, which was also prohibited. The date could be a misprint. After all, Hugo Weisgall had left Europe when he was a young boy of eight.

Despite such a long and successful career in music, Professor Weisgall does not appear in *ČSHS*, whereas he has almost two full pages in the *New Grove's on American Music*.

Eytan Otto Lustig was born in Brno in 1899, and was a well-known choral director in Prague before his emigration to Israel (1939), where he died in Tel Aviv in 1970. He founded and directed the Tel Aviv Collegium Musicum. His choir performed the premiere of Mordechai Seter's (originally Starominsky) *Sabbath Cantata* (1940) which was awarded the Tel Aviv [Joel] Engel Prize in 1945. This composition, using the traditional melodies of the Sabbath service, has been described as "one of the first significant works of Israeli art music ... evoking a religious fervor that heralds a spiritual awakening in the new Holy Land." To become that well accepted, a musical work naturally must be very well performed. In that sense, Lustig's choir undoubtedly contributed to the success of the premiere.

In the 1950s, various operatic companies were founded in Israel, but for technical and financial reasons the standard operas usually had to be performed in concert form only. Eytan Lustig's Collegium Musicum also presented several earlier operas in that manner. Unfortunately, more details on the choral director's career have not been found, and Eytan Lustig does not figure in the main lexicographical sources.

Another successful Brno-born musician living in Israel is Yaacov Shilo. He was a student of the pianist Bernard Kaff, who later often performed in Terezín and eventually perished in Auschwitz. The late Hans Hollander and Pavel Haas taught him music theory. One interesting detail Mr. Shilo remembers is that Haas, a personal student of Janáček's, did not use with his own pupils the harmony textbook of his renowned teacher. A preserved certificate from Haas, stating this young student had completed the study of music theory and was a talented pianist, is a document Mr. Shilo cherishes to this day.

In his youth Professor Shilo dreamed about a medical career, but in the late 1930s he was recommended for an audition and was chosen to study at the conservatory in Jerusalem. There he specialized in piano with Alfred Schroeder, a former assistant of Artur Schnabel (b. Lipnik, 1882; d. Switzerland, 1951). He also studied conducting with Jiří Georg Singer. After his graduation, Shilo served in the British Armed Forces, the only member of his family to survive the Holocaust.

In his recitals, Yaacov Shilo likes to perform Smetana, Janáček, Suk and Haas, but he has also premiered works by contemporary composers from Israel and other countries. Such premieres are sometimes sponsored by the Kol Israel Broadcasting Authority. Besides his concert work - as a soloist, with various orchestras or in chamber music ensembles - he was a founder of the Jerusalem Rubin Academy of Music and Dance, at which he has taught for many years and whose Vocal Department he coordinated. He also writes letters in excellent Czech. He lives on Masaryk Street in Jerusalem.

During a recent visit to Brno in 1990, Yaacov Shilo was interviewed for the Czech music journal *Opus musicum* by its editor, Dr. Eva Drliková, and plans were made for his participation in the 27th International Music Festival of Brno in 1992. Mr. Shilo's very successful piano recital took place on Sunday, October 4, 1992, at the Dietrichstein Palace. He played two works by the American composer George Rochberg (b. 1918) and a substantial sample of Israeli music in so-called Mediterranean style by Paul Ben Haim (1897-1984), Abel Ehrlich (b.1915), Josef Tal (b. 1910), Hanoch Jacoby (1909-1990) and Yinam Leef (b. 1953). Program notes in Czech and English were available, and the audience as well as the music critics warmly greeted the pianist after many years of absence from his home town.

Hans Hollander, music critic and writer, was born in Břeclav, on October 6, 1899. After graduating from the high school in his home town, he studied with the musicologist Guido Adler in Vienna. His doctoral dissertation was devoted to Schubert's Lieder. Moving to Brno, Dr. Hollander taught music theory and history at the school of the local Musikverein (1928-1938) and was active as music director of the German-language Brno Broadcasting Service. He escaped to England in time and became a tutor at the University of Exeter and a life fellow of the International Institute of Arts and Letters.

Hans Hollander contributed larger studies and articles to many leading British international music reviews. He specialized in Schubert, Mahler and Janáček. He knew Janáček personally and integrated his memories into his biography of the composer, published in England and the United States in 1963. Dr. Hollander died in England on August 6, 1986. He is mentioned in *ČSHS* but his biography needs updating.

Another promoter of Czech and Slovak music who enjoyed recognition abroad was Jan Popper. He was born in Liberec, studied in Vienna, conducted at the Prague German Opera, and came to the United States in 1939. He is remembered as the "opera man" of Stanford University and UCLA. He organized, taught and conducted opera workshops in Los Angeles since 1949, presenting operas of all eras by American and other modernists, in addition to the standard classics. Under his direction Janáček's *Jenůfa* and Kůrka's *The Good Soldier Švejk* were performed in California. In his lectures and concerts, his wife sang Czech and Slovak folksongs in the original languages.

Professor Popper was named chairman of the Music Department at UCLA. June 6, 1975, the day marking his retirement, was declared "Jan Popper Day" by the city of Los Angeles. After that date, he became more intensely involved in bringing opera to the Orient, i.e., Japan, Taiwan, Thailand and Malaysia. He conducted the Singapore Symphonic Orchestra in October 1986. He died of cancer on September 3, 1987, at the age of 79.

Peter Herman Adler, born in Jablonec on December 2, 1899, is another operatic conductor educated in Czechoslovakia. He very early showed his musical talent, starting to play the violin at the age of five. His father, a physician, was against a musical career, particularly that of a Wunderkind, but Peter Herman managed to learn music theory on his own. Later, as a law student in Prague, he became a pupil of Vítězslav Novák, and later studied of composition and conducting at the Prague Conservatory under Alexander von Zemlinsky. He conducted the local orchestra in Jablonec for a time.

While still in his twenties, Adler went to Brno, where he conducted such Czech operas as *The Bartered Bride, Dalibor* and *Jenůfa.* After a short stay in Teplice, Adler was engaged by the Bremen Opera House, with opportunities to guest-conduct in many other places. He then accepted an invitation to conduct operas in Kiev (1937), teach at the Kiev conservatory, and perform also in Moscow and other Russian cities. A year later he was guest-conducting in Prague, at the New German Theater and with the Czech Philharmonic and the Radio Orchestras. When war with Germany threatened and the Czech army was mobilized, he left music for service in the Czechoslovak army. After the Munich crisis, he left Czechoslovakia, arriving in the United States in 1939.

Peter Herman Adler made his American debut with the New York Philharmonic Orchestra in a concert benefiting the Czech Relief, on January 24, 1940. That concert made an excellent impression and received a very favorable press. After touring the United States, Maestro Adler became music director of the NBC Opera Company for the decade 1949-1959, working closely with Arturo Toscanini. Between 1959 and 1968, he held a similar position with the Baltimore Symphony Orchestra. In 1959 he joined the National Educational Television, debuted at the Metropolitan Opera in 1972, and directed the American Opera Center at the Juilliard School until 1981. Even after his retirement, he continued to participate in the operatic activities in New York until his death in Ridgefield, Connecticut, on October 2, 1990, at the age of 91.

During his association with NBC, Peter Herman Adler commissioned a number of operas by contemporary composers, suitable for television, among them Martinů's *The Marriage* (1952). He was a pioneer of opera in English to make the stories understandable to the listeners the way it has been traditionally done in European opera houses, and today is accomplished by the projected supertitles, while the singers use the original language, be it Italian, German or even Czech.

It is interesting to note that the short paragraph on Adler in *ČSHS* ends abruptly with the year 1938, saying simply: "Afterwards in New York."

In England, we have Vilém Tausky, born in Přerov in 1910, educated in Brno and Prague. He was engaged at the National Opera House in Brno (1929-1939), before serving as a soldier in France and England during World War II. He became music director of the British Carl Rosa Opera (1945-49), guest conductor of the Royal Opera House (1951), Sadler's Wells Opera (1953), and other opera companies, as well as the BBC. Mr. Tausky also composed and wrote on music. He premiéred Janáček's opera *Osud* (Fate) and published *Leoš Janáček, Leaves from His Life*. For his war service, he received the Czechoslovak Military Cross (1944) and the Czechoslovak Order of Merit (1945). That may explain why this Czechoslovak patriot does not appear in *ČSHS*. However, the City of London honored him by giving him the status of a "Freeman" (1979); other honors followed.

Paul Stefan (originally Gruenfeld) was a musicologist and writer. He was born in Brno on November 25, 1879 and died in New York on November 12, 1943. He studied at the University of Vienna and composition also with Arnold Schoenberg. However, he kept close contact with many contemporaneous musicians of Czechoslovakia. He became the editor of the journal *Musikblätter des Anbruchs*, which was published between 1919 and 1938 and systematically reported on premiéres of avant-garde Czech musicians. The journal was always open to news on musical events in Prague or Brno received from writers such as Alois Hába, Max Brod, Josef Bohuslav Foerster, Jan Löwenbach, Ervin Schulhof, and others. This journal is a valuable source for Czechoslovak music of the 1920s and 1930s. Stefan was one of the founders of the International Society for Contemporary Music and President of its Vienna section, as well as a correspondent for several foreign newspapers and music periodicals, including *Musical America*. After the Anschluss in Austria, he eventually arrived in the United States, following short stays in Switzerland and France.

Paul Stefan has several biographies of famous composers to his credit, including Dvořák (1934). He and Czech musicologist Otakar Šourek worked together to condense Šourek's original four-volume edition to one authoritative volume for English-speaking readers.

As we discuss musicologists who dedicated much of their efforts to Czech music, we must not forget Edith Vogl-Garrett of Boston who was born on December 9, 1904, in Nýrsko, Bohemia. She earned her doctorate in philosophy, in musicology and classical archeology from the University of Prague, but also studied piano at the Academy of Music in Prague and was active as a music critic.

Dr. Vogl-Garrett came to the United States in 1938. She taught piano, musicology, German and Italian at various colleges and universities, including Harvard University. Bohemian pre-Classics have been one of her special interests. She has participated in many annual meetings of the American Musicological Society, reading papers on Ryba, Benda and other composers of that time, but also on Smetana and Haydn, when their anniversaries occurred. She has been a member of the International Musicological Society and has known well many of her colleagues from many countries. She demonstrated sincere concern about several musicologist friends during the Communist era in Czechoslovakia and offered them practical support. She also was helpful to her American friend, the late Nicolas Slonimsky, editor of several revisions of *Baker's Dictionary*.

Her publications include the article "The Influence of 18th Century Czech Composers on the Development of Classical Music" (in *The Czechoslovak Contributions to World Culture*, ed. Miloslav Rechcígl, 1964). She contributed to the *Harvard Dictionary of Music* and to the *Festschrift, Studies in 18th Century Music: A Tribute to Karl Geiringer*, to mention only a few of her writings.

Edith Vogl-Garrett, interestingly, is not written up in those dictionaries to which she contributed data related to Czechoslovak music, nor is she to be found in the *Czechoslovak Music Dictionary* in which many musicians of similar status are included. However, to the students who became interested in Czechoslovak music through her work and to her friends she has been "Madam Czech Music" just the same.

Editor's note: This article evolved from the paper which Dr. Fischman read upon her return to Prague and Charles University after the Velvet Revolution, as a participant in the 16th Congress of the Czechoslovak Society of Arts and Sciences, June 26 - July 2, 1992.

Notes

For the purposes of this study, Czechoslovakia is defined in the territorial rather than historical sense as comprising Bohemia, Moravia, part of Silesia, Slovakia and Subcarpathian Ruthenia, and including all the nationality groups inhabiting those regions. However, it should be noted that quite a number of the musicians mentioned in this study were born during the era of the Austro-Hungarian monarchy. Even though they developed at least a part of their careers during the period of the first Czechoslovak Republic (1918-1939), these individuals may have identified themselves in the census of 1930 as members of Czech, Slovak, German, Hungarian, Jewish or some other nationality group. Such formal identification is immaterial, as are their language preferences, religions practices or political views. This study is focused on their creative achievements and personal life stories.

1) *The Jews of Czechoslovakia. Historical Studies and Surveys,* Vol. 1, Philadelphia, 1968, pp. 539-57. See also review essay of all three volumes by Z.E. Fischmann in *Kosmas. Journal of Czechoslovak and Central European Studies,* Vol. 5, No. 1, Summer 1986 (published by the Czechoslovak Society of Arts and Sciences).

2) Rietsch (1869-1927), a native of Cheb, was a half-Jew; his real surname was Löwy. His teacher was Guido Adler (b. Ivančice, Moravia, 1955; d. Vienna, 1941), who remained a practicing Jew until his death at the age of 86. Cf. Nettl (1968), pp. 550, 551).

3) Becking (1894-1945) was a leftist at first, but then became a Nazi. He met his death on May 8, 1945, during the Prague uprising at the end of the Nazi occupation. Cf. *Baker's Biographical Dictionary of Musicians,* fifth ed., 1958; sixth ed., 1978; seventh ed., 1984. Hereafter referred to as *Baker's.*

4) Among Paul Nettl's English works are *The Book of Musical Documents,* New York, 1948 (reprint 1969); *The Other Casanova.* New York, 1950 (reprint, 1970); Forgotten Musicians. New York, 1951 (reprint 1970); *National Anthems,* New York, 1952 (enlarged second ed., 1967); *Mozart and Masonry,* New York, 1957 (reprint, 1970); *The Dance in Classical Music,* New York, 1963. He also edited the *Beethoven Encyclopedia.* New York, 1956 (republished in 1963 in a revised edition as the *Beethoven Handbook*).

5) Komma, born in Aš in 1913, studied composition at the German Music Academy and musicology at the German University in Prague. The subject of his doctoral dissertation was Jan Zach. The quotation in this study is from his book *Das böhmische Musikantentum,* Cassel, Hinnenthal-Verlag, 1960, p. 190. Interestingly, he states in the introduction to his book that musicologists from the Sudeten region are nowadays identified in Germany as "Bohemian musicians."

6) *Musik-Barock in Böhmen und Mähren* (Baroque Music in Bohemia and Moravia), Brno, Verlag Rudolf M. Rohrer, 1927; p. 71. Cf. Hana Rothova, "Co všechno František Škroup netušil" in *Židovská ročenka 5749,* in which the author reviews Škroup's activity in Prague synagogues from 1836 to 1845. She mentions the purchase of an organ for Sabbath eve services.

7) Ansorge (b. Silesia, 1862; d. Berlin, 1930) was a concert pianist and composer who taught in Berlin. In 1920 he was appointed head of the German Music Academy in Prague. He toured the United States in the 1880's.

8) Bruno Nettl's many publications include *North American Indian Musical Styles,* Philadelphia, 1954 (based on his doctoral dissertation); *Music in Primitive Culture,* Cambridge, Massachusetts, 1956; *An Introduction to Folk Music in the United States,* Detroit,

1960 and 1967 (a third, thoroughly revised edition appeared as *Folk Music in the United States: An Introduction* in 1976); *Theory and Method in Ethnomusicology*, New York, 1964; *Folk and Traditional Music of the Western Continents*, Englewood Cliffs, New Jersey, 1965, 1973; *The Study of Ethnomusicology: 29 Issues and Concepts*, Urbana, Illinois, 1983, and *The Western Impact on World Music*, 1985.

9) *Československý hudební slovník osob a institucí*, two volumes; Prague, Státní hudební nakladatelství, 1963 and 1965, hereafter referred to as *ČSHS*. Some of the musicians named in Nettl's article are not included in this dictionary, while others that do not appear in Nettl's study are mentioned. Some of the biographical data in both works need updating, especially as to recent dates of death.

10) Another former student of Professor Auspitzer is the soprano Lída Brodenová, a native of Brno, who later emigrated to the United States and promoted Czech opera in New York City and Washington, D.C. Editor's note: Auspitzer also taught Anna Hanusová-Flachová in Terezín during her ninth and tenth years. Anna is a professor of voice at the Janáček Academy in Brno.

11) Joža Karas, *Music in Terezín 1941-1945* (New York, Beaufort Books, 1985). Ludmila Vrkočová, *Hudba terezínskeho ghetta* (n.d., a Prague Jazz Section publication).

12) *ČSHS* confirms the death date of October 17 only for Haas and Kaff. The death data given for Ledeč is "Auschwitz, 1944." Krása and Ullmann are not mentioned at all. In the case of Schächter, the dictionary states that he was in the transport that left Terezín on October 16, 1944, and that he did not return. Bedřich Borges' biography of Schächter, published in *Židovská ročenka 5749* (Prague 1988), claims that Schächter perished in 1945 during a death march from Auschwitz.

13) A small phonograph record enclosed in the English version of *Terezín*, published by the Council of Jewish Communities in the Czech Lands in 1965, provided only a few musical examples: Ilse Weber's song *I Wander Through Terezín*; an anonymous *Lullaby; Song on an Old Chinese Text* by Pavel Haas (from his song cycle *Four Songs on Chinese Verses*) ; a fragment from Gideon Klein's *Piano Sonata*, and *Bread*, sung by Karel Berman. By comparison, a full-size Pantheon record produced in Czechoslovakia in 1985 to mark the fortieth anniversary of the end of World War II included Gideon Klein's complete *Sonata* and his *Trio for Violin, Viola and Cello*; Viktor Ullmann's *Piano Sonata* No. 6; Hans Krása's *Dance* (for a string trio); and two of Pavel Haas' *Four Songs on Chinese Verses*. The opera *Brundibár* has been filmed and *The Emperor of Atlantis* has appeared on television in Europe. [Editor's note: many additional recordings have been released since this article was written.]

14) Sincere thanks go to the founders of the Mecklenburgh Opera for kindly sending programs, copies of reviews of the performances and other data on Ullmann's *Emperor*.

15) Entries for Juliette Arányi are included ČSHS and in the Karas book, but is mentioned only by name in Nettl's study. The Joachim family connection is explained in Joseph McLeod, *The Sisters d'Arányi*, 1969).

16) In addition to the entries in *ČSHS*, information was provided by Konrad Wallerstein's younger daughter, Hana Orsten, of Los Angeles, California. Names of singers and a copy of František Kafka's article were particularly helpful.

17) Biographies of Karel Ančerl and Walter Susskind were appended to this writer's study, "Oskar Morawetz: Humanitarian Composer," in *Review of the Society for the History of Czechoslovak Jews*, Vol. II, 1988-89, pp. 141-54. Editor's note: this article is rerpinted in this volume.

18) Adler's seminal books, particularly *Theresienstadt 1941-45* (1955; second ed., 1960) and *Die verheimlichte Wahrheit: Theresienstädter Dokumente* (1958) are sources on the fate of the Jews of Bohemia and Moravia, and also of Austria and Germany. *Der verwaltete Mensch* (1974) is an analysis of the bureaucratically-run Nazi death machine. *Nachruf bei Lebzeiten* (1974) is more autobiographically oriented.

19) Editor's note: reprinted in this volume.

20) In Czechoslovakia, Jan Löwenbach was music critic of the Prague *Hudebni Revue*. In America, he contributed articles to numerous music journals in Czechoslovakia and later to *The New York Times*, *The Musical Quarterly*, the British *Slavonic Review*, the *Encyclopedia Americana* and other periodicals, mainly on the music of his native country. His many larger publications include *Music in Independent Czechoslovakia*, Prague, 1931 (in Czech); *Czechoslovak Music*, New York, 1941; *B. Smetana-Genius of a Freedom-Loving People*, Washington, D.C., 1943, and *Music in America*, Prague, (in Czech). After the death of Jan Löwenbach and his wife, their daughter Věra Bála of Ottawa, Canada, donated the books and written material from Jan Löwenbach's literary legacy to the Malcolm A. Love Library of the San Diego State University, where the Department of Music established, in 1981, the Jan Löwenbach Graduate Scholarship in Musicology for students of Czechoslovak music.

21) *The New Grove Dictionary of Music and Musicians*, 1980 [first] edition, is referred to as *New Grove* (1980). Kraus is not listed in any of the other English dictionaries of music consulted for this essay, nor in *ČSHS*.

22) Max Brod (1884-1968) is the subject of two essays by this writer. "The Max Brod Centennial," in *Cross Currents 4* (1985), pp. 2999-307, is more biographical and focuses on Brod's literary achievements. "Max Brod's Life in Music" appeared in the *Review of the Society for the History of Czechoslovak Jews*, Vol. I, 1987, pp. 101-20. Editor's note: these two articles are reprinted in this volume. An essay by Herman Zvi Carmel, "Max Brod's Way to Judaism and Zionism," was published in *Bitzaron, Quarterly Review of Hebrew Letters*, Vol. IX, No. 41-42, 1989, pp. 24-32, to commemorate the twentieth anniversary of Brod's death in Israel.

23) Brod's work has five chapters. Chapter I, "Three Theses," offers definitions and analyses of what Jewish music is and what it is not; Chapter II, "Firm Ground Beneath the Feet," is devoted to synagogue music and traditional Jewish music; Chapter III is entitled "Folksong;" Chapter IV is a compilation of data on "Jewish Musicians in the Diaspora," and Chapter V deals with "The Music of Israel." Since Brod wrote in German, it was only natural for Yehuda Walter Cohen to continue the work in the same language.

24) The information about the Weinberger archive is appreciated, as are the dates that were provided or confirmed by the joint efforts of Yehuda Poláček and Dr. Avigdor Dagan, both of Israel.

SOME JEWISH MUSICIANS FROM CZECHOSLOVAKIA

Twenty years ago, on January 8, 1972, a world-known musicologist, born in what later became Czechoslovakia, died at the age of 83. He was born in Vrchlabí on January 10, 1889, and lived, wrote and taught in Prague, until September 1939, when he escaped to the United States, with his wife and a son. He thus avoided the fate of his elderly parents, who perished in the Holocaust. His name was Paul Nettl; his scholarly work was centered on research and promotion of the music of Czechoslovakia.

In America, particularly during his tenure at Indiana University in Bloomington (1946-59, part time to 1963), Paul Nettl continued to call attention of his numerous colleagues and students to the neglected and little known area of Czech music. Today, there are United States and Canada born and educated musicologists who have specialized in this field because of Nettl's teaching.

In 1968, Paul Nettl wrote the article "Music" for the first volume of the trilogy *The Jews of Czechoslovakia. Historical Studies and Surveys*, published in Philadelphia by the New York based Society for the History of Czechoslovak Jews. Several years after the third volume came out in 1984, the same society (SHCJ) started a new periodical, *Review for the Society for the History of Czechoslovak Jews.*

Asked for some contribution for the *Review*, I wrote a study on Max Brod's musical activities and another on Oskar Morawetz. Then I concentrated on other Jewish musicians active in the Czechoslovak Republic and elsewhere, updating and complementing some of Nettl's data, and adding new information available since 1968.

An interesting aspect of this research was a comparison of sources, i.e.: different editions of standard music dictionaries (*Grove's, Baker's, Československý hudební slovník, Thompson Cyclopedia*, etc.); encyclopedias (*Britannica, Judaica*), *Who's Who in Music*; books on Jewish musicians (Holde, Saleski, Lyman); articles in music journals, collected current news, and so on. One fact came across clearly: that the writer's, editor's or compiler's nationality or ethnicity played a role in the selection of who was included; and that more research of the Jewish musicians from the area of ČSR was needed and should be done by scholars with Czechoslovak roots, whatever their subjects' linguistic or religious background had been. For many musicologists of other backgrounds the cultural history of the Central Europe is often somewhat confusing. There may ensue a debate of how to know who should be called a Bohemian and who should figure in the music history as a Czech composer or performer. The concept of historical multiculturality sometimes appears difficult to understand or tolerate.

Returning to Paul Nettl: Although his education and primary language were German and later he published in English - both he and his prominent son, the ethnomusicologist Bruno Nettl who was born in Prague - are to be found in the *Czechoslovak Music Dictionary* of 1963 and 1965. However, the names and careers of other musicians are missing from this reference work, despite their interesting achievements and basic allegiance to their home country. I will mention some of them.

Hugo Weisgall of New York was born in Ivančice on October 13, 1912. He recently visited Prague, not as a musician but as President of the exclusive American Academy and Institute of Arts and Letters, founded in 1889, to deliver in a ceremony at the Castle a certificate of honorary foreign membership to President Václav Havel for his literary achievements as a playwright. This, of course, was not a first in Weisgall's diplomatic career, for he served in Prague as cultural attaché in 1946-47. I do not know if his music has been performed in Prague.

The Weisgall family settled in Baltimore in 1920. Their son studied music at the Peabody Conservatory and sutdied composition privately with Roger Sessions; he earned diplomas in composition and conducting at the Curtis Institute and his Ph.D. in 1940 from Johns Hopkins University. After World War II, he was a frequent guest conductor in Europe. He founded the Chamber Society of Baltimore and the Hilltop Opera Company. He taught at Johns Hopkins, Queen's College, and Juilliard, and was composer-in-residence at the American Academy in Rome. Since the 1930s, he has composed 10 operas, among them *Six Characters in Search of an Author*, after Pirandello (1959), ballet music, cantatas, songs, instrumental and chamber music, in an expressionistic atonal style. His music is frequently performed and is well accepted by the public. Despite his long and successful career in music, professor Weisgall does not appear in the Czechoslovak Music Dictionary. However, he has almost two full pages in *New Grove Dictionary of American Music*.

Several Jewish musicians from Czechoslovakia emigrated before World War II and went to Palestine, now the State of Israel. Some of these emigrés, though recognized in Israel, are less known abroad, and are not listed in *ČSHS* nor in Nettl's study. Max Brod's short monograph *Musik in Israel* (1951; 67 pages in the current reprint) is an important source. Yehuda Walter Cohen, also a native of Prague, revised and expanded Brod's essays, adding nearly 100 pages of text, with indexes, bibliography and informative lists. The new book was published under the title *Die Musik Israels* (1976) by Bärenreiter, Cassel. Brod and Cohen are named as co-authors.

Yehuda Walter Cohen was born in Prague on March 14, 1910. Since his parents did not consider music a stable profession, he earned a degree in engineering at the Technical University in Prague. At the same time, he studied violin with František Vohanka and composition with Theodor Veidl. In Prague, he founded and conducted a Jewish Symphonic Orchestra and composed several plays in the style of the future musicals.

Following his arrival in Tel Aviv in 1936, eventually Cohen worked as music program editor for the Israeli Broadcasting system, wrote music reviews for *Yediot Hadashot*, the German language newspaper for which Brod also wrote; was music correspondent for foreign press, lectured in Israel and other countries, and composed more music. In 1964, for example, he gave a course on Israeli music in Bayreuth, and was awarded various honors by West Germany and Italy.

Yehuda Cohen's compositions include an opera on the theme of the Maccabees, and *Ballad of Lieutenant Trumpeldor*, the Israeli national hero, which has been frequently performed. In the book mentioned above, he carefully documented all his additions to Brod's text, but does not reveal anything about himself or his own creative work. He wrote two articles on Brod's music for the *Ein Gedenkbuch* (a book "in memoriam"), originally planned as a Festschrift for Brod's eighty-fifth birthday. He based one of them on Brod's list of his own compositions. Cohen died during the 1980s.

Georg (Jiří) Singer (1909-1983], another Prague-born musician and a student of Zemlinsky, was a conductor. He was also a fine pianist, who could easily sight-read the most difficult orchestral scores. Arriving in Palestine illegally in 1939, he became the conductor of the Palestine Symphonic Orchestra (later the Israel Philharmonic). He also frequently conducted the Israel Opera Orchestra and the Israel Broadcasting Orchestra and appeared as guest conductor with many orchestras in Europe and the United States. His specialty was the music of Czechoslovak and Israeli composers. In 1947, he conducted at the Prague Spring Festival two movements of Paul Ben Haim's *Second Symphony* (1943-45), dedicated to Max Brod. One of his important achievements was conducting the world premiere of Darius Milhaud's opera *David*. The premiere took place on June 1, 1954 in Jerusalem, during a festival celebrating the establishment of Jerusalem by King David as the capital of Judea.

One of the older Bohemian-born composers who settled in Israel was Baruch (Berthold) Kobias. Born in Český Krumlov in 1895, he studied in Vienna with Guido Adler and in Prague with Fidelio Finke. In Israel he played the viola in a string quartet, and from 1941 on was the violist in the orchestra of the Palestine Opera. His compositions include ten string quartets, some 100 songs, a *Serenade* for five wind instruments (performed at the Israel Music Festival of 1950); two *Israel Suites*; *Suite 1948*, consisting of "Pastorale" and "A Call to Battle;" *Seventeen Variations on the Israeli Folk Song 'On the Shores of Lake Kineret,'* premiered by Georg Singer, and Violin Concerto (1956). Kobias died in Tel Aviv in 1964.

Two musicians went to Israel from Slovakia. Jakob Gilboa was born in Košice on May 2, 1920. He has lived in Israel since 1938. Among his teachers were the Israeli composers Paul Ben-Haim and Josef Tal, and Karlheinz Stockhausen of Germany. Gilboa has composed a number of piano miniatures for children (1955); *The Twelve Chagall Windows in Jerusalem* (1966) and

Tau for harp and a children's voice-band (1968), which received a special prize. The ballet scenes *Horizons in Blue and Violet* (1970), *Bilder zur Bibel*, premiered by Zubin Mehta in 1973; and many more works followed. His style has been described as neo-impressionistic.

Yehoshua Lakner was born in Bratislava on April 24, 1924 and settled in Palestine in 1941. He studied music in Israel, in the United States at the Berkshire Center with Aaron Copland, and electronic music in Germany. Since 1965 he has been teaching in Switzerland. Among his compositions are a *Sonata for Flute and Piano* (1948), *Sextet for Woodwinds and Piano* (1951) and a *Toccata for Orchestra* (1958) for which he was awarded the Joel Engel prize. His *Kaninchen* (1973) uses a speaker, percussion and tape; *Umläufe* (1976) is written for flute, bass clarinet, piano and two tapes. The City of Zurich cultural award was bestowed on him for his contributions to music and theater in Switzerland, to "test the application of the computer to compositions, improvisations and incidental music with special regard to the interaction of visual and aural elements."

One interesting but not clearly determined connection between Prague and present-day Israel is suggested by the name Zemánek. Vilém Zemánek (1875-1922) who was the conductor of the then newly-organized Czech Philharmonic Orchestra is included in ČSHS. Another conductor with the same family name lives in Israel - Arie (Erich) Zemánek, who was born in Prague on March 20, 1918. He studied piano from the age of eight, and studied harmony privately with Viktor Ullmann during his teens. He played piano at the Prague Mozarteum at the age of ten, and at 17 conducted the chorus and orchestra of his school at Lucerna Hall. He later enrolled in the law school at Charles University. In 1939 he received an immigration certificate to enter Palestine as a student at the Jerusalem conservatory. He studied conducting with Jiří (Georg) Singer.

Arie Zemánek performed on the radio, accompanied the world-renowned tenor Herrman Jadlowker, and in 1941 joined the band of the Yugoslav army. After being demobilized in 1943, he was a member of the Palestine Police Band for two years as a second conductor, pianist and bass player. He served in the future Israel Defense Force from 1947 to 1949, then went to Holland for advanced studies of music theory and conducting. Returning to Jerusalem, he taught and coached at the Music Academy and frequently appeared as guest conductor with the Israel broadcasting service. For several years he conducted the Police Band and was repeatedly invited to coach the summer master courses for opera singers at the Salzburg Mozarteum.

Zemánek has demonstrated an affinity for Czech music in his programs. In 1965, he recorded (with Zlata Glueck) vocal works by Dussek, Rössler, Janáček, Martinů and Novák for the first program broadcasting of Kol Israel. He retired in 1986 and now lives in Jerusalem.

Another successful musician from Czechoslovakia living in Israel is Yaacov Shilo, born in Brno. He was a student of the pianist Bernard Kaff - who later often performed in Terezín and perished in Auschwitz. The late Hans Hollander and Pavel Haas taught him music theory. An interesting detail Mr. Shilo remembers is that Haas did not use the harmony book of Janáček, his own teacher. A preserved certificate by Haas stating that his young student finished the study of theory and was a talented pianist is a document, which Mr. Shilo has cherished until today.

Professor Shilo dreamed about a medical career during his youth, but in late 1930s he was chosen to study at the conservatory in Jerusalem. In Palestine he specialized in piano with Alfred Schroeder, but also in conducting, with Jiří (Georg) Singer, and in that manner he survived the war, the only one of his family to do so. After his graduation, he served in the British Armed Forces.

Mr. Shilo likes to perform Smetana, Janáček, Suk and Haas in recital, but he has also premiered works by contemporary composers from Israel and other countries. These premieres have sometimes been sponsored by Kol Israel Radio Broadcast. Besides his concert work - as a soloist with different orchestras or in chamber music ensembles - he was one of the founders of the Jerusalem Rubin Academy of Music and Dance, at which he taught for many years and coordinated its Vocal Department. During a recent visit to Brno in 1990, Yaacov Shilo was interviewed for the Czech music journal *Opus musicum*. He also writes letters in Czech and lived on Masaryk Street in Jerusalem.

Yehuda (Julius) Poláček, born on April 18, 1920, at Kosová Hora in Southern Bohemia, belongs to the group of Czechoslovaks admitted to then Palestine just before World War II began. He played violin from the age of seven, graduated from the Business Academy in Prague, passed the state exam in violin, and after 1939 continued his studies of clarinet and saxophone at the Jerusalem Conservatory and Academy. As he says, he survived the war because of music; his entire immediate family was killed in the Nazi camps.

In 1941 he volunteered to serve in the Jewish Brigade and was assigned to its orchestra. After his demobilization, he joined the Palestine Police Band in Jerusalem for the next thirty years, though he also played with the Radio Orchestra. Until his retirement ten years ago, he also taught at the conservatory and Rubin Academy.

Mr. Poláček still teaches part time and keeps busy with special projects. He is a nephew of the composer Jaromír Weinberger (1896 - 1967) and inherited his uncle's musical memorabilia and documents, including some manuscripts. He catalogued the materials and keeps them in his home as the Weinberger Archive, which is private but recognized by the State of Israel. His biographical study of Weinberger was published in *Review of the Society for the History of Czechoslovak Jews* (IV). Other writers on music history have sought Mr. Poláček's assistance in order to explore the creative legacy of this rather neglected composer, born in Prague, who died in Florida, USA, 1967.

All of these musicians - and those who will still follow - deserve to be better known in Czechoslovakia, as Frank Pelleg, the pianist and harpsichordist (1910-1968) and Leo Kestenberg, music educator, music director of the Israel Philharmonic Orchestra (IPO) and pianist are – they have entries in ČSHS. Or, of course as Max Brod (1884-1968), though his literary fame overshadows his quite intensive composing. Brod's musical work from the decade after he left Czechoslovakia on March 15, 1939, has been neglected in his home country, which he could visit once only, in 1964.

Many other Jewish musicians did not enjoy the international fame of a Dvořák, but influenced the development of musical taste and music education in the countries where they found safety and a chance to use their skills and knowledge. We will briefly mention some who promoted Czech music in their new careers.

Jan Popper, born in Liberec studied in Vienna and conducted at the Prague German Opera, then came to the United States in 1939. He is remembered as the "opera man" of Stanford University and UCLA. He organized, taught and conducted opera workshops in Los Angeles since 1949, presenting operas of all music eras, and by American and other modernists, besides the standard classics. Under his direction Janáček's *Jenůfa* and Kurka's The *Good Soldier Švejk* were performed in California. In his lectures and concerts, his wife sang Czech and Slovak folk songs in the original languages. He was named Music Department chairman at the UCLA, and June 6. 1975, the day marking his retirement, was declared "Jan Popper Day" by the City of Los Angeles. Then he got more intensely involved in bringing opera to the Orient, i.e., Japan, Taiwan, Thailand and Malaysia. He conducted the Singapore Symphony in October 1986 and died of cancer on September 3, 1987, at 79.

Another operatic conductor, educated in Prague under Zemlinsky, was Peter Herman Adler, born in Jablonec on December 2, 1899. He was active in Bremen, Kiev and elsewhere in the USSR and Europe before he arrived in the USA in 1939. He debuted in America with the New York Philharmonic Orchestra on the occasion of a concert benefiting the Czech relief. For a decade he was director of the NBC Opera Company, then became a successor of Toscanini with the NBC Symphonic Orchestra, conducted at the Metropolitan Opera since 1972, and directed the American Opera Center at the Juilliard School until 1981.

Adler distinguished himself in presenting operas on the National Educational Television, among them some Czech works, such as Martinů's *The Marriage* and several of Janáček's operas, including *From the House of the Dead*. Mr. Adler died on October 2, 1990 at the age of 91 in Ridgefield, Connecticut. In *ČSHS*, his career ends with his emigration to the U.S.!

Franz Allers, born in Karlovy Vary in 1905, conducted Strauss' *Fledermaus* in California as recently as February 1988. In an interview for the *Los Angeles Times* (February 24. 1988) he commented that, strictly speaking, he should not be identified as a Czechoslovak musician because Czechoslovakia was not yet in existence at the time of his birth. Allers had lived and worked in Germany for some time, before Hitler came into power. About his return to Czechoslovakia he said: "After the *Reichstag* fire, I knew what was going to happen. In *Mein Kampf*, Hitler had announced his timetable, to which he adhered. The book was so revolting I could not finish it ... Being from Czechoslovakia, it was easier for me to leave. I took the train and went *home...*" He conducted opera in Prague until his departure for London in 1938. He later had a very successful carreer in the United States; for example, he conducted the musical *My Fair Lady*.

While a good number of musicians from Czechoslovakia emigrated to America and Israel, others represented their home country in more unusual places.

Walter Kaufmann of Karlovy Vary (b. April 1, 1907) directed European music programs for Radio Bombay, India from 1938 to 1946. He later taught at Indiana University as a colleague of Paul Nettl, and died in Bloomington on September 9, 1984.

Riccardo Pick-Mangiagalli was born in Strakonice on July 10, 1882, and died in Milan, Italy, on July 8, 1988. He was a concert pianist but preferred to compose. In 1936, he was chosen to succeed Ildebrando Pizzeti as the director of the Milan conservatory, and some of his operas were performed at the La Scala. In 1920, his short opera *Il Carillion Magico* was premiered in New York at the Metropolitan Opera along with another one-act opera. He apparently was not persecuted for his Jewish ancestry in Italy.

In 1956, the gala African premiere of *The Bartered Bride* took place in Bulawayo, Rhodesia. The role of Jeník was sung by tenor Walter Janowitz, born in Stará Boleslav in 1913 (Jan. 18) and trained in Prague by his relative, Konrad Wallerstein. After 1939 he lived and performed in Palestine, England and Egypt, returned to Czechoslovakia and left again for Ireland, Rhodesia and, finally in 1961, for the USA.

After Walter Janowitz settled in Southern California, he made contact with a long-lost distant cousin, the pianist Hans Janowitz, born in Rumburg in 1910. Hans was a student of August Stradal, who had been a pupil of Leschetitzky and Liszt. The family of Hans Janowitz emigrated in 1939 to Panama City, and he became "the pianist" of the Republic of Panama, teaching at the conservatory, performing in some neighboring Latin American countries, accompanying many renowned singers and instrumentalists who gave concerts and recitals in Panama on their tours. He recently died in Portland, Oregon.

Hans Janowitz's mother, Anna Fischerová, sister of Otakar Fischer, was married to Irma Ledečová, sister of the violinist Egon Ledeč, the concertmaster of the Czech Philharmonic, who perished in Auschwitz after being musically active in the Terezín ghetto. It sounds a little strange to talk about such family connections, but it illustrates the ramifications of the cultural ties in pre-World War II Czechoslovakia.

In England, there was Vilém Tausky, born in Přerov in 1910, educated in Brno and Prague, engaged at the National Opera House in Brno (1929-39), before he served as a soldier in France and England during the war. He became music director of the British Carl Rosa Opera (1945-49), guest conductor of the Royal Opera House (1951). Sadler's Wells Opera (1953), and other opera companies, as well as of the BBC. Mr. Tausky also composed and wrote on music. He premiered Janáček's opera *Osud (The Fate)* and published the notical book *Leoš Janáček, Leaves from His Life*. He received the Czechoslovak Military Cross (1944) and Czechoslovak Order of Merit (1945) for his war service. That may explain why this Czechoslovak patriot does not appear in ČSHS. The City of London honored him by giving him the status of a "Freeman" (1979); other honors followed.

In London also lives the pianist Alice Sommer, born in Prague in 1903, who is well known to all who had heard her in Terezín, later in Czechoslovakia, and in Israel from 1948. Her son, Rafael Sommer, born in 1937, who played the role of The Sparrow in performances of the children's opera *Brundibár* in Terezín, became an excellent cellist, taught in Prague by Pravoslav Sádlo and in France by Paul Tortelier. He has won several international cello competitions and has been music professor at several British schools of music. Neither mother nor son appear in *ČSHS*.

And thus we come to the serious question why certain musicians born in the area of Czechoslovakia and integrated in the musical life there, were omitted in the mid-1960s when the two-volume Czechoslovak Music Dictionary was published. It seems inconceivable that, e.g., Hans Krása, the composer of *Brundibár*, or Viktor Ullmann, whose anti-fascistic opera *The Emperor of Atlantis*, prohibited in the Terezín ghetto, has been performed the world over, were not given any space in the dictionary. I know that by now they are "persons" again, but the inconsistency and lack of objectivity have been intriguing. In a way, this question seeks some answers about the criteria the censorship applied in different cases: Was it their mother tongue, their Jewishness, their political views, their esthetic orientation for we talk about modern creative artists), family skeletons, personal antagonisms or a combination of all such factors? The answer could be important and interesting, even for this modest sample of musicians who left their home and often reached the ranks of internationally recognized masters in their specialties.

OSCAR MORAWETZ: HUMANITARIAN COMPOSER

In January 1987, the Canadian musical world celebrated the seventieth birthday of Oscar Morawetz, the Czech-born Jewish composer whose best-known works include memorial tributes to Martin Luther King Jr. and Anne Frank. The latter composition received a special award from the Segal Fund in Montreal as "the most important contribution to Jewish culture and music in Canada."

Since he has lived in Canada since the age of 23, Morawetz is generally viewed as a Canadian composer. [1] However, his music has been performed in countries throughout the world, including Czechoslovakia, which he and his family left before the Nazi occupation. On January 5, 1987, William Littler, music reviewer of *The Toronto Star*, wrote, "Mind you, the [coming] week is a special one, in that Morawetz will celebrate his seventieth birthday [on] January 17, 1987. But [then] most weeks are Morawetz weeks somewhere around the world..." [2] During that one week, the composer's works were performed in Edmonton, in Winnipeg, at the University of Toronto, on television, over the Canadian Broadcasting Company and in Cleveland, Ohio. He personally attended quite a few of these live performances, flying back and forth. Later that year, his music was featured elsewhere in Canada and the United States, as well as in England, France, West Germany, Guatemala and Israel.

On May 6, 1987, his merits were officially acknowledged by the Province of Ontario. In a special ceremony, the newly-established Order of Ontario was awarded for the first time by Lieutenant Governor Lincoln Alexander to twenty residents of that province. [3] The recipients had been chosen from among four hundred nominees who had achieved distinction in many fields of endeavor, including politics, social volunteerism, the fine arts, music, literature, science sports and others. Morawetz, the "Toronto composer," was among those chosen in the category of music.

This recognition of his achievements and of his secure position as the most frequently performed composer in Toronto, in Ontario and indeed in all of Canada has added another chapter to the success stories of Czech-born musicians who left their native country and made outstanding careers for themselves in other lands.

Oscar Morawetz was born in 1917 in Světlá nad Sázavou, an ancient Bohemian town in a region that has been described as very scenic and romantic. One local writer, Jan Morávek, extolled the town's river Sázava in these enthusiastic terms: "Our river...! I think you cannot really understand what this word 'our' connotes. I would say it in three words: love, pride and gratitude." [4] Many Czech literati, artists and others who achieved eminence in nearby Prague came from that area.

Perhaps the natural beauty of the environment in which he was born provided Morawetz with his earliest musical and esthetic inspiration. About nineteen months old when the first Czechoslovak Republic came into existence, he belonged to the "Masaryk generation" for whom a sense of justice and social responsibility, no less than the quest for freedom of expression, were the daily bread and a natural prerequisite for life.

His father, Richard Morawetz, was a well-known Bohemian textile manufacturer, who, until 1939, was the president of the Juta Company in Prague. [5] Young Oscar attended *gymnasium* in Prague, where he also began his serious musical studies, particularly piano (1929-36) with Karel Hoffmeister (1868-1952). It is said that his very first teacher expressed some doubts about the youngster's future as a performer but, encouraged by another mentor, Oscar blossomed, and he soon won himself a place among the young musical prodigies of the early 1930s. Between 1933 and 1936, his composition teacher was Jaroslav Křička (1882-1969).

The mid-1930s seemed to be an auspicious beginning for this ambitious student who wanted to become a conductor, a composer and a concert pianist - all three, no less. His first opportunity to ascend the conductor's podium came in 1937, thanks to George Szell (1897-1970), who was then the conductor of both the Vienna and Prague opera houses.

However, the Nazi annexation of Austria in the spring of 1938, followed by the Munich crisis of Czechoslovakia that fall, made it clear to Oscar's parents that they would have to emigrate. Some time before the Germans entered Prague on March 15, 1939, the family left Czechoslovakia and settled in Toronto. Oscar was then still in Paris, where he had been studying piano with Julius Isserlis (1888-1968) and Lazare Lévy (1882-1964). He subsequently fled from France to Italy and in 1940 sailed for Canada, via the Dominican Republic, aboard one of the last boats to leave Italy before that country entered World War II on the Nazi side. [6]

In 1944 Morawetz received the degree of bachelor of music from the University of Toronto. *His String Quartet No. 1* not only won him his degree but also a prize in the competition sponsored by the Composers, Authors and Publishers' Associations of Canada. The second piece that gained him the same prize and nationwide recognition was his *Sonata tragica* (1945) for piano solo. This work was Morawetz's first musical response to the end of World War II. It expressed his feeling of survivors' guilt after he learned of the horrors of the death camps, in which European Jewry was almost annihilated while he had been studying music in the peace and safety of Canada. Years were to pass before he was able to deal creatively with this problem. [7]

From 1946 Morawetz taught theory and composition at the Royal Conservatory of Music in Toronto. In 1953 he, received a doctorate in music for his *Symphony No. 1*, which consisted of three movements - *Fantasy*, *Dirge* and *Scherzo* - each suitable for separate performance. In 1958 he was appointed professor of composition at the University of Toronto. He has retired from teaching, but continues to add new works to his output of compositions, and remains active as a conductor and pianist. According to those who are in direct contact with him, he is as busy as ever with his music, but is enjoying his freedom from teaching schedules.

As already noted, Morawetz's composition teacher in Prague during the mid-1930s was Jaroslav Křička. The fact that Křička, a highly appreciated and prolific composer and educator, is little known outside Czechoslovakia may be one reason why the entry on Morawetz in the *New Groves Dictionary of Music and Musicians* (1980 edition) categorically states that "as a composer Morawetz was completely self-taught." [8] Even if that statement were based on fact, Morawetz would be in very good company, since quite a number of composers, including Leoš Janáček, have been labeled as autodidacts. Indeed, it could be said that all truly creative artists are self-taught in the sense that, after acquiring solid knowledge of basic techniques and musical literature, every composer must find the mode of musical expression most congenial to him and develop his mature imagery, taste and style. That an effective composition "has to come from a deeply felt experience," as the Groves entry quotes Morawetz's personal credo, will explain his preference for certain subjects which he shapes musically in an individual fashion.

The *New Groves Dictionary* describes Morawetz as a neoromanticist. On the other hand, the terse description of Morawetz's style in *Baker's Biographical Dictionary of Musicians*, coming from the astute pen of Nicolas Slonimsky, says it better. He characterizes Morawetz's music as "classical in format, romantic in spirit, impressionistic in coloring, and modernistic in harmonic usage." [9] This combination of qualities may explain why Morawetz's music has been readily accepted for performance by many noted conductors and soloists while other contemporary composers often lack opportunities to hear their works performed. It also suggests why audiences have responded favorably to his creations which are serious, often tragic, but always emotionally sincere. It seems that Oscar Morawetz has been able to preserve some golden mean between avant-garde exaggeration on the one extreme, and an over-avoidance of contemporary musical developments, on the other. This middle way apparently suited his Canadian milieu, enabling him to give of his talents to the land that had offered a refuge to him and his family at their hour of peril.

The following is a list of Oscar Morawetz's compositions, in chronological order and grouped by genres.

Among his earliest compositions are such orchestral works as the *Carnival Overture* (1946) and *Divertimento for Strings* (1948; revised 1954); two groups of solo songs based on the poetry of William Blake and other English-language poets (1947 and 1949); the *Duo for Violin and Piano* (1947) and the above-mentioned *String Quartet No. 1;* chamber music; the *Sonata tragica* (1945) was followed by *Fantasy in d* (1948), *Tarantelle* (1949), *Ballade* (1950) and the *Scherzo* (1947) which has been the Morawetz composition most frequently performed by Canadian pianists.

During the 1950s, Morawetz composed his *Symphony No. 1* (1953), *Overture to a Fairy Tale* (1956); the *Second Symphony* (1959); *Keep Us Free* (1951) for chorus with orchestra; *String Quartets No. 2 and 3* (1952-55 and

1959); *Violin Sonata* (1956); *Fantasy on a Hebrew Theme* (1951); and *Scherzino* (1953) for piano solo; *Fantasy, Elegy* and *Toccata* (1958); and several songs, including a work based on Robert Browning's *Sonnets from the Portuguese* (1955).

The 1960s saw Morawetz's gradual transition from basically traditional musical forms to his highly original masterpieces. This was a very fruitful period in his career. In the orchestral group, he composed *Capriccio* (1960), *Piano Concerto No. 1* (1962), *Sinfonietta for Strings* (1963), *Passacaglia on a Bach Chorale* (1964), another *Sinfonietta for Winds and Percussion* (1965), *Two Preludes for Violin* and *Chamber Orchestra* (1965), *Concerto for Brass Quintet and Orchestra* (1968), *Memorial to Martin Luther King*, (an elegy for cello, winds and percussion (1968), and *Reflection after a Tragedy* (1969). His other compositions were *Four Songs* (1966) for solo voice; *Two Contrasting Moods* (1966) and the spiritual *Crucifixion* (1968) for unaccompanied chorus. There were also a *Trio for Flute, Oboe* and *Harpsichord* or *Piano* (1966), *Two Preludes for Violin and Piano* (1965); *Two Fantasies for Cello and Piano* (1962) and, for piano solo, *Ten Preludes* (1966) and *Suite* (1968).

The 1970s began with *From the Diary of Anne Frank for Soprano or Mezzo-soprano, Chorus and Orchestra* (1970); *Who Has Allowed Us to Suffer?*, based on words from the Anne Frank diary (1970); *A Child's Garden of Verses*, after Robert Louis Stevenson (1971); *The Song My Paddle Sings* (1975), for unaccompanied chorus; *Psalm for Strings* and *Symphonic Intermezzo* (both 1970); *Improvisations for Cello and Orchestra* (1973), *Fantasy for Cello and Orchestra* (1974) and *Concerto for Harp and Chamber Orchestra* (1976); *Suite for Flute and Piano* (1972).

Morawetz's symphonic poem, *The Railway Station*, his *Sonata for Trumpet and Piano* and his vocal *The Weaver* (the latter premiered in London shortly before his seventieth birthday) were composed in the 1980s.

Unfortunately even the latest editions of the standard dictionaries of music have not yet listed all of his most recent works, such as his *Second Violin Sonata*; *Fourth String Quartet*; his sonatas for horn and piano, tuba and piano, clarinet and piano, bassoon and piano, and piano and oboe, all of which were commissioned by principal players from Canada's foremost orchestras. In addition, it should be noted that the composer has kept revising a number of his earlier works, and that he has orchestrated the accompaniments of several of his own songs and transcribed five of Antonín Dvořák's *Biblical Songs* for a choir *a capella*. In any event, the list of Morawetz's compositions is impressive and still growing. The only genre to which he has not yet contributed is music for the theater - opera and ballet.

It is interesting to mention the time span that elapsed between the dates given for the creation of Morawetz's works and their premiere performances. Frequently his works, particularly those commissioned by performers, chamber music ensembles and orchestras, or those works created to mark a special occasion, were performed in Canada and other countries not much later than one year after they were finished. His *Divertimento for Strings* (1948, revised 1954), for example, was chosen to represent Canadian music at the Brussels

World's Fair in 1958; his *Concerto for Harp and Chamber Orchestra* (1976) had been commissioned by the Guelph Spring Music Festival, and his *Concerto for Brass Quintet and Chamber Orchestra* (1968) had been written for the New York Brass Quintet. In 1979 the contralto Maureen Forrester had commissioned from Morawetz a setting of *Psalm 22* with piano accompaniment. It was not until January 1984 that Forrester performed it, with a rescored orchestral version of the accompaniment. This world premiere, with the Toronto Symphony Orchestra under the baton of Andrew Davis, was an outstanding success.

As already noted, Morawetz was the recipient of numerous awards for his compositions. In addition to the *Sonata tragica* mentioned earlier, his *First Piano Concerto* won first prize in a national competition sponsored by the Montreal Symphony Orchestra in 1962. The prize was awarded by Zubin Mehta, who also conducted the premiere of the concerto a year later. Morawetz's *Sinfonietta for Winds and Percussion*, one of the 104 entries in the International Competition for Contemporary Music held in Italy in 1966, won the Critics' Award for that year. The world premiere of this composition, too, was conducted by Zubin Mehta. The American premiere of the *Sinfonietta* took place in Aspen, Colorado, under the baton of Walter Susskind, a native of Prague. Morawetz's frequently-performed *Overture to a Fairy Tale* and received the 1987 Juno Award of the Canadian Academy of Recording Arts and Sciences in the category of "best classical composition."

In 1960, 1967, and 1974, Morawetz received the Canada Council's Senior Arts Fellowship. In celebration of his sixty-fifth birthday in 1982, and in recognition of his long teaching career, the University of Toronto organized a festival concert of his works and the Canadian Broadcasting Company prepared a seven-record anthology of his compositions.

Two of the works which have been very meaningful to the composer are the *Memorial to Martin Luther King* and *From the Diary of Anne Frank*. These compositions, which were performed during the 1987 Morawetz celebrations in Canada and the United States, have an interesting background.

In 1957 the virtuoso violoncellist Mstislav (Slava) Rostropovich, who was then still living in the Soviet Union and was permitted to travel abroad only for government-sanctioned concert tours, suggested that Morawetz write a composition for cello and some unusual orchestral combination. [10] Morawetz kept Rostropovich's request in mind but could not find the right inspiration. The stimulus for composing the work came in the spring of 1968, while he was watching the funeral of Martin Luther King Jr. on television. The mood of the event brought to his mind all the funeral marches in Gustav Mahler's music. [12] He developed this idea into a work for Rostropovich for solo violoncello accompanied by winds and percussion. The cello has been traditionally regarded as the string instrument most nearly capable of reproducing the eloquent quality of the human voice through musical sound. Thus, Morawetz considered it a most suitable instrument to portray the spirit of Dr. King, who spoke on behalf of his people at the cost of his own life.

Morawetz's *Memorial to Martin Luther King* was to become a permanent document of King's legacy.

In composing this *Memorial*, Morawetz ran into a problem. He conceived the concluding part of the *Memorial* as a funeral march based on King's favorite spiritual, "Free At Last." However, he did not know the tune of this spiritual, and when the Black concert singer Dorothy Maynor sang it for him over the telephone he found that it was anything but funereal. Indeed, "Free at Last" is a somewhat joyful melody. However, Morawetz succeeded in stylizing it. The work was completed in time for a planned world premiere intended for performance by Rostropovich himself. Unfortunately, Rostropovich's American tour was suddenly canceled. As a result, the *Memorial* was performed somewhat belatedly by the cellist Zara Nelsová and the Montreal Symphony Orchestra. She also recorded the work.

In 1979, to honor the fiftieth anniversary of Martin Luther King's birth, the *Memorial* was broadcast simultaneously by the Canadian Broadcasting Company with some thirty radio stations the world over. On February 14 and 15, 1980, it was performed for the first time in Prague by the Czech Philharmonic, conducted by Henryk Czyz of Lodź, Poland with the cellist Josef Chuchro.

The music critic and musicologist Eugene Cramer described the *Memorial* as a "very effective and moving piece," comparing it in significance and craftsmanship with Alban Berg's *Violin Concerto.* [13] In January 1986, during the "Canadian Salute" to Martin Luther King, Morawetz first met King's widow, Coretta Scott King, and his eldest daughter. Thirteen years earlier, in 1973, Mrs. King had sent her thanks to Morawetz for his *Memorial*, along with the last picture taken of the entire family before her husband's assassination.

From the Diary of Anne Frank had its world premiere in Toronto, on May 26, 1970, with Lois Marshall, soprano, and Lawrence Leonard, conductor, under the aegis of the Canadian Broadcasting Company. The American premiere came two years later, on April 14, 1972, at New York's Carnegie Hall, during the International Festival of Visiting Orchestras. The concert was repeated the following day at the Kennedy Center in Washington, D.C. On both occasions, the performance by the Toronto Symphony Orchestra was conducted by another native of Czechoslovakia, Karel Ančerl, who had survived Terezín and Auschwitz. Since then, *From the Diary of Anne Frank* has been performed in Israel, Australia, Czechoslovakia and many other countries around the world. Following the premiere, Anne's father, Otto Frank, began a correspondence with Morawetz, and the two men met several times in Europe. Another noteworthy encounter was that between Morawetz and Golda Meir, who had expressed a wish to meet the composer of the tribute to Anne Frank.

It is interesting to note that, by his own admission, Morawetz's initial attitude toward the *Diary of Anne Frank* had been one of avoidance. In an interview for *MacLean's magazine*, [14] he is quoted as saying that for some twenty years he had refused to read the *Diary*, or even to hear about it, not even after it had been made into a play and a film and had been read by millions all over the world, in many languages. He felt he would not be able to bear such a direct confrontation with the Holocaust and its victims. But when he finally brought himself to read the book in 1967, he found both inspiration and solace in the thoughts and words of the young girl. He used passages from Anne's *Diary* referring to her friend Lies Goosens, who had been deported by the Nazis. Anne was to see Lies one more time, for a few moments in January 1945, through a barbed wire fence at Bergen-Belsen. Anne and her sister perished, but Lies survived. The references to Lies were included neither in the play nor in the TV version of the *Diary*.

In the *Diary* (entry for November 27, 1943), Anne tells of a dream she had about Lies one night. The Frank family was still hiding out in a presumably safe place, but Lies had already been sent East. Anne records her concern about Lies and prays for her safety. The passage (based on Anne's entry for December 29, 1943) that Morawetz incorporated into his composition ends with these words: "Lies seems to be a symbol to me of the suffering of all my girl friends and all the Jews. And when I pray for her, I pray for all the Jews and for all those in need." This simple but profound message, from a girl who did not live to reach her sixteenth birthday and herself became a symbol of everyone's little sister or brother or daughter or any child lost to the inhumanities of the twentieth century, is eloquently echoed in Morawetz's nineteen-minute composition.

It was Anne's father who later told Morawetz that Lies had settled in Israel and was in contact with him. Morawetz eventually visited Lies in Israel and learned more details about the friendship between the two girls, and their final, unexpected encounter at the death camp. Otto Frank considered Morawetz's choice of text most felicitous. In a letter dated February 24, 1970, he wrote in English to Morawetz from Switzerland: "From your letter and the one you wrote to Doubleday [the American publisher of the *Diary*] I can make out the deep impact Anne's *Diary* had on you ... You are the first to be struck by the feelings Anne expresses about the fate of her friend Lies and the suffering of so many other Jews. Lies survived, however, and is living now in Jerusalem. She is married and has three children ..." [15]

In Morawetz's *Memorial to Martin Luther King*, which won him recognition from advocates of human rights throughout the world, and *From the Diary of Anne Frank*, which was honored for its contribution to Jewish culture and music in Canada, we can sense the composer's deep-felt humanitarianism and his compassion for oppressed individuals and minorities everywhere. The concept of music as an expression of ethics and moral force, which is shared also by Jewish tradition, places upon the creative artist a special responsibility toward his community. We believe that, besides giving his audiences purely musical enjoyment, Oscar Morawetz has shared with them the humanist philosophy that has shaped his life and work.

Morawetz's works have been performed by many eminent conductors, soloists, chamber ensembles, and first-rate orchestras and choirs. We will append to this article biographical sketches of only two conductors who have been linked with the works of Oscar Morawetz. Both were natives of Czecho-slovakia, both were Jews, and both settled in North America. They were Karel Ančerl and Walter Susskind.

Karel Ančerl

Karel Ančerl (1908-73), who, as noted earlier in this article, survived Terezín and Auschwitz, studied with Herman Scherchen in Munich and Václav Talich in Prague. During the late 1930s he conducted - among his other activities - the band of the Osvobozené divadlo, the famous theater of Voskovec and Werich. After the war, he returned to Prague, where he con-ducted the orchestra of the Prague Radio and the Opera of May 5. He briefly taught at the Prague Music Academy (AMU) and in 1950 was appointed con-ductor of the Czech Philharmonic Orchestra. He made several tours with the Czech Philharmonic, and was a guest conductor in many countries, often per-forming at festivals of contemporary music and conducting foreign premieres of older and modern Czechoslovak music. He made his Canadian debut in 1967 and a year later decided to settle permanently in Canada, becoming the conductor of the Toronto Symphony Orchestra. His last contract with the To-ronto Symphony would have run until 1975, when he intended to retire; but he died in 1973 after a long illness at the age of 65.

While in Terezín, Ančerl managed to organize a string orchestra, using instruments smuggled into the ghetto (twelve first violins, ten second violins, eight violas and one contrabass), and conducted a program of Handel, Mozart and Bach. He wrote a short chapter on musical activities in the *Terezín* ghetto for the book *Terezín*, which was published in English by the Council of Jewish Communities in the Czech Lands (Prague, 1965):

"Our 'public' awaited our first concert with great excitement. The hall in which we were allowed to play was overcrowded, the corridors were crammed with people who wanted to hear the whole program for the first time. Our success was so great that we were afraid our activities might become em-barrassing for the ghetto commander. But things went on. We repeated our first program as often as possible, meanwhile rehearsing a new one, dedicated to Czech music. It was Dvořák's *Serenade for Strings*, the *Meditation* based on *St. Wenceslas' Chorale* by Josef Suk, and the *Fantasy for Strings* espe-cially composed for us by the ghetto prisoner Paul Haas. When we had fin-ished rehearsing this program, orders came to hold the concert in the half of the so-called café. Surprised, knowing that no good could come of it, we were let into the flower-decorated hall. We were all issued black suits, my conduc-tor's stand was lined with flowers to hide my clogs. Soon a high official visitor in SS uniform appeared to inspect if everything was going all right. Czech Quislings with film cameras appeared. I was told to introduce the composer Paul Haas after the first performance of his music to an invisible, cheering audience. This farce was filmed to show the world outside the ideal conditions of our ghetto life. The following day the normal concert of our second program took place and two days later, in October 1944, all of us, together with 2,500 other ghetto inmates, were sent in a transport to Auschwitz.

"That was the end of the short history of the Terezín orchestra. Only a small fraction of the entire transport survived... Of the orchestra, only three colleagues, besides myself, survived this transport."

Ančerl's conducting in New York and Washington undoubtedly contributed to the emotional impact of Morawetz's *From the Diary of Anne Frank.*

Walter Susskind

Walter Susskind (1913-80) is listed in the most recent editions of *Baker's Biographical Dictionary of Musicians* as a Czech-American conductor, but an obituary in California described him as "the globe circling conductor of dozens of the world's principal orchestras." Born in Prague on May 1, 1913, he studied piano with Fidelio Finke and Roman Veselý at the Prague Conservatory of Music, graduating as a concert pianist in 1931 from Karel Hoffmeister's master class. He studied theory and composition with Josef Suk and Alois Hába, and conducting with George Szell. He left Czechoslovakia as a result of the Nazi occupation. His numerous engagements as conductor or music director include the German Opera in Prague (1934-37), the Carl Rosa Opera Company in London (1943-45), the Scottish Orchestra and Scottish National Orchestra in Glasgow (1946-52), the Victoria Symphony Orchestra in Melbourne (1953), the Toronto Symphony Orchestra (1956-65) and the St. Louis Symphony Orchestra (1968-75). His final appointment, as musical advisor and principal guest conductor of the Cincinnati Symphony Orchestra, came in 1978 and lasted until his retirement to Berkeley, California. Even after retiring, he occasionally accepted engagements as a guest conductor and was scheduled to conduct the Los Angeles Chamber Orchestra in May 1980, but he died in Berkeley on March 26 of that year.

Susskind was one of the most frequently recorded conductors of his day. His currently available records include Czech music (such as Dvořák's *Piano Concerto* with Rudolf Firkušný, Dvořák's *Violoncello Concerto* with Zara Nelsová and Smetana's *Má Vlast*), standard classics, twentieth-century composers and contemporary works. He conducted Morawetz's *Overture to a Fairy Tale* at the Stratford Music Festival in 1956, and Morawetz's *Sinfonietta for Winds and Percussion* in 1966.

Susskind composed for piano, chamber ensembles and voice. Some of his compositions were performed when he was still active in Prague. Known for his keen interest in young musicians, he enjoyed conducting American youth symphony orchestras whenever he had an opportunity to do so, and was acclaimed as "the patron saint of youth orchestras."

His love of the piano in particular remained with him even during his final illness. He reportedly played Bach and Mozart for a visiting friend while wearing an oxygen mask only two weeks before his death.

His brother, Charles Susskind, an educator and historian teaching at the University of California at Berkeley, published a book, *Janáček and Brod*

(New Haven and London: Yale University Press, 1985), which dealt with the relationship between the Czech composer Leoš Janáček and the Czech-born Jewish author and composer Max Brod, [16] and which he dedicated to the memory of Walter Susskind. Susskind's son, Peter Susskind of St. Louis, Missouri, is a musician and occasionally conducts.

These biographical sketches reveal similarities among these muisicians. They were all born in the first two decades of the present century, Morawetz being the youngest. They had teachers in common. They cooperated with one another to promote Czech music, old and new, and all three made excellent careers in other lands.

Notes

1) Paul Nettl, "Music," in *The Jews of Czechoslovakia*, Vol. I (Philadelphia and New York: The Jewish Publication Society of America and the Society for the History of Czechoslovak Jews, 1968), p. 549.

2) William Littler, "Canadian Composer Wins World-Wide Fame," in *The Toronto Star*, January 5, 1987.

3) "First Twenty Winners of Order of Ontario," in *The Globe and Mail*, April 25, 1987.

4) Vladimír Kovařík, *Literární toulky po Čechách* (Prague: Albatross, 1977), p. 458.

5) There is a brief reference to Oscar Morawetz's father in Joseph C. Pick, "The Economy," in *The Jews of Czechoslovakia*, Vol. I, p. 413, 435.

6) These details about Morawetz's escape from Europe come from an unsigned article, "Tragic Inspiration," in the Music section of *Time Magazine*, vol. 95 noo. 23, June 8, 1970.

7) In his book *Creativity: The Magic Synthesis* (New York: Basic Books, 1976), the late Silvano Arieti, an Italian-Jewish psychoanalyst active in the United States, describes various "Simple Attitudes and Conditions for Fostering Creativity" (pp. 372-79). One of the prerequisites he names is the "rememberance and inner replaying of past traumatic conflicts" by transforming them into creative work, be it music, arts, literature, philosophy or technical invention.

8) Entry on Oscar Morawetz by Dorith R. Cooper.

9) *Baker's Biographical Dictionary of Musicians* has carried the same article on Morawetz in the sixth through tenth editions.

10) This date is given in an article by the music critic Robert Finn, "Composer Inspired by King's Funeral," in *The Plain Dealer*, Cleveland, Ohio, January 15, 1987. However, Morawetz himself, in "Thoughts on the Memorial to Martin Luther King," *in Toronto Symphony News*, 1979/80, Issue Six, gives 1966 as the year when Rostropovich first became acquainted with Morawetz's *Two Fantasies for Cello and Piano* and requested him to compose another cello work, "not a concerto, neither a work with the usual form and content nor with the standard size orchestra." The discrepancy between the two dates is striking and, unless one of them is a misprint, they seem to suggest that an aura of myth has already begun to surround Morawetz's music.

11) Mahler (1860-1911) was born in Kaliště, not far from Morawetz's birthplace, Světlá nad Sázavou, where other branches of the Mahler family lived. Mahler studied in Jihlava and was active in Olomouc, Prague and elsewhere before his career as a conductor led him to the Vienna Opera and the Metropolitan Opera in New York. During his lifetime, his activities as a composer were overshadowed by his fame as a conductor. Today he is highly

appreciated as a composer who influenced future generations of musicians. He did much to promote Czech music.

12) *Toronto Symphony News*, 1979/80. Issue Six.

13) Gaynor Jones, "Anne Frank's Diary: The Epilogue," in *MacLean's*, Vol. 93, No. 39, September 29, 1980.

14) Dr. Morawetz very kindly sent me a copy of Mr. Frank's letter for this article, along with other material, which is herewith gratefully acknowledged.

15) See Zdenka E. Fischmann, "Max Brod's Life in Music," in *Review of the Society for the History of Czechoslovak Jews*, Vol. 1, pp. 101-20, reprinted in this volume.

RAFAEL KUBELÍK AT 75

Rafael Kubelík, son of the celebrated violinist Jan Kubelík (1880-1940), was born on June 29, 1914. He studied violin, composition, and conducting at the Prague Conservatory from 1928 to 1933. He made his conducting debut with the Czech Philharmonic Orchestra at the age of 20. His career began in Czechoslovakia at the Brno State Theater (1939-1941) and developed further when he served as director and conductor of the Czech Philharmonic Orchestra in Prague (1942-1948). After escaping to the West in 1948, Kubelík never again looked back to his own country. His wife Lála Bertlová, a well-known violin virtuoso, who died in Switzerland in 1961, also did not return to Czechoslovakia. Kubelík became a Swiss citizen in 1967, but his activity was world-wide.

In exile, he was the principal conductor of the Chicago Symphony Orchestra (1950-1953); musical director of the Covent Garden Opera in London (1955-1958). In 1972, he was named musical director of the Metropolitan Opera in New York, but resigned after the death of Gentele. His most important position was with his own orchestra, the Bavarian Radio Symphony Orchestra in Munich, which lasted from 1961 to his retirement. Kubelík made the city where he lived famous: he founded the yearly festival in Lucerne; he was guest conductor with the best orchestras in American, Europe and Israel, and frequently recorded with them. In addition to the standard repertory, he featured less known compositions and contemporary music on his programs, even which his audiences and administrative colleagues did not always fully agree with his choices.

Kubilik's discography encompasses merely a part of the works which he interpreted at the podium during his long career, but they demonstrate his interests. He performed entire symphonic cycles, for example, all nine of Beethoven's symphonies, each with a particular orchestra; the nine symphonies of Dvořák with the Berlin Philharmonic Orchestra. And the complete cycle of Dvořák's symphonic poems, *Slovanic Dances*, and *Stabat Mater* with the Bavarian Radio Symphony Orchestra; Dvořák's *Legends* and *Serenade* with the English Chamber Orchestra; three complete recordings of Smetana's *My Country* with the Viennese Philharmonic. With the Bavarian Radio Symphony Orchetra, he recorded Smetana's symphonic poems; Janáček's *Sinfonetta, Taras Bulba* and *Glagolithic Mass*; Mahler's first, fourth, fifth, and eighth symphonies, in which his second wife, the Australian Elsie Morison, was vocal soloist. With baritone Dietrich Fischer-Dieskau he recorded Mahler's *Songs of a Wayfarer*. He also recorded Handel's *Royal Fireworks Music* and *Water Music*; all four symphonies of Robert Schumann, his piano concerto in A major, *Konzertstück* and *Manfred*; clarinet concertos by Weber and Mozart; Grieg's glorious piano concerto; Borodin's second symphony and *Polovetzian Dances* with the Vienna Philharmonic; Bartok's

Concerto for Orchestra; Wagner's *Siegfried Idyll* and various preludes from Wagner operas with the Boston Symphony Orchestra.

His requiem *Pro memoria Patris* was premiered with the Czech Philharmonic Orchestra in 1942, and the first performance of his opera *Veronika* took place in Brno in 1947. He also composed in exile. His oratorio *Libera nos* was first given in West Germany (1965). His opera *Cornelia Faroli* on a Czech text was intended for the cultural events of the 1966 Olympics. Its world premiere took place on August 15, 1972 in Augsburg, and it was repeated in Albany, New York the following year. The librettist was Dalibor C. Faltis, who also wrote the librettos of *Veronika* and the earlier opera *Chodská svatba*.

Rafael Kubelík is an important Janáček specialist. For example, he reconstructed the original version of the opera From the *House of the Dead*, which was performed according to his interpretative ideas in Munich during the Lucerne festival, in Vienna, and also in New York in a concert version.

Despite decorations, honors, prizes for recordings and international recognition, Kubelík describes himself as "a simple Czech musician," whose principal goal in life is and always had been "to fight for music and the expression of freedom." Rafael Kubelík was among the first vice-presidents of SVU and became an honorary member in 1966.

His meritious service in preserving Czech music is immense and deeply valued by his countrymen as he disseminates this music throughout the world - and surely, also in his own country. Perhaps we could say "like father, like son;" both artists of international scope, proud of their origin and always willing to serve music.

Editor's note: this article was written in 1989 to celebrate Rafael Kubelík's seventy-fifth birthday.

CZECH MUSIC IN TEXAS

The strength of the Czech folk music tradition in the state of Texas was convincingly demonstrated November 14-16, 1986, as over 1500 people crowded into a conference center in Bryan to attend a program entitled *Czech Music in Texas: A Sesquicentennial Symposium*. Performances of Czech music and dance are commonplace in Texas, but the symposium was a special event. It was designed to illustrate the full range of this musical heritage through varied performances as well as a series of scholarly presentations and panel discussions. Performances were given by soloists, ensembles, choral groups, dance groups, and concert orchestras, all of them made up of Texas residents, with the notable exception of the folk orchestra and dance ensemble Podlužan, from Břeclav, Czechoslovakia, which was invited to symbolize cultural ties between the Texas Czechs and the "Old Country." [1] It was perhaps the dance orchestras, which played for two evening dances - the Vrazels and the Jodie Mikula Orchestra - that best represented the real status and function of Czech folk music in Texas. These two orchestras, currently the most popular of their kind in the state, inherit a tradition that preserves Czech-American ethnic identity in its unique, provincial way.

Next to the Czech language, music has always been the single most important cohesive force in Texas-Czech culture. From the beginning of their settlement in Texas, almost all of the Czech communities had at least one orchestra. Scores of Texas-Czech bands and orchestras have been organized throughout the years, many of them existing today with third and fourth-generation family members. The Bača family provides a striking example of the Czech musical families in Texas. Joseph Bača, whose family was associated with a musical tradition, settled near Fayetteville in 1860. The first formal Bača band in Texas was organized by the immigrant's son Frank and eventually consisted of his entire family, including thirteen children, all of whom played musical instruments. Several of these children formed new Bača orchestras after they established their own families, and, in addition, other descendants of the immigrant Joseph formed Bača orchestras in various parts of the state. In addition to the Bačas, traditionally musical Czech family names in Texas include Adamčík, Adámek, Beseda, Boháč, Černý, Červenka, Diviš, Dlabaj, Drozd, Dušek, Dybala, Gerik, Honza, Ilse, Janečka, Ježek, Jurečka, Kohut, Kostohryz, Kovář, Křenek, Křivánek, Kubala, Kubín, Kučera, Mača, Majek, Marek, Matocha, Matuš, Menšík, Mikula, Milan, Motl, Mráz, Nesvadba, Němec, Paták, Pátek, Pavelka, Pavlas, Pokladník, Rejček, Řepka, Ripl, Ripplo, Šebetka, Shiller, Šimek, Šlampa, Slováček, Sodek, Stránský, Vaněk, Vrázel, Vrla, Vytopil, Zbránek, Zdrůbek, and others.

Most of the early ensembles played music of a type known as brass, military, picnic, or, sometimes, German. A typical arrangement of such a band is one or two clarinets or saxophones, two or more trumpets or cornets, and an accordion or hammered dulcimer in the front row; a trombone, baritone, and perhaps a French horn in the second row; the drums, bass horn, and, more rarely a piano, in the rear. The band would play waltzes, polkas, overtures, and military music at public concerts and - dropping some of the brass instruments - waltzes and polkas for dances in the evening. When playing dance music, they would call themselves an orchestra rather than a band. Today, daytime public performances for the groups are rarer, and the distinction between a dance band and an orchestra has become blurred.

It would be difficult to overestimate the influence of the music itself. I will always remember my vain attempt to coax an elderly Texas Czech lady into telling me one of the *pohádky* [fairy tales] she had heard in her youth. She could not remember even one--but she spontaneously broke into song and sang the words to *Louka zelená* [Green Meadow, a traditional waltz] a cappella. The singing of Czech folk songs had always been a popular pastime among Texas Czechs, and today, as the 1986 symposium demonstrates, numerous choral groups, and even a few folk dancing troupes, are still active (often organized by fraternal or religious institutions). However, the dance bands which continue to play polka and waltz arrangements of the traditional songs, singing the lyrics in Czech, are, by far, the most important single factor in keeping alive the folk music tradition. A few of the more popular folk or traditional numbers are *Louka zelená, Nemelem, nemelem* [We Aren't Milling], *Škoda lásky* [better known as *The Beer Barrel Polka*], *U studánky seděla* [She Was Sitting By the Fountain], *A já sám* [I Alone], and *Pode mlejnem* [Under the Mill].

Traditional Czech music is being perpetuated in Texas as a cultural expression and as an aesthetic link with a pastoral past. Although it fulfills immediate emotional needs, it is essentially archaic and ritualistic, unsuitable for adaptation to an industrial and urban age, new ways of life, changing values. And, most obviously, few young Czech-Americans (past the second generation) today really understand the Czech lyrics. The surprising fact is not that the music of the Texas Czech dance band is changing but that it is changing so slowly. The nature of that gradual change, that evolution, is my particular interest. Most striking is the adoption of elements from American country (or "country and western") music. Not only is country music an important component in the popular majority culture of Texas, but one might even say that country music is the closest thing in America to a living tradition of Anglo, rural, folk music, and the Texas Czechs are a predominantly rural-oriented people, even today.

About ten years ago, it was estimated by a record producer specializing in Czech ethnic music that approximately fifty percent of the standard repertoire performed by the Czech bands at dances could be classified as "country and western." On the other hand, only about twenty-five percent of the songs being recorded on the bands' albums could be thus classified, and about one-third of all songs recorded by the bands were being sung in Czech. [2]

The manner in which country music is being incorporated into the Czech ethnic music is illustrated clearly and forcefully by the liner notes from a Red Ravens album released in late 1976: "This album could easily be de-

scribed as the 'Now Sound' of Polka ... To understand completely how important the above statement is, let's return in time to only a few short years ago,
when to be a recognized polka band, you played with a bass horn or the bass
on records was derived strictly from the bass portion of the drums... Guide
records was one of the first Polka labels in the United States to start using ... a
guitar. At that time, which was only nine short years ago, the words 'country
and western' [were] not spoken in the same sentence as Polka Music. However ... we presented the first Polka LP on the market with the country sound,
calling it the 'New Country Polka Sound.' Also... we started using from two to
three songs on each album that were strictly country and western songs even
though this was not accepted outside of Texas. However, we felt that country
music was going to be the accepted sound of the future so we encouraged
Texas Polka Bands to use the songs that were most requested at their dances.
We went on to use more country and western songs with our never forgotten
'Old Time Polka Tunes' which people will never forget and always love, and
the fact...remains that a polka band that presents some country and western
tunes in their dance presentation is the most in demand and has the largest
following today....The big difference [in the Red Ravens style] is the country
flavor that is used on the 'Czech vocals.'" [3]

In this passage, one can see that changes in repertoire are closely related to changes in instrumentation (especially in the increased use of electric
guitars) and musical styles (even the delivery of Czech lyrics in a "country"
manner). Of equal significance is the rhetorical stance: change is inevitable,
change is necessary to ensure the popularity of a band. With, of course, the
nostalgic bow to tradition, the core of love for the old music that will "never
be forgotten."

It seems reasonable, then, to treat this process of musical change as one
measure of cultural assimilation and, on the other hand, the persistence of traditional forms as a measure of resistance to assimilation. Naturally, issues related to this process are somewhat controversial within the Texas Czech community - and the resultant Czech-American ambiguities regarding assimilation
and pluralism are reminiscent (though not nearly so profound or volatile) of
those regarding the retention of the Czech language fifty years ago. The issue
of repertoire is more controversial than those of style or instrumentation. Both
the Vrazels and the Jodie Mikula Orchestra in their dance performances at the
1986 symposium exhibited musical styles much like that described in the Red
Ravens liner notes, in spite of the fact that they played Czech music exclusively (largely as a symbolic gesture appropriate to the occasion).

A panel discussion on the present status of Czech dance music in
Texas, held as part of the 1986 symposium, reinforced the idea that the traditional ethnic music continues to decline in popularity. The five panelists and
moderator have all had long careers as hosts of Texas radio programs featuring
Czech music and extensive contacts with both the bands and the Czech-
American audience throughout the state. The comments by Rudy Sefcik, host
of a polka show on KHBR - Hillsboro, were typical: "In this week's copy of
the *Věstník*, a Mr. Malina from Houston writes how SPJST Lodge 45 used to

host polka dances that the entire family would attend. That was fifty years ago. Now, the lodge has disbanded and is used as a hay barn. In the West area, the young people attend country western dances. I don't know why they won't attend a polka dance." [4]

Sefcik's remarks underscore the generational dimension of the problem and thus its relation to the larger issue of assimilation. Even more poignant was the anecdotal evidence by a lady from the audience who identified herself as a resident of the Dallas area. "Why don't the children go with their parents? Why has a lot of our own generation stopped going to the dances?... We can go to Lodge 84 [of the SPJST, in Dallas], and we might see six people there that we know. We can go to the Sokol Hall, which is a big hall, and we might see two people that we know there.

"Yet we were raised there, and we attended these halls all of our lives.... If you go to the Dallas Sokol hall, you will find that its attendance is 98% other nationalities. The hall manager definitely has a problem ... they've got to make a certain amount of money ... So who do they attract? They attract people of other nationalities, and those people who don't want to hear polka music. They go to the hall manager and ask why the band doesn't play ballroom music or *Cotton-Eyed Joe* or country and western music."

Much of the discussion among the panelists and members of their audience focused on strategies for *teaching* young people to dance the polka and enticing them in various ways to attend the polka dances. Perhaps the fraternal and ethnic clubs and organizations will have some success in this project. As pointed out earlier, Czech choral (folk song) groups and folk dancing troupes continue to survive and even grow in popularity in Texas today. Of course self-conscious preservation it not identical with a spontaneous, living folk culture but those who advocate ethnic institutional support for such programs undoubtedly see it as an inevitable compromise. Even with the Texas Czech music losing ground to Anglo-American country music, however, it is difficult to imagine a time when the Czech polka in Texas will be classified, along with the artificially preserved and archaic *beseda* as a "folk dance."

Notes

1) For an entertaining description of the symposium events, with an emphasis on the Podlužan performance, see Josef Škvorecký, "Neroztavení" *Západ* 9 (April 1987), 12-14. Podlužan went on to perform in eight additional towns and cities in Texas during the following months, probably the first cembalon orchestra to tour this part of the United States.

2) This information was furnished by Ray Doggett, of *Guide Records*, Houston, Texas, in private correspondence of 1 February 1977.

3) *Guide* 1045 (1976). The Red Ravens is still an active band.

4) Sefcik, in addition to his position as radio host, is editor of the *Věstník* (Herald), an official publication of the SPJST, the largest Czech-American fraternal organization in Texas. (In spite of its name, about three-fourths of the journal is now printed in English.) The city of West, which has a large Czech-American population, is north of Waco, Texas. Other panelists were Lada Cerny (KSKY-Dallas), Al Kozel (KULP-El Campo), Helen

Pavelka (KSIX-Corpus Christi) and Alfred Vrazel (KMIL-Cameron). Bernard M. Gebala, the moderator, is a former host of a Czech music program on KTEM-Temple and is the current Vice President of the SPJST.